31

Social History of Canada

H.V. Nelles, general editor

GEOFFREY BILSON is a member of the Department of History at the University of Saskatchewan.

From its first appearance in 1832 until the last scares of 1871, cholera aroused fear in British North America. The disease killed 20,000 people and its psychological effects were enormous. Cholera unsettled governments, undermined the medical profession, exposed inadequacies in public health, and widened the division between rich and poor. In a fascinating and disturbing book, Geoffrey Bilson traces the story of the cholera epidemics as they ravaged the Canadas and the Atlantic colonies.

The political repercussions were extensive, particularly in Lower Canada. Governments, both colonial and municipal, imposed various public health measures, including quarantine. These actions were always temporary and poorly enforced, and they sometimes met with violent opposition, especially among the poor and the immigrants, hit hardest by cholera. Even the panic that ensued from the periodic onslaughts of the disease could not overcome the prevailing laissez-faire attitude towards public health legislation.

The medical profession was equally helpless. Doctors could neither cure the disease nor isolate its cause, and public sentiment against them ran high.

A Darkened House is important reading for those interested in Canada's social, political, and medical history.

GEOFFREY BILSON

A Darkened House: Cholera in Nineteenth-Century Canada

UNIVERSITY OF TORONTO PRESS
Toronto Buffalo London

© University of Toronto Press 1980
Toronto   Buffalo   London
Printed in Canada

Canadian Cataloguing in Publication Data

Bilson, Geoffrey.
  A darkened house
  (Social history of Canada ; 31 ISSN 0085-6207)
  Bibliography: p.
  Includes index.
  ISBN 0-8020-2367-3 bd. ISBN 0-8020-6402-7 pa.
  1. Cholera, Asiatic – Canada – History – 19th
  century. 2. Public health – Canada – History –
  19th century. I. Title. II. Series.
  RC132.C2B54   616.9'32'00971   C80-094409-7

Social History of Canada 31

The cover illustration is a detail from Joseph Légaré's *Cholera Plague, Quebec* (1832), reproduced with permission of The National Gallery of Canada, Ottawa.

TO BETH, MAX, AND KATE

Contents

viii Contents

Acknowledgments

I am grateful for the help given to me by members of the staffs of the archives and libraries in which I have worked on this project. From the Public Archives of Nova Scotia in Halifax, where I began, to the Wellcome Institute for the History of Medicine in London, England, where I was able to complete and revise the manuscript during a leave, I was met with courtesy and efficiency. Living in western Canada makes research in the east a slow and, increasingly, expensive business. Grants from the University of Saskatchewan helped meet some of the costs of my work in the Maritimes and of typing the manuscript. Grants from the Canada Council helped me to visit Quebec and Ontario. Some of the material in this book has appeared in different form in articles published in various journals, including *Historical Papers, Acadiensis, Medical History,* and *Ontario History.* Professor Michael Cross read part of an earlier version of this book and encouraged me to continue and Professor Viv Nelles made a number of suggestions which improved the final draft. That draft was typed by Peggy Hillel, who reduced chaos to order with skill and good humour.

This book has been published with the help of a grant from the Social Science Federation of Canada, using funds provided by the Social Sciences and Humanities Research Council of Canada.

A DARKENED HOUSE

From south to north hath the cholera come,
He came like a despot king;
He hath swept the earth with a conqueror's step,
And the air with a spirit's wing.
We shut him out with a girdle of ships,
And a guarded quarantine;
What ho! now which of your watches slept?
The Cholera's past your line!
There's a curse on the blessed sun and air,
What will he do for breath?
For breath, which was once but a word for life,
Is now but a word for death.
Wo for affection! When love must look
On each face it loves with dread.
Kindred and friends, when a few brief hours
And the dearest may be the dead!
The months pass on, and the circle spreads
And the time is drawing nigh
When each street may have a darkened house
Or a coffin passing by.

ANON. 1832

Introduction

Cholera originated in Bengal where it was endemic for many years. In 1817, it began to spread through Asia and Europe in a series of pandemics which lasted into the twentieth century.[1] Moving through Russia to western Europe, the disease reached the British Isles in 1831. The next year saw it in Canada for the first time, and between 1832 and 1871 epidemics occurred in various parts of British North America. On each occasion, cholera was imported from outside and it usually reached Canada with immigrants from Europe.

The disease is caused by a micro-organism which enters the body through the mouth. It can multiply without producing symptoms, and can cause minor disturbances, or severe illness which can kill more than one-half of those affected. The disease's worst effects are caused by a toxin which makes the gut wall more permeable to water. It causes vomiting and massive purging of liquid which quickly produces dehydration and upsets the chemical balance of the body. In its course it produces a number of symptoms including severe spasms and cramps, a sunken face, blue colour, husky voice, and further consequences, including kidney failure, as the bodily processes collapse. Cases can develop very quickly in apparently healthy people, and death can occur in a matter of hours or a few days at most. The patient passes through a number of stages from 'premonitory symptoms' to 'collapse,' the last stage before death, and the speed of passage varies with the particular case. Antibiotics and intra-venous transfusions now make it possible to cure many cases but in the nineteenth century no cure was possible.

Cholera made a massive impact on the imagination of people in the nineteenth century. They feared its sudden, painful, and arbitrary attack. They were horrified by the rapid course of the disease which did not allow a gentle decline into a peaceful death. They were baffled by the pattern of spread of the disease which fitted no known model of contagion. They grew contemptuous of the doctors who could do nothing for the victims and in some places they turned on the doctors and accused them of spreading the disease. The death rate, often approaching 60 per cent of those affected, helped to create panic. 'May the cholera catch you' became a curse.

The disease continued to mystify doctors until late in the century. From the start, there seemed to be some affinity between dirt and the disease but the connection was not clear. In the 1840s and 1850s a number of doctors suggested that the disease was spread by something which escaped from the victim and affected the water supply. In time, this would prove to be the main means by which the disease was spread but, until the germ theory developed in the 1880s won general support, this suggestion did not convince most of the profession. Outbreaks of cholera did strengthen the demands for public health and sanitary measures which were becoming issues in urban politics in Europe and North America in the nineteenth century. Any society suffering from an epidemic of the disease found its people under a strain which exacerbated existing tensions. In Canada, the disease had an impact on politics, medicine, and society during the middle part of the nineteenth century.

1

'Scrape, wash and cleanse'

As cholera spread through Russia and eastern Europe in the late 1820s, the British government watched its progress. It sent doctors to eastern Europe to investigate and it called on the experienced men who had seen the disease in India. No measures of quarantine appeared to check the spread of the disease and some doctors argued that the disease was caused by changes in the atmosphere. When the disease reached western Europe, however, the British government decided that some action had to be taken. It acted on the assumption that cholera was contagious and ordered that a quarantine be set up against it. Boards of health were established to enforce rules of cleanliness which it was hoped would protect people from the disease. Information about these preparations was sent to the colonial governments in circulars from Whitehall.[1]

Canadian newspapers followed the progress of cholera across Europe and its arrival in the British Isles. In fact, it was from the newspapers and not from any official correspondence that Lord Aylmer, the governor-general, first learned that the disease had reached Great Britain. He immediately asked the executive council to recommend defensive measures. Late in 1831, a quarantine was established at Quebec under the authority of the Quarantine Act of 1795 to deal with ships arriving at the end of the season. Aylmer next turned to local medical men for advice on what to do to prepare for the disease.

The Quebec Medical Board, the main function of which was to examine candidates who wished to practise medicine in the province of Lower Canada, met in the autumn of 1831 to discuss cholera. It reviewed all the material which could be found on the disease and noted that opinions were divided. Given the division, it recommended that the disease be treated as it if were contagious and suggested a scheme for a quarantine station. It also recommended that boards of health be set up to enforce the rules of cleanliness laid down by the Privy Council in London. The information sent from Britain should be translated into French and sent out to the country doctors so they would be familiar with the symptoms of cholera.[2]

The House of Assembly, on the basis of this report, passed a bill to enforce a quarantine and to establish boards of health in Quebec and Montreal. The bill also provided that boards could be set up wherever they were needed. The assembly appropriated £10,000 to meet the costs of quarantine and of the boards of health. In most years, some immigrants arriving in Lower Canada needed help with housing, food, and transport, and it seemed likely that cholera, if it came, would increase what was already a heavy burden on the province. To meet this expense, the assembly adopted a suggestion made by the British government and imposed a tax of five shillings per head on immigrants. There were protests from Upper Canada that the tax would hinder British immigrants, but the money was needed, according to the assembly, to help the sick and to forward indigent immigrants to Upper Canada.[3]

There were, of course, a number of members of the house quite happy to hinder British immigration. Since 1815, immigration had been increasing and had changed in character. Disruptions in the European economy forced large numbers of poor people to emigrate. The developing Atlantic shipping trade brought tens of thousands to Lower Canada each year. The numbers who stayed in Lower Canada dropped sharply after 1825 and the vast majority pushed on to Upper Canada and the United States. Those who did remain, however, combined with the growing population of Lower Canada to place increasing strains on the resources of the province. The result was a sharpening of social tension and conflict.[4] French-Canadian nationalists feared the impact of English and Irish settlers on the French community and there were some who would say that immigration was being used to introduce cholera into Lower Canada to destroy the French.

In 1831, 50,000 immigrants entered Canada and 70,000 or 80,000 were expected in 1832.[5] The Quebec Emigrant Society warned immigrants of the difficulties which they would face in Canada. It argued that too many people were being thrown into the province by a badly operated traffic. They arrived in a country where prices were high, job prospects poor, the climate severe, and private charity limited. A.C. Buchanan, the Chief Emigrant Agent, denounced the society as a body made up of French Canadians who wanted to end British immigration and others who wanted to end Irish immigration. He preferred to emphasize the opportunities Canada offered the immigrants and the wealth which they brought to the country and created by their labour.[6]

Buchanan's arguments were sound when applied to Upper Canada but the immigrant traffic placed a huge strain on Lower Canada. In 1832 immigrants arrived at Quebec in numbers ranging from 600 to 10,000 per week. Many were self-reliant and had the money to continue their journey and to establish themselves in Upper Canada or the United States. Many others were penniless and had spent their last few pounds on the passage. All steerage passengers arrived tired or near exhaustion after a voyage of six to nine weeks in ships which were often crowded and filthy. If the voyage had been particularly slow they might be close to starvation on arrival. Those who could afford lodgings found themselves jammed into overcrowded houses while they waited to continue the journey. Those who could not afford shelter found themselves penniless and exhausted on the wharfs at Quebec and Montreal.

One newspaper, writing of the annual inundation of immigrants likened it to 'the passage of an immense army, much exposed and ill-equipped, and leaving the inhabitants to take care of and provide for the sick, wounded and disabled, and bury their dead.'[7] To meet these needs, charitable groups built sheds to shelter the travellers and arranged to forward them up river. In weeks when very large numbers of immigrants arrived these facilities were overwhelmed and the waiting passengers were forced to sleep in the open on the wharfs, on the beaches, and in the fields. Any interruption in the traffic up river intensified the difficulties as the stranded immigrants came to rest in Montreal.

The immigrant traffic brought a threat to the residents' health in any year, but in a cholera year that threat was increased immeasurably. Fear of cholera did not bring a ban on immigration, but immigration shaped the quarantine recommendations made by the Quebec Medical Board. Awareness of the danger to public health may have muted the protests against the inconvenience and expense of quarantine. The scheme proposed that a quarantine station be established down river from Quebec under the supervision of the Quebec Board of Health established by the Quarantine Act. There, passengers arriving from overseas could be examined and the sick detained in a lazaretto. Passengers would be required to clean themselves and their baggage while their ship was cleaned before proceeding to Quebec. The scheme was put into effect early in 1832. Grosse Isle, a small, hilly island thirty miles below Quebec, was chosen, over the objections of its resident farmer and his seigneur, to be the site of the station. Despite its unsafe landing and limited facilities the island was to be the first landfall in Canada for tens of thousands of immigrants in this and many future years.[8]

The pilots on the St Lawrence were ordered to bring all vessels to anchor at Grosse Isle. There, the health officer would examine the ship, and decide if it should proceed to Quebec. No one was to land between Grosse Isle and Quebec. At Quebec, the medical officer would examine the vessel before allowing passengers to land.[9] The Quebec Board of Health then laid down its regulations for operating the quarantine. They were elaborate, and quickly overtaxed the resources of Grosse Isle. At first, the board made distinctions between ships which had sailed from infected ports, ships which had had sickness on board during the voyage, and ships which had had cholera on board during the voyage. Ships from infected ports served a three-day quarantine, ships which had had sickness were to be cleaned before proceeding, ships which had had cholera cases performed a fifteen-day quarantine, and ships arriving with cholera on board were quarantined for thirty days. Steerage and hold passengers from infected ships had to land and clean themselves and their baggage while their ships were purified. Cabin passengers were not required to land or clean their baggage as they had not been subjected to the same squalid conditions as their fellow passengers. These first regulations threw an enormous strain on the island. Early in July, with cholera well established in Quebec, the board required nearly all steerage passengers to land at Quebec to clean themselves and their baggage. On some days in July, more than a thousand passengers struggled for space and washing water on Grosse Isle.[10]

These schemes to isolate victims of cholera from the residents of Lower Canada had obvious shortcomings. Much of the information had to be given by the ships' masters who had an interest in playing down reports of sickness on board. At Quebec, for example, the medical officer made his decision on whether to allow a vessel to dock or return it to Grosse Isle on the basis of reports from the ship's master and by questioning the relatives of any passengers who had died. He asked the survivors what they thought their relatives had died of and he asked them to describe the symptoms.[11] Even if the passengers and crew were completely honest the system could do nothing to recognize cholera carriers with no symptoms. In practice, what was quarantined was illness which could not be disguised and dirt which was visible and measurable. The quarantine system made no provision in 1832 for keeping passengers of the different vessels separate on the island. Passengers from healthy ships mingled with those from diseased vessels before moving on up river.

The board of health recognized from the start that the problem of regulating hundreds of ships and thousands of passengers would be very great. They therefore put Grosse Isle under military command. After the Royal Engineers had erected a hospital, and sheds to shelter the immigrants, the island passed under the command of Captain H. Reid. His establishment included an inspecting physician, a marine boarding officer, a medical superintendent, an assistant medical superintendent, a sergeant in charge of the emigrant sheds, and a complement of clerks, labourers, nurses, and troops. The station was under military command but not under martial law. The board of health did suggest that the commandant be given power to inflict summary punishment for breaches of regulations. In reply, the solicitor-general gave his opinion that the commandant could use his military power and control over property to 'produce obedience' and to restrain people until they were brought to trial. He had no judicial power to inflict summary punishment.[12]

Captain Reid had asked for power to punish passengers in an effort to maintain discipline on the island. As the hundreds of passengers poured ashore conditions quickly deteriorated. The women fought for water to boil on open fires and for spaces to dry and air their clothes. Despite objections from the pious this work went on seven days a week. While on the island, the travellers bought their food from shops and stalls set up by private traders and there were frequent complaints about the quality and cost of the supplies. The board of health fed those who were destitute. Theft was widespread. Once their work was done, the immigrants crowded together in the sheds to wait until their ships were fit to reboard. They celebrated the end of their ocean voyage, according to the sergeant in charge of the sheds, with 'singing, drinking, dancing, shouting, and cutting antics that would surprise the leader of a circus. They have no shame – are under no restraint.' He described his problems to Mrs Susanna Moodie and her party, who had arrived as cabin passengers and were sightseeing on the island: 'they are such thieves that they rob one another of the little they possess ... we could, perhaps, manage the men but the women, sir! The women! Oh, sir!' he said.[13]

It was against this background of crowding, hardship, and crime that the staff of Grosse Isle attempted to enforce the quarantine. Dr George Griffin, an assistant surgeon of the 32nd Regiment, had to visit the hundreds of vessels which arrived at the island. It was no work for a soldier who hated sailing in small boats. Griffin became more reluctant to do the job after a boat sank under him. As the number of vessels arriving increased, he was overwhelmed. He began to neglect his duties, failed to visit ships, and finally suggested that the masters of vessels came to him on shore. Reid complained of the surgeon's 'indolence, negligence and disobedience in the performance of his duties.' Dr Francis Fortier was appointed to assist Griffin.[14]

Even if the inspecting physician at Grosse Isle had been more energetic than Griffin, the quarantine could not have worked, given the state of knowledge about contagion at the time. As it was operated, quarantine was permeable. From the beginning of the season, ships passed the island without stopping for inspection by sailing beyond the reach of the guns. While the regulations provided that ships reaching Quebec without a clearance from Grosse Isle should return to the island it was not clear that they could be forced to do so. In July, the brig *Fanny* reached Quebec and passengers and crew landed. When the health officer ordered the vessel back to Grosse Isle the master refused. The passengers who had been rounded up and returned to the *Fanny* helped the crew to resist when efforts were made to tow the brig out of port. Had the master not relented, military force might have been used against the vessel.[15] Less dramatic breaches of quarantine, but breaches nonetheless, were cases where passengers hid sick members of their families to avoid long delays. Sometimes cholera would develop on board a ship after it had left Grosse Isle. When Mrs Moodie's vessel reached Montreal, the captain's brother fell sick. Deeming it advisable to avoid the health officers, Mrs Moodie went ashore, put up in a hotel, and left town on a stage-coach the next day.

Grosse Isle itself was not isolated from contact with the shore. Supplies had to be brought in, and Robert Nelson, health commissioner of Montreal, suggested that there was some clandestine trade in passengers between the island and the city. The quarantine station at Grosse Isle did not do the job it was set up to do and its failure was plain at the end of June. With cholera raging in Quebec, the board of health set up a committee to consider the suggestion that quarantine be abandoned as an expensive and disruptive failure. The committee recommended, however, not only that quarantine continue but that it be extended to all ships with more than 15 steerage passengers. The justification offered was that quarantine 'is adequate to the removal of a particular and known cause of evil ... it will enable us to disinfect a ship ... whereas if there be no such place as Grosse Isle or yet any substitute for it that evil is without remedy.'[16] Grosse Isle would continue to operate as a place to isolate the obviously sick and to clean the dirty throughout the cholera years. Some changes would be made in its operation to prevent sick and well mixing indiscriminately. Limited medical knowledge, uncertain administration, and the nature of disease ensured that quarantine would never become a certain means of protecting Canada from contagious diseases.

Quarantine against travellers from overseas did not stop cholera, and some communities within Canada tried to protect themselves once the epidemic had begun. Both Lord Aylmer and Sir John Colborne, governor of Upper Canada, disliked these local quarantines because they disrupted normal patterns of travel and trade. However, they found themselves in the politically difficult position of supporting the quarantine at Grosse Isle while appealing to Canadians not to set up quarantines to protect their separate communities. Colborne rejected a suggestion that immigrants entering Upper Canada be kept together in quarantine as 'very injudicious.' He argued that the arrangement would force those most susceptible to the disease to crowd together. It was better for the public health, he thought, to keep traffic flowing normally and quickly distribute the immigrants throughout the region. Local arrangements would have to be made for those who fell sick while on the move.[17] It was difficult for many people to understand why quarantine was useful at Grosse Isle – but undesirable once the immigrants had left the island.

Despite the arguments made by the executive, therefore, magistrates in both Lower and Upper Canada did experiment with local quarantine and travel restrictions. Trois-Rivières imposed stringent regulations on landings. In Upper Canada, the first days of the epidemic brought travel to a halt as boatmen fled from the rivers. Magistrates in a number of communities imposed regulations which were intended to keep traffic at a standstill. At Bytown, the lock-keepers on the Rideau Canal were ordered to stop the traffic and to prevent cargo being carried around the locks. The magistrates also suggested that the residents of Bytown prevent boats or canoes from leaving town or approaching it by the Rideau and Ottawa rivers. In the Western District, the magistrates of Kent were ordered to stop people 'suspected of being infected with cholera' from entering the district. At Belleville, boats were forbidden to land goods or passengers and armed guards were posted on the roads to keep out strangers. On both sides of the international boundary, communities tried to prevent cross-border visits by their residents and to bar entry to sick strangers.

For a short time, early in the epidemic, these and similar efforts at Kingston and Cornwall brought passenger traffic to a halt. The immigrants were forced to wait in Montreal while the Emigrant Society and others appealed to the magistrates of Upper Canada to lift their blockade. A combination of official and semi-official protest and the need to continue trade and travel despite the epidemic soon broke down the bans. The magistrates, in fact, had no legal power to close the Rideau Canal and river traffic and they could not refute the argument that their efforts were illegal and made them liable to penalties. Early in July travel along the rivers and on the lakes resumed its usual course. There was some popular support for regulating the traffic and a number of towns did continue to inspect vessels coming to their quays despite the objections of the boatmen. Sometimes the resentment of the boatmen could provoke violence as it was to do in Niagara during the summer, but Sir John Colborne asked the boat captains to co-operate with the authorities. He suggested that if they did not do so he was prepared to support legal measures to force proprietors to obey local inspection regulations.[18]

When the measures taken failed to check the spread of cholera in 1832, it became vital to make preparations to deal with the disease. Those preparations were few enough. To begin with, the medical resources of Lower Canada were limited. There were few doctors and even with the help of their apprentices or medical students they remained a small force. Most professional medical men were found in urban centres. The profession was a quarrelsome one and frequently divided over questions of medicine and professional politics. Laymen tended to be sceptical about the claims of medical men to special skill and the cholera epidemics would help to feed that scepticism. Many people, however, could not afford to pay doctors and preferred to employ unqualified medical men or to take the advice of apothecaries from whom they bought their medicines. For many of the poor the only medical advice to be had was given by the clergy or neighbours. The problem of getting medical aid to the poor was one which all communities began to consider – but usually not until after the cholera had developed.

There was agreement among medical men and magistrates before the epidemic began that should many of the poor fall sick they would need hospital care. Hospitals were normally institutions for the care of those too poor to help themselves. In Quebec, the four civilian hospitals had fewer than 300 beds and the military hospital was restricted to military use. A new marine hospital was begun in 1832 but it was not completed until 1834. The fever hospital at Point Levi alone would admit patients with contagious diseases – but it was across the river from the city and was frequently inaccessible. The Montreal General Hospital, the chief one in the city, was closed to those with infectious diseases. It remained closed to them during the cholera epidemic by a unanimous decision of the governors taken at a special meeting.[19] One of the functions of a hospital was to protect society from the dangers of large numbers of sick poor; boards of health now had to find accommodation for patients barred from most existing hospitals.

This need was so clear that providing hospital space became one of the chief tasks of boards of health. In Quebec, the board of health considered the question when it went to work in March 1832. The city's doctors suggested that Point Levi hospital be closed as it was inaccessible. They argued that a cholera hospital could be safely operated inside the city. The board agreed to close Point Levi and to extend accommodation at the Emigrant Hospital by hiring a nearby house. They also debated opening a temporary hospital and decided to ask the government for tents to serve as a hospital at the King's Wharf. News of these discussions soon leaked out and the fact that the board intended not only to use the Emigrant Hospital for cholera cases, but also to increase its size, caused fear and anger among the hospital's neighbours. In past years, they had objected to the use of the hospital for smallpox cases and now they protested against its use for cholera victims. The residents of St John suburb presented a petition to the board of health. Among the nineteen double columns of signatures were the marks of many illiterate residents. These poor people expressed their fear that the 'destroying scourge of the human race which has been and still is inflicted upon their fellow subjects in Great Britain' made the presence of the hospital even more dangerous than in previous years. The board disingenuously read the petition as a fresh one against using the hospital for smallpox cases and replied that a well-run hospital was less danger to the public than 'the crowded and ill ventilated apartments of the very poor.[20] The board's experience in Quebec showed the difficulties of providing hospital space; elsewhere in Lower Canada solutions were sought only after the epidemic had begun.

The Privy Council in London had concluded that a well-run community could reduce the impact of the disease by cleanliness. Consequently it had laid down regulations which Canadian legislators had accepted as a standard. While the nature of cholera remained a mystery, there did seem to many to be some connection between dirt and the disease. If that were the case,

the disease could be checked by cleaning towns and their inhabitants. The practical problems of achieving cleanliness were very
great even if widespread indifference to the question could be
overcome. Few communities in Lower Canada made any attempt
to improve public cleanliness before the epidemic began. Residents of Quebec were more conscious of the need to do so than
were those of Montreal and other towns. In Quebec, most of the
population lived below the cliff that dominated the city and they
crowded together more closely than did the inhabitants of Montreal. In Montreal the inhabitants were better housed than in
Quebec, and Robert Nelson, the health commissioner, claimed
that there were few tenements in the city and that 'each French
Canadian had his own house, small, neat, clean and comfortable,
with at least a yard, and often a small garden.'[21] Perhaps Montreal was not quite as salubrious as Nelson remembered it thirty
years later, but its population does seem to have been more complacent early in 1832 than was the population of Quebec.

There was little to be complacent about in the towns at that
time. Many urban dwellers lived in houses which were small,
dirty, and often overcrowded in the immigrant season. Cellars
and yards were filled with refuse and the streets were piled with
garbage left untouched by the superintendent of highway's
workers. Water came from wells which were often shallow and
easily contaminated by run-off from the surface. Those who had
no well drew their water from the St Lawrence or bought it from
water-carriers who themselves took it from the river. The river
water was famous for its evil effects on the digestion of those
who drank it. Conditions of life made it difficult for many people
to keep clean or to keep a house clean and the sudden call for
action in 1832 could not be met even by those who saw any
convincing reason for responding.

In March the Quebec Board of Health began, in the face of
difficulties, indifference, and hostility, to clean the city's streets.
It laid down a scheme for enforcing the public health measures it
adopted. The scheme was one many large foreign cities had
adopted and one which would become standard in Canada. The
city was divided into wards and health wardens appointed for

each ward. In Quebec there were fourteen wards with two wardens appointed for the lower town and one for each of the other wards. It took over a month to fill the positions – the work was heavy and it exposed the wardens to abuse and sometimes to danger.

The health wardens were the police force of the board. Each was given a sign to nail up outside his house and a silver badge engraved 'Health Warden/Gardien Sanitaire' to be worn around his neck on a red ribbon. Thus identified they set out to enforce the public health regulations and to 'denounce delinquents' so that penalties could be invoked. They were required to list all the houses and apartments in their ward and to note the names of the occupants. They were to visit every house three times a week and report daily to the board. Their badge allowed them to inspect private property while acting 'with discretion and civility' and without 'extend[ing] your researches beyond what is strictly requisite.' If they met resistance, the wardens could call on 'all Constables and other officers' for help. When investigations showed faults of hygiene, the warden was to point them out to the householder. After the epidemic broke out, the wardens took on the additional tasks of distributing medicine to the poor and removing squatters from condemned buildings. The wardens were paid five shillings a day – and were quickly overwhelmed by the work.

In its early enthusiasm the board of health laid down a daunting list of regulations which attempted to correct a whole range of civic problems at a stroke. Buildings were to be cleaned and everyone was required to 'scrape, wash and cleanse their premises and carry away all filth which may have collected' during the winter. The buildings were then to be purified with lime or chloride of lime. All apartments were to be numbered and new tenants reported to the board by the owner within twenty-four hours. Tavern keepers, boarding and lodging house keepers, and sellers of beer and wine had to register their premises, display the board's regulations in the entrance hall, and report all sick boarders to the board. To improve the city's cleanliness regulations were made concerning the dumping of rubbish, emptying of privies, and keeping of hogs. Offensive trades such as those of tallow-chandlers (candle-makers), soap-boilers (soap-makers), and sausage-makers were regulated. Slaughterhouses, butchers, and meat sellers were also covered by regulations under a penalty of £100 currency. In providing for the public health of Quebec, the board laid down regulations which were elaborate and largely unenforceable in the face of public hostility and indifference. That long-standing customs could not be changed overnight soon became clear, and the board was forced to extend the deadline for complying with its regulations into early May.[22]

Quebec established an elaborate code of regulations as it prepared for the influx of immigrants, but Montreal did nothing. In March the Special Sessions, which were responsible for governing the unchartered city, considered a report from Dr Robertson. He found that there had been widespread sickness during the winter, with twice the usual number of fever cases admitted to the general hospital in the period since November. Dirt and crowding were common and would invite cholera if not dealt with before the spring. This is, perhaps, a more accurate picture of Montreal than Nelson's memories noted earlier. The magistrates resolved to clean up the city 'especially those quarters occupied by the Indigent classes of our population' and to ask Lord Aylmer to set up a board of health. The board was established in May but did not meet until 8 June; consequently, no precautions were taken in Montreal before cholera struck the city.[23]

If the miles between Quebec and Montreal helped to reduce the urgency of preparation, those between Lower and Upper Canada reduced it even more. There was no public health legislation in Upper Canada. No preparations were made there until cholera had broken out in Lower Canada. When the news reached Upper Canada, the responses included efforts like those discussed earlier to close traffic and block immigrants. Some communities, such as Kingston and Hallowell, held public meetings to recommend precautions, appoint boards of health, and raise funds. In Brockville the board of police took on the functions of a board of health, and in Prescott the citizens set up a board of health which was later recognized by the magistrates.

These local initiatives occurred before Sir John Colborne responded to the news. In mid-June, he offered aid to those communities most likely to be exposed to the disease because of their place on the immigrant routes. He first offered £200 to the magistrates of Brockville and other 'exposed stations' but he revised his plans on hearing that cholera had reached Prescott. He then put £500 at the disposal of the magistrates of each district to provide hospitals and to take measures for the public health recommended by the boards of health which they were asked to establish. A circular letter announcing this decision was sent to all magistrates on 20 June along with the request that they be careful about spending the money. These actions were taken solely on the governor's initiative. Sir John refused to call a special session of the legislature and preferred to gamble that it would retroactively approve of his actions. While this perhaps meant a politically quiet summer for Sir John it did mean that the boards of health operated in a legal limbo which undermined their effectiveness.

The fact that so little was done before June did not mean that people were totally indifferent to the danger of cholera. The bishop of Quebec called for the proclamation of a day of humiliation and fasting. 4 May was proclaimed a day of humiliation 'to avert the judgment earned by our sins.' While most people assumed that cholera would probably come with the immigrants, some doctors saw no reason why it should not come earlier – and a few claimed to have seen cases early in the year.[24] The first great scare of 1832 showed the extent of the tension that existed in Canada as it awaited cholera.

In March, 'a most virulent and contagious disease' erupted at Lundy's Lane and Chippewa near Niagara. A public meeting held on 1 April at Niagara heard that twenty workers had been attacked and eleven had died. The meeting resolved to ask Sir John Colborne to send medical men from York to make a diagnosis of the disease which one correspondent said was 'worse than any account I have read of the cholera.' Medical men had already been sent to the district when this request was made, but they differed over the nature of the disease. Dr W. Telfer believed it to be 'Spasmodic cholera which is now prevailing in England and has of late been so fatal in Europe and Asia.' However, a military surgeon denied there were any symptoms of cholera. There is no evidence that he had ever seen cases of cholera, but he was satisfied that the outbreak was one of 'Bilious Remittant Fever.' Rumours that cholera was at Lundy's Lane quickly reached York and were denied in the press. The rumours spread to Lower Canada where they created wide alarm. There, too, the press denied that it was cholera and urged people to keep calm.[25]

There was news other than that of cholera in the press early in 1832. In Lower Canada, the news was dominated after 21 May by the events of that day. British troops had fired into a crowd at an election meeting in Montreal, killing three men and wounding others. The incident helped to focus opposition to the executive through the spring and summer. The political life of Lower Canada was growing more heated and more radical – and cholera would play a part in the process. The tension with which it was awaited, so clear in the reaction to the Lundy's Lane incident, helped to shape events. The response to cholera after it arrived affected politics directly. Political attitudes did colour people's responses to the threat of cholera. In England, radicals in 1832 dismissed the scare over cholera as a humbug of corrupt politicians eager to build an elaborate public health machinery to provide jobs for their friends. In Canada, William Lyon Mackenzie echoed the English radicals and scoffed at reports from England of the extent of the disease. He agreed with William Cobbett that the panic was being encouraged 'to frighten us out of reform.' He enjoyed poking fun at the division and confusion in the medical profession.[26] As he was in England when cholera attacked Upper Canada he could make no comment on its progress in York, but as first mayor of Toronto he would later be directly involved in the second epidemic.

21 Scrape, wash and cleanse

Canadians lived for more than six months with the expectation that the summer would bring cholera. They were months marked by political division and rancour. Few communities had taken any precautions against the disease despite the fear it produced. The towns were not clean, there were few hospitals, and little medical aid was available for those who could not pay. The quarantine at Grosse Isle was clearly inadequate. These shortcomings were due in part to the lack of any clear evidence that the suggested precautions could avert cholera, and in part to inertia and the hope that the disease might not appear. Despite their inertia people were not indifferent to the disease. That had been shown once already in the scare over Lundy's Lane, and it would become very clear when cholera broke out in June 1832.

2

'Calculated to unman the ... strongest': Lower Canada 1832

Spring brought the transatlantic ships back to Quebec. By the end of the first week of June about 25,000 immigrants had arrived in 400 ships from the United Kingdom. As most of the precautions taken against cholera had been directed toward the immigrants it was natural that the residents of Lower Canada watched their arrival with anxiety. They knew that ships were passing Grosse Isle unexamined and many must have heard of cases of sick passengers being hidden. Even if one accepted, as many did not, that quarantine could prevent cholera entering the country, it was obvious that the quarantine as it was operating was a feeble defence. In early June, numerous rumours began to spread in Quebec that there were cases of cholera in the Emigrant Hospital.

At the same time, the board of health received reports of cholera at Grosse Isle. On 6 June Dr Joseph Morrin, health commissioner of Quebec, and Mr T.A. Young, secretary to the board of health, went to the island. The next day, the board heard from Dr Griffin that passengers had landed at the station from the brig *Carricks* 'under undoubted suspicion of the cholera morbus.' Dr Fortier reported that ships were passing the island and evading examination. In the face of these reports, the board chose to wait for Dr Morrin's report. On 8 June, he told the board that the passengers from the *Carricks* were victims of an epidemic 'in many particulars resembling cholera' but that the '*fever* [was] in no particular different from many now in the Quebec Emigrant Hospital.' Did that mean that the disease at Grosse Isle was *not* cholera or that the disease in Quebec *was* cholera? The board preferred the first explanation and Secretary Young issued a denial of the rumours that there was cholera in the city.[1]

The board had grounds for its action. No ship with cholera on board was known to have reached Quebec. The first victim of the disease which resembled cholera was a resident, not an immigrant. By denying the rumours for these reasons the board was accepting that cholera had to be imported and that it did not develop, for example, through atmospheric changes. The natural reluctance of leading citizens of the city to confirm the rumours was increased by the fact that the doctors did not agree that cholera was present. Not until 9 June, according to Dr J. Skey, chief military medical officer in Lower Canada, did 'the truth flash on our minds.' When he and some colleagues visited the Emigrant Hospital that day 'several of the cases were so far advanced in their progress that it was impossible not to decide upon the true nature of the disease in that very instant.' In less than a week 161 people died in Quebec. On the same day, the *Quebec Mercury*, after having talked to members of the board of health, published the news that 'this disorder has actually appeared in this city' and reported that eleven doctors had agreed that eight cases of the disease had occurred that day. The same issue carried Young's statement denying that there was cholera in the city and asserting that 'the rumour of death by cholera at the Emigrant Hospital in Quebec, now in circulation, is also entirely without foundation.'[2]

These first acknowledged cases of cholera occurred among passengers from the steamer *Voyageur*. By the time doctors in Quebec had diagnosed cholera, the steamer had reached Montreal where the first cholera death was reported on 9 June. The board of health at last began to meet. After a delay, it issued a denial that cholera existed in Montreal. On 12 June the board issued a bulletin announcing that 94 cases had been reported. On 13 June it issued no bulletin. The board's behaviour helped to fuel the panic which marked the first days of the epidemic. While the board was denying that cholera was present, people could see that each afternoon a number of burials were performed without a church service. That was unusual and very disturbing. When the board announced a large number of cases and then issued no further bulletin many people jumped to the conclusion that the truth was too horrible to reveal. The *Canadian Courant* reported that 'a panic of an almost indescribable nature seemed to have taken hold of the whole body of citizens and to have deprived them of presence of mind to an extent exceeding anything of a similar nature which had ever been witnessed in Montreal.'[3] Popular anger turned against the slothful and inept members of the board of health.

The panic which marked the end of the long period of waiting was intensified by the nature of the epidemics which struck the two cities. Both cities experienced explosive epidemics of great virulence with deaths mounting rapidly in the first few days. In Quebec, the daily toll climbed quickly past 70 and into the 90s to peak at well over 100 on 15 June. For a week, the daily toll exceeded 100 before beginning to decline. In Montreal the number of deaths mounted daily, passing 100 on 17 June and reaching a peak of 149 on 19 June. The next day showed a sharp drop to below 100 and for weeks after that the deaths ranged between 10 and 40 per day. These deaths stunned the population of the two cities and Lord Aylmer reported that they had been hit 'with a degree of violence far surpassing anything that has occurred in Europe, and officers now serving here assert that even in India (so far as they have had opportunities of observing it in that country and here) the disease was neither so rapidly fatal nor so universal in its seizures as during the first days of its prevalence in this place.'[4]

The apparent randomness with which the disease spread added to the fear. In Quebec, the first cases were reported at Roache's boarding house on Champlain Street. Four cases occurred there in twenty-four hours and the board of health declared the house a public nuisance and shut it. After the first outbreak cases developed all over town and across the river at Point Levi, although the poorer and dirtier parts of town, such as Buade Street, Cul-de-Sac, St John Street and St John suburb, were worst affected. In Montreal, the first cases were discovered near the old market house but the next were a half-mile away in the St Lawrence suburb. The disease then spread through the suburbs and only after a short delay did it erupt in the town and on streets near the river among the immigrant crowds.[5] These widely scattered outbreaks could not be explained by any then current ideas about contagious disease, and hence it was suggested that the whole atmosphere of the cities had been poisoned. Doctors had no success treating the early cases and the death rate in the early days seemed to be approaching levels which would depopulate the cities.

Gloom and panic spread with the disease. On the morning of the day when deaths reached their peak in Montreal, Alexander Hart wrote that most shops were shut and no business was being done except in one-inch boards which were in great demand for coffins. 'We none of us go into town, numbers are moving into the country yesterday 34 Corps passed our house today till this hour 23 – besides what goes to the old burial Ground and the Catholic ground 12 carts are employed by the Board of Health to carry away the dead who are interred without prayers ... all the schools are broke up and it is dreadful to see the immense number of carts with yellow flags.'[6]

In the face of scenes like these, those who could do so fled. On the river, the boatmen abandoned their crafts and passengers and fled inland. Many people fled from the cities to shelter with relatives and friends in the country. The *Montreal Gazette* appealed for calm in an issue reduced to a half-sheet because many of its workers were absent. There were many who criticized those who fled and warned them that they were increasing their own danger by getting out of touch with the doctors. Lord Aylmer, however, approved of flight. He thought that reducing the numbers of people in the cities would reduce the incidence of the disease. In fact, the flight from the towns actually helped to spread the disease into the nearby communities and those closest to

Quebec and Montreal were soon affected. The *habitants* refused to come to town with produce and the price of food began to rise.[7]

The panic was particularly hard on the immigrants who inspired suspicion and fear. River traffic was disrupted at first by the flight of the boatmen and then by the restrictions imposed by the magistrates in Upper Canada. In Quebec, the board of health opened a camp on the Plains of Abraham which housed immigrants and local residents who were moved while the board cleaned their houses. The camp was frequently overcrowded but it did offer some shelter. In Montreal, the board of health seized the Emigrant Society's sheds for a cholera hospital and many immigrants were forced to bivouac on the beaches. Conditions were at their worst in the short period when the boatmen had returned to work before travel to Upper Canada reopened. The distress would have been greater had cholera broken out a few days earlier. In the week ending 9 June 10,000 immigrants arrived. When the panic was at its height, the number of immigrants reaching Grosse Isle was less than 2,500 per week and the demand on resources was reduced.[8]

The panic began to subside as the death toll fell. Once the first explosive phase of the epidemic was over, and it became clear that cholera was not going to destroy everyone in its path, life resumed a more normal pattern. Toward the end of June a correspondent, writing from Quebec to York (Toronto), noted that there were still two of three cases per day among the people he knew and that 'the deaths among the lower orders are perhaps 10 to 15 a day.' The figures were uncertain because the papers deliberately played down the numbers to reduce alarm. There was, however, a noticeable change in mood from the first days when 'the state of things was really frightful and calculated to unman the ... strongest.' Few people could afford to give up their trade or profession and they had to adjust to life in towns now suffering from a stubborn and persistent epidemic. By early July, life had returned to normal sufficiently that men resumed political activity which they had abandoned earlier. Lord Aylmer ruefully noted that an end had come to the lull which had begun when 'the cholera appear[ed] to give full occupation to the minds of those who were busily engaged at the period of its appearance in fitting up meetings concerned with the Events of the recent Elections of Montreal.[9] Soon cholera itself would become a political issue.

With hundreds of the poor population falling sick, the need for hospitals became acute. In the first days of the epidemic, Quebec began to send cholera patients to the Emigrant Hospital which was expanded as the board of health had planned. The neighbours again petitioned in large numbers to plead for an end to the practice. They claimed that their neighbourhood was in danger from both the hospital and the victims who had to be carried through the streets of the town to reach the hospital. The *Quebec Mercury* agreed with the protest and said the city was being disheartened by the sight of the sick being carried into the hospital and dead being carried out. The alternative which the board and many other people preferred was to open small hospitals in the worst hit areas. That would still produce complaints from the neighbours but it would spare the city from the danger associated with carrying cholera victims through the streets. The problem with this solution was that prejudice against the cholera hospitals was so strong that people feared to rent their buildings to the board. An owner of two buildings near the East India Wharf, for example, refused to rent them to the board 'on any terms whatsoever' because 'public opinion has been strongly announced against making choice of such a locality.' After a search the board did succeed in renting buildings at a brewery at Pres-de-Ville. It faced new protests and claims for compensation from the neighbours but was able to open the hospital under the charge of Drs O'Callaghan and A. van Iffland. Later, it opened a hospital in tents in St John Suburb.[10]

In Montreal no plans had been made for hospitals before 9 June. In the first panic of the epidemic the board of health seized the emigrant sheds at St Anne Common. One of the sheds had no floor and for days patients lay 'on straw ... exposed indiscriminately to the open windows and doors – men, women and children, the convalescent, dying and the dead laid in an irregu-

lar line along the sides of the building.' According to another
commentator the hospital offered its patients only the chance to
'die beneath a roof instead of the canopy of heaven.' In the second week of the epidemic a cholera hospital was opened on rue
St Denis. It was a hastily constructed shed 'closed in with rough
deals, with here and there a hole to serve as a window and in
most cases straw for bedding ... they might be more properly
called dying houses than hospitals.' The Montreal General Hospital maintained its refusal to admit cholera patients. The man-
agers also refused a request to open a shed for convalescent
patients on its grounds because they did not think they could
find a full-time attendant.[11]

In both Quebec and Montreal, especially in the first days of the
epidemic, the hospitals were swamped by patients and came
near to chaos. Towards the end of the epidemic a committee of
doctors in Quebec produced a report on the operation of the
hospitals. The committee had been set up during a feud with the
board and it blamed the conditions it described on inadequate
preparations. The doctors claimed that, early in the epidemic, the
Quebec Emigrant Hospital became so crowded and filthy that
the doctors had to wear clogs as they walked the wards. Dr William Lyons resigned from his post because of interference from
the board, and the running of the hospital passed into the hands
of a matron who abused the staff and robbed the dead. Dr Van
Iffland recorded his experiences, which suggest some of the difficulties hospital staff faced, especially early in the epidemic. For
the first two weeks he worked without taking off his boots, and
'when he did, the flesh adhered to the sole leather.' Overwhelmed by the numbers of patients, van Iffland found it almost
impossible to keep the staff at work. Many left after a day preferring to sacrifice their pay than to work in the hospital another
hour.

In Montreal conditions were always worse than in Quebec; it
was late June before any adequate bedding was provided for the
cholera hospitals and they remained under the supervision of
part-time, non-resident, physicians. It is hardly surprising that
people refused to go to hospital – one man's relatives refused to

let him go 'being able to pay.' The Quebec board's claim that two out of three cases went to the hospital must have been an exaggeration.[12] No one went willingly to the cholera hospitals. They were intended to serve only those severely ill whose homes offered inadequate shelter or who were a threat to the community.

For the less severely ill, but poor, victims some extraordinary provision had to be made. The boards of both Quebec and Montreal set up depots marked with yellow flags where medicine could be had. The health wardens of Quebec were given medicine to distribute 'to the poorer classes.' The resident physicians appointed by the board were expected to visit the sick poor. These men were quickly overworked and sometimes grew careless. Dr Joseph Painchaud complained to the Quebec Board of Health that when he had asked Dr Hall to visit a sick sailor at 11 o'clock one night, the resident physician had refused. Painchaud claimed that 'many hundreds of poor persons have died of cholera in this manner.' The board agreed that Hall's conduct was 'reprehensible' and pointed out that physicians were 'bound to visit without delay all patients labouring under cholera when reported to them.' This statement suggests the board thought there was an obligation on all physicians to offer help during the epidemic. Many did, some more reluctantly than others. Early in the epidemic, for example, Dr Drolet of St Roche wrote to the Quebec board to say that he had been overwhelmed by poor patients. His practice was suffering and he asked the board for an indemnity, failing which he would 'attend to nothing but my private practice.' The board could offer him no money and could only appeal to him to 'continue to give his charitable assistance to the poor.'[13]

The few medical men employed by the cities, and the charity work performed by private doctors, could not meet the demands for help during the epidemic. In normal times many people looked to the apothecary for advice and many did so now. Dr Robert Nelson, acting as prosecuting member of the Montreal Board of Health, ordered apothecaries to stop selling medicines, prophylactics, or nostrums 'for cholera or otherwise.' He claimed that the advice and prescriptions given out by apothecaries had made some people who were suffering only from fear 'really ill.' The early days of a major epidemic were not the best time for Nelson to take up the old battle between doctor and apothecary. The press rounded on him, one paper accusing him of 'an act of unparalleled tyranny ... at a time when physicians cannot attend the half, we might believe, nay fifth of the sick in our city.' A correspondent writing to *La Minerve* pointed out that many people waited four or five hours for a doctor to come and that others preferred to take the advice of an experienced druggist over that of a young fellow just out of school. The regulation would be particularly hard on country districts where there were rarely two doctors to a parish. Others took up the theme that doctors were baffled by the disease but still claimed expertise in treatment. There was criticism of one doctor who was alleged to have told patients to take one opium pill and do 'absolutely nothing' but to do it under medical advice at £5 per visit.[14] Nelson's regulation could not be enforced and he brought no one to court.

If the doctor did not come and there was no money even for an apothecary people turned to their neighbours or to the clergy. In Quebec, the residents of St Roche and St John petitioned for a reward for Jacques Hamel, a blacksmith who had given up his forge to help cholera victims. He had worked among the indigent and the working classes. The board gave him nothing.[15] There were no doubt other men and women who did what Hamel had done. The clergy, too, did what they could to help the sick. During the epidemic, the seminaries were closed to free the clergy for this work.

The search for help and comfort led many of the poor of Montreal to Stephen Ayres. He became the most famous of all the unofficial helpers of the poor and was known as 'the cholera doctor.' His recipes against cholera passed into folklore. Ayres had a showman's flair but he sold nothing and gave his services freely. That added to the air of mystery which surrounded him and which he was content not to dispel. He had arrived in Montréal, soon after the epidemic began, on foot and leading two thin horses. Some observers said that he looked like a gipsy with a long black beard, long hair tied behind, and a pair of shrewd and bright eyes. His clothes were shabby, his coat ragged, and his hat worn. He immediately began to treat victims of cholera with a remedy made of lard, charcoal, and maple syrup and with massage to ease the cramps which were one of the most painful results of the disease. News quickly spread that he was treating the sick and refusing any payment. Within days, he was spoken of as a saint and large crowds followed him as he moved from house to house. A new rumour began – he would leave the city on 29 June, taking the cholera with him.[16]

He did not leave, but continued to work among the sick. In July he became a more controversial figure, denounced by medical men and caught up in a quarrel with the church. Ayres became involved with Joseph Lancaster, a Quaker educator and controversialist, who began to act as his agent. Ayres opened an office next to Lancaster's house at the corner of Craig and Bleury streets. There, Ayres offered to treat all 'without regard to name, origin, party or religion' and without charge every day from 8 am to 7 pm. Doctors called him a charlatan but that did his reputation no harm. He was on more dangerous ground when Lancaster involved him in his feud with the Catholic church.

The quarrel arose from Ayres's visit to the Indian reserve at Caughnawaga. There had been a severe epidemic among the Indians with 70 deaths from 187 cases since 18 June. Lieutenant-Colonel William MacKay had visited the reserve, reported it 'generally clean and neat and remarkably well ventilated' and had left the missionary, Father Marcoux, instructions on how to treat cholera. Shortly afterwards, Ayres arrived at the reserve, allegedly by invitation of the chiefs, and paid a short visit. On Ayres's return to Montreal, Lancaster published a pamphlet, praising his work among the sick at Caughnawaga, which incensed Father Marcoux. The missionary denied that Ayres had had any part in stemming the disease at the reservation. Lancaster's reply was to stage a parade in Montreal on 3 August featuring Ayres supported by Indians carrying British, American, and other flags in a salute to the cholera doctor. After this bizarre display, *La Minerve* warned Ayres that his association with Lancaster and the attacks on the church would lose him public confidence.[17] His popularity, however, survived these indiscretions and he remained an object of devotion, curiosity, and mystery until he left the city after the epidemic.

Mrs Moodie saw him on her arrival in Montreal and thought, from the shrewdness of his eye, that he was a Yankee. Her surmise was correct. In a petition to Lord Aylmer after the epidemic, Ayres privately unravelled the mystery which had enfolded him during the summer. He claimed to be a licensed physician from New Jersey. He had been travelling to Montreal on non-medical business but on his arrival the 'distress and mourning' which he found persuaded him to abandon his business and help the sick. He claimed to have cured eight of ten patients, although he excluded from his reckoning those too weak from hunger and disease, those who had been patients of other doctors, and those 'already given up by other doctors.' Some patients whom he had cured of cholera died of hunger and exhaustion. Certainly Ayres sounded like a regular physician when making up his statistics. He did not claim to have found an infallible cure but he did argue that his 'visit to this City is generally acknowledged to have dissipated panic and restored confidence.' He now asked for compensation for himself and his 'death daring assistant' for their work in Montreal and among the Indians. He got nothing. It would be hard not to credit Ayres with helping to dissipate some of the panic in Montreal. He was a man of mystery who seemed to have a remedy for a disease wrapped in mystery. No one made anything like this impact on the popular imagination in later years when cholera had become more familiar and a little less feared.[18]

Cholera remained a mystery even as people adjusted to living in cities riddled by the disease. The months of the epidemic were marked by debates over the nature of the disease and the mechanism by which it chose its victims. The Montreal Board of

Health considered the question of physical causes in the spread of cholera. 'Perhaps there are few other cities,' it reported, 'more exposed to the operation of all the causes which create or aggravate such disease. Low and marshy grounds, stagnant waters filled with all the elements of miasma (pestilential effluvia), in circumstances most favourable to their malignant influences meet us in every part of this city, and even in its very centre, while in many of the vacant lots we find substances in a state of putrescence, and acted on by all the fiercest power of a burning sun.'[19] Montreal was dirty and it seemed, at first, that those closest to the dirtiest parts of town were the most likely victims. The first victims all seemed to have lived in squalor and filth.

There were some difficulties, however, with this explanation of how the disease arose and spread. The obvious one was that similar conditions in other years had not produced cholera. That was an objection which sanitary reformers would hear again in future years. Even if one accepted a connection between dirt and the disease, how did cholera choose its victims from among those living, for example, in Roache's boarding house? In what ways had the victims predisposed themselves to the disease? The boards of health, in their instructions to citizens, emphasized cleanliness and moderation as the keys to health. People were urged to maintain their usual diets, avoid too much fresh fruit and raw vegetables, be sparing in their use of alcohol, and keep themselves and their clothing clean and dry. It was good advice and in looking for predisposing causes people looked to see if it had been ignored. Dr Skey noted that the first victims in Quebec had been mainly among immigrants, sailors, and poor Canadians. The virulence of the disease was to be expected because 'Quebec at this season abounds in an enormous number of persons who from a combination of moral and physical causes, were just of the description likely to suffer the extreme violence of the disease.'[20]

Because so many of the early victims came from among the poor it was easy for those better off to slide toward moral judgments when asking how victims had rendered themselves liable to the disease. The Irish passion for drink, the French Canadian's love of raw cucumbers, the lower orders' apparent pleasure in squalor and filth suggested moral failings. These comfortable judgments were shaken when the disease began to claim victims in the higher ranks of society. The deaths of Louis Lagueux, MPP, and Judge Taschereau made a great impact in Lower Canada, and demanded an explanation of deaths among those as Dr Skey said, 'less likely to suffer than one would have imagined.' The list of predisposing causes began to lengthen to include the personality of the victim. Perhaps fear predisposed one to the disease. Judge Taschereau was said to have been fearful of the disease, but Lagueux had been resolute, 'boasting ... that people should stand it *en grenadier*. At midnight he was attacked and at seven this morning he was a corpse.'

The idea that fear predisposed the victim to cholera was current for many years and each epidemic brought reminders to stay calm and resolute. It was hard to do so when as the same writer pointed out 'a thousand causes seem to be the first source of the disease. A sprain like a clerk at Hardie's while fitting on a shoe, a little cold caught by the falling off of the bed clothes, an alarm such as in the case of Lemond tinsmith Champlain St. who after hearing a long frightening sermon at the Weslyan church walked down and met the hearse in Champlain street. His feelings were shocked, a pain in the breast followed, at 12 o'clock he was in the last stage of the disease.'[21]

There was no clear-cut moral or psychological explanation of how the disease chose its victims which could offer a guide to safety. The temptation to look for moral failings among poor victims, however, continued to influence the better off for some years.

Boards of health, once the disease was upon their communities, had to concentrate on removing what might be the physical causes of the disease. In Quebec, barrels of tar were given to the poor to be burned outside their homes between 6 and 10 pm each day. All residents were asked to burn 'anti-contagion combustibles.' In Montreal, the artillery fired a barrage to clear the air and the board arranged to burn rosin each night. The blazing barrels and columns of smoke added to the dread in the cities as each night fell. While tar and rosin might improve the air the best solution was to remove the filth which was thought to be poisoning the atmosphere.

The Quebec Board of Health showed vigour in its efforts to clean the houses of the poor and the streets of the city. Meeting daily, and sometimes twice a day, through June and July, on alternate days in August, and less frequently into November, the board had time to hear reports on the state of the city. The reports of the health wardens were catalogues of overcrowded houses, of rooms sublet until dozens of people were crammed into one building, of buildings reopened by their landlords after being closed by order of the board, and of immigrants squatting in derelict buildings. The board heard complaints of nuisances in front of buildings, behind houses, and under houses. They heard complaints against the location and operation of slaughter-houses and against those who kept pigs and cows in houses within the city. They heard protests from people who objected to the actions of the health wardens as they made their inspections and tried to enforce the regulations.

People from all levels of society resented the work of the health wardens as they entered houses and pointed out sanitary failings. There were some health regulations that touched on very emotional questions and these were the most deeply resented. From 14 June until the end of the epidemic the bells did not toll for the dead in Quebec. The board feared that the constant sound would depress the living. There were other regulations which disrupted the customary courtesies to the dead. Those who died on the river were to be sewn into tarpaulins and dropped into the water at least twenty miles from major settlements. Those who died in town were to be buried within six hours if they died during the day, or twelve hours if they died at night. There was no time allowed for mourning or holding wakes and resentment was very high. The health wardens occasionally had to call on the constables to help them enforce this regulation. The widespread fear of premature burial added to the resistance to these measures. Those who could not afford to pay the $4 or $8 fee to hire a hearse saw their relatives carried off by the board of health's carters to be buried, without prayers, in one of the cholera grounds.[22] Burial in unconsecrated ground provoked a number of protests.

The carters employed by the board of health appear to have had great power. Alfred Perry recalled that his father fell ill with cholera soon after the family arrived in Quebec. The father 'was sinking under the disease [when] a man with a cart came to the house and insisted he was dead, and, in spite of my mother's remonstrances, carried him away, put him in the cart and conveyed him to the Point St. Charles where a trench had been dug for the burial of immigrants.' Mrs Perry followed, still protesting that her husband was not dead. He was just about to be flung into the trench when he moved and was found to be alive. While the party was returning to town, Mr Perry died. The only way Mrs Perry could persuade another carter to take her husband's body to the English burial ground was to give him the suit from the corpse.[23]

Callous carters, an absence of customary courtesies, fear of premature burial, and interment without prayers in unconsecrated ground all added to the horrors of the epidemic. The horror could provoke anger and violence. In the rural community of St Eustache, the magistrates ordered that no person dying of cholera was to be buried in the plot which lay in the centre of the village. Two people who died were buried as ordered outside the village. Many of the villagers were greatly upset by this action and some days later 'a tumultuous assembly took place, when horrid to relate, they proceeded to dig up the bodies ... the putrified carcasses were placed on open carts, and carried in savage triumph through the village, communicating a stench intolerable as they passed along.' The corpses were left in the sun for hours despite the protests of the curé and the magistrates.[24] This was not the only case of its kind in 1832 and it suggests the depth of fear and anger which could be provoked when health regulations were seen to be arbitrary.

Attempts to control drinking, while not as profoundly disturbing as the regulations on burial, also provoked opposition.

The whole question of drink and drunkenness of course touched on the issue of the connection between moral failings and disease. Some reformers saw the epidemic as an opportunity to make their point. The temperance societies claimed that they lost very few members during the epidemic. There seemed to be solid arguments for a link between drink and cholera. The Montreal Board of Health noted that Monday was the day on which most cases were reported. This they put down to the 'excesses ... too frequently committed by the lower orders and labouring classes, on the evenings of Saturday and Sunday.' The *Montreal Gazette* noted an increase in the number of cases on 20 August and linked it to a cruise on the *Canadian Patriot* the Sunday before. That cruise had been 'a bacchanalia which culminated in a general melee involving hundreds on the wharf on Sunday night.'[25]

The boards of health had decided that some control of drinking was necessary even before this kind of direct link had been claimed. Montreal regulated taverns but the Quebec Board of Health went further and ordered all taverns shut on 16 June. It was an order which met widespread resistance. The magistrates began to hear cases against tavern-keepers, some of whom were fined and jailed. The tavern-keepers objected that while they were prosecuted and 'exposed to ruin' the grocers were still allowed to sell liquor. The board then ordered the grocers not to sell liquor in quantities less than two gallons. This regulation was intended to advance temperance by preventing sales by the glass to the poor. Both the English and the French press objected to this new order because it would prevent the poor from buying liquor in the medicinal quantities which doctors were prescribing – the public health required the poor to have access to liquor in moderation. In the face of these arguments and of the widespread opposition, the Quebec board virtually gave up its attempts to control the drinking of the poor. In the second week of July it repealed its regulations, insisting only that there be no drunkenness and that taverns shut at 9 pm.[26]

The boards felt that their efforts to improve the health of their communities were hindered by public opposition and by their own inadequate legal powers. The boards of Quebec, Montreal, and Trois-Rivières all asked the executive to allow them to use extraordinary procedures against those who broke the regulations. Lord Aylmer refused to accept any deviation from normal procedure. One difficulty that arose from his decision was that prosecutions for breaches of regulations were difficult to bring. The boards of health used private lawyers to bring actions for summary judgments before the justice of the peace. The law officers of the Crown objected to this and argued that cases should be prosecuted by one of the law officers. When the Montreal Board of Health resolved that the use of law officers was 'totally inexpedient' they were reprimanded for 'a want of respect to the Representative of His Majesty' whose instructions were not to be called inexpedient. In August, a prosecution by the Quebec Board of Health was declared illegal by the solicitor-general because it had not been brought by the solicitor-general or the attorney-general who alone had the right of action. When the board protested that the usual procedures were slow, expensive, and unsuited to an emergency, the most that the solicitor-general would concede was that a 'professional gentleman' could be appointed to act for the law officers. The executive insisted that all cases not urgent were to be referred for approval before being prosecuted.[27] Under these narrow constraints the boards did what they could but the courts played a small part in enforcing regulations.

The work of the boards was made no easier by conflicts with the medical profession. Doctors were willing to work for the boards, and there were always more applicants than positions. The doctors, however, were sensitive to lay interference in their duties. Dr Lyons resigned from the Emigrant Hospital for that reason. His successor, Dr Mills, was involved in an altercation with a member of the Quebec Board of Health which illustrates some of the difficulties that could arise between board members and their appointees. Dr A. Harkness, a Presbyterian minister and member of the board, found a patient bleeding from a vein from which the bandages had slipped. Harkness went in search of Mills to rebandage the wound. The hospital porter reported that Harkness had found Mills at tea and that Mills said he

would come when he had finished his tea. Harkness 'then said
Dr. Mills should obey his orders as he was a member of the Board
of Health ... the Devil take you and your tea, and said by (something), I forget what oath he took, that Dr Mills should not take tea
there tomorrow Evening.' At the patient's bedside another argument developed and Dr Harkness waved his stick at Dr Mills.
The board of health told Harkness to be more circumspect on
future visits to the hospital but he replied that the board had no
power to censure him.[28]

In this case right lay with the medical doctor but the Quebec
board also had difficulties with Dr Tessier, the health officer. He
was charged with failure to perform his duties before and during
the epidemic. In September the board asked Lord Aylmer to sus-
pend Tessier, and accused him of giving the board faulty information which caused prosecutions to fail, neglecting his duties,
ignoring regulations of the board, and giving certificates of
health to outward-bound ships for a fee of £1 or £2. The board
believed that he deserved to be dismissed on the last charge
alone, for making a private gain from his public office. Tessier's
defence provides a glimpse at the difficulties the summer of 1832
brought. He was required to inspect hundreds of ships and
thousands of immigrants some of whom did not welcome him.
On one occasion, he wrote, he was driven away from a vessel
when the passengers and crew poured dirty water into his boat.
'The people continuing to pour water over my head, I conceived
the insult to be intentional, and I left the vessel.' His duties were,
he claimed, 'the most laborious, the most dangerous and the
most invidious of all those engaged in the Health Department,'
but he was judged to have neglected them and he was dismissed
in February 1833. When the House of Assembly called for the
papers in the case, Aylmer refused to forward them as the dismissal was 'in the exercise of the undoubted prerogative of the
Crown.'[29]

The board had difficulties not only with the health officer but
also with the profession at large. The board required doctors to
report cases of cholera in order to keep a check on the progress of
the disease and to arrange that victims' houses be disinfected.

Doctors often failed to supply the information under the press of work. When the board was criticized for inefficiency it tried to share the blame with the doctors by telling them to conform with its regulations. To enforce this point it took two doctors to court for failing to report deaths. One case was dismissed as there was no evidence that the patient had died of cholera. The other case was set over. These prosecutions enraged many doctors. Drs Holmes and William Marsden called a meeting which attracted fourteen doctors. They appointed a committee to publish the facts about the board of health and to watch over their professional interests while the board was in existence. The meeting also set up a defence fund. The board continued to criticize doctors and in September brought cases against a doctor and surgeon which were dismissed on the grounds that there was no requirement under the quarantine act that reports be made. After the epidemic, the doctors' committee published a report critical of the work of the board.[30]

The Montreal board had difficulties with Dr Robert Nelson. Nelson felt insulted because the government paid money for the expenses of the board directly to the chairman rather than to Nelson, who was health commissioner. The money could only be spent, however, in the form of cheques drawn on the health commissioner. In August he refused to pay a bill which he thought was an unnecessary expense. The board resolved that his action put it 'in the preposterous situation of subjection to its officers.' In September, Nelson brought the work of the board to a halt by refusing to have the board's money transferred to his account. Lord Aylmer had to intervene to end this impasse.[31]

The quarrels between doctors and the boards, and the boards' limited power, made them less effective than they might otherwise have been. The boards met hostility and indifference in their attempts to enforce their regulations but they were criticized also for not enforcing them effectively. The critics demanded action.

A voluntary movement was started in Montreal to supplement the work of the board of health. Soon after the board had seized the emigrant sheds to use as a hospital, a public meeting was called to discuss the problems of the immigrants. It heard reports of immigrants dying on the wharfs and in the open fields. Peter McGill reported that his offer to build sheds in the suburbs of St Ann had been resisted by people in the neighbourhood. The meeting set up a Committee for Emigrant and Sanitary Purposes, thus establishing a significant link between the problems. A public subscription was opened for the relief of immigrants. At this time, the ban on travel to Upper Canada was in effect and the committee asked Aylmer for money and the use of tents or government barracks to house the immigrants held up in Montreal. The executive suggested that the £500 allocated to the Montreal Emigrant Society should be applied to the relief work and it sent a further £300 for supplies for widows and orphans. It was also prepared to give £150 to any society established to relieve dependants of residents.[32]

With this support the committee set to work. It had two sheds built at Ogilvie's Point on land owned by the Grey Nuns. It rented a store in town to house immigrants. The residents of Griffintown in St Ann objected to the sheds being built there by gentlemen who did not live in the neighbourhood. They cited the danger of bringing dirty and possibly diseased people to a spot near the city water-supply and close to the point from which boats left for Upper Canada. The committee ignored the protests. By the time traffic to Upper Canada had reopened early in July the committee had spent nearly £1500 of the £2000 subscribed for relief.[33]

The committee also offered to help the board of health enforce its sanitary regulations. The board was glad to accept this offer and also the help of committees established in the suburb of St Lawrence and the East and West wards. The volunteers offered to act as health wardens and to relieve some of the strain on the paid wardens. The movement attracted a number of men from the 'middling' ranks of Montreal society and it put some of them into closer contact than they had ever been before with poorer Montrealers. Much of what they saw shocked them deeply. Benjamin Workman, editor of the Canadian Courant, reported after a week as health warden that 'never till now were we aware of the extreme filthiness of the houses and yards occupied by the poorer classes.' The *Montreal Gazette's* editor, on reading the reports of the wardens, was 'harrowed at the frightful details which they contain and certainly could scarcely imagine that such accumulated filth could remain in the city after what had been so repeatedly urged on the necessity of cleanliness ... Thirteen deaths have occurred in some houses and yet no cleaning or purifying has followed.' The paper soon after reported that 'immense quantities of filth and manure' had been removed from Montreal.[34]

The discovery of the conditions in which some of the poor lived merely confirmed prejudices already held about their character. The voluntary health wardens, in fear for their own safety, could act brutally. In the East Ward they thought that some people were 'refractory' about cleaning their houses. They therefore brought up a fire engine and 'played it into the houses in question, till they were thoroughly drenched from the garret to the cellar.' The action may have relieved their frustrations but it was not a very constructive contribution to public health. Bullying and officiousness might be used against the anonymous poor, although the wardens were taking chances when they did so; but it would not work against better established members of society. John Campbell, a bookseller, wrote to the *Canadian Courant* to complain of grossly improper behaviour by a warden, James Young, whom he had ordered out of his house following a sharp disagreement. The health wardens' most useful work was the providing of evidence which allowed a number of prosecutions to be brought in a regular manner in August.[35]

The sanitary committee helped to overcome some of the failures of the Montreal Board of Health. Its campaign against dirt could not solve all the sanitary problems of the city. The limits to what could be done were seen in the case of the Craig Street creek. The creek ran through a district badly hit by cholera and the board ordered an investigation in response to public complaints. Dr Robert Nelson reported that there was a 'strongly offensive' odour coming from the creek at night that might be reduced by spreading lime, although that alone would not solve the problem. The board did nothing. The residents along the creek then formed the St Lawrence suburb sanitary committee to deal with the problem. In August, a public meeting considered the state of the creek. They heard that it was lined with tanneries, soap factories, and houses, all of which dumped rubbish in the creek. The flow of water was rarely strong enough to carry it all away. The best solution was to cover over the creek. That was also an expensive solution, and Peter McGill pointed out that there were problems which he, as a magistrate, saw in adopting the proposal. It was a big decision which ought to be left for the city government which would be set up by the charter due in 1833. McGill felt that the city government should, in any case, not adopt the proposal because it was too expensive and because it would use public money to benefit only one part of the city. He felt that the only acceptable way of financing the scheme was by a public subscription, but he thought it would fail because of the many demands already put on private funds. After hearing that speech, the meeting did the only thing it could do, and appointed a committee.[36] The Craig Street creek continued to fester for years. Public attitudes, the structure of local government, and the problem of expense all played a part in the question of sanitary reform.

In Quebec, the voluntary movement was slower to begin and it was late August before some of the citizens took up the idea. Mr Justice Kerr chaired a public meeting on 20 August which established the Quebec Sanitary Committee. Within three days, nearly 200 volunteers had been named to serve in the various wards. A further group was named on 1 September. The volunteers were told how to disinfect houses with chloride of lime. They were to work with the health wardens on their rounds and were also to report any lapses from duty by the salaried wardens.[37] The late organization of the movement meant that the volunteers played a lesser role in Quebec than they did in Montreal.

If sanitary investigation was a new line for volunteers, relief of widows and orphans was a traditional object of private charity.

The epidemic greatly increased the need for this relief. Widows of men well established in the community could be left in poverty. Mrs Green, for example, whose husband had been for twenty years clerk of the peace and seven years clerk of the court at Quebec, had to petition for part of his salary as a pension after his death from cholera. For the dependants of immigrants and the poor, things could be desperate. The emigrant agent was able to arrange for some widows to return to Britain, but most families which lost their father and husband had to be helped in Canada. Many of these survivors had few or no resources and once the early panic had died down the question of caring for them was raised in the press. The government had allowed the Quebec Board of Health £150 to buy 'blankets, clothing or necessaries of life' but some more permanent solution had to be found. The clergy led the movement and *La Minerve* reported early in July that in the parish of St Roche not a single Catholic orphan remained unplaced. The rector of Quebec called a meeting on 5 July which set up a committee to raise funds for the relief of widows and orphans and to open an asylum for orphans who could not be placed.[38]

A committee of ladies was established to help the Beneficent Society created at that meeting. It prepared lists of widows and orphans with the help of the local clergy and restricted its relief to survivors with children. Those eligible for relief could choose to go back to Britain, to go on to Upper Canada, or to stay in Lower Canada where they would receive a weekly allowance through the clergy. Orphans would be placed, with their surviving parent's consent, with respectable families of their own denomination 'either gratis or on paying what the discretion of the persons undertaking to place them shall suggest.' The society's services were badly needed, for by the end of July it was helping nearly 200 widows and almost 350 children.[39]

In Montreal, efforts to help the survivors opened in controversy. A number of newspapers made an issue of the fact that Louis-Joseph Papineau refused to subscribe to a relief fund for orphans. The *Canadian Courant* raged 'Hear this Canadians! The fattest pensioner of the Province, who receives nearly £1000 per annum for doing almost nothing, refuses to give a farthing to relieve the starving, perishing orphan because forsooth as we opine men opposed to him in politics took part in this work of charity ... Irishmen is this the man for whose party tool you lately were so violent, who now refuses your perishing country-man a farthing of relief?' Fortunately for the widows and orphans relief work did not collapse in feuding and partisan-ship. The immediate stimulus to action was an appeal from the orphan asylum for funds to hire a house to accommodate the overflow from the 60 to 70 children jamming its building. The seminary and the Grey Nuns who normally supported the poor and housed the younger orphans were strained beyond capacity – at least 150 women had been widowed in the epide-mic by the first week of July.

The asylum was intended to help residents of Montreal. To meet the needs of immigrants the Montreal Ladies Benevolent Society was set up late in August. The ladies expressed the hope that 'a Female Society, whatever may be their deficiency in other qualifications, will be enabled to devote more time, while they bring no less zeal and affection to the work than one composed of the other sex.' Having made their modest protestations, the ladies soon laid down some strict rules. They would help only those in real need and then for the shortest time possible. All who could work were excluded from aid to avoid 'affording un-merited indulgence to the indolent and improvident.' Those who were sheltered must work and those given support would be given goods, not cash. An asylum would be opened but residents would be dismissed if inquiry justified such action, and the insti-tution would be connected with 'a soup kitchen and a Register Officer for the encouragement of domestic servants, a class so important to every community.'

The asylum opened in September to deal with a temporary need. The ladies carried out investigations of those who applied for indoor or outdoor relief and 'committees of Ladies were appointed to visit their abodes of wretchedness, and went for the purpose of detecting fraud and imposture, as well as to select the most worthy object' for charity. The committees exposed 'mendacity and idleness' and their investigations encouraged some applicants to work and others to leave the city. Despite all this care and selection, the society was quickly in financial trouble and it advertised in October for 'broken victuals' with which to feed those who came for outdoor relief. People who sent their scraps to the society were assured that any widow who came for help had to send her children to school and take them to church each Sunday.

The asylum operated throughout the winter despite continued financial strain which forced it to cut off outdoor relief in March. It did not succeed in placing all orphans with families and began to fill a permanent need in the city. Rather than close down, as had originally been planned, the asylum expanded and began to operate an infants' school. It drew funds from donations, legislative grants, and fund-raising efforts, and was still in operation over a decade later. When the new asylum went into operation, the Montreal orphan asylum confined its aid to children who had lost both parents, and housed between 40 and 70 of them during the winter. The children were 'supported on a plan at once frugal, healthful and abundant' and they received 'daily moral, religious and mental instruction, suited to their age.' The combined efforts to help widows and orphans in Quebec and Montreal gave some support to approximately 250 widows and about 700 orphans selected rigorously from among the most desperate cases.[40]

Cholera spread into the smaller towns and villages of Lower Canada as the summer passed. In the 1830s most travellers moved by water and the disease followed the river and canal system toward Upper Canada. The first towns affected were staging posts on the river. Trois-Rivières had its first cases four days after the disease was confirmed at Montreal. At Chambly, immigrants travelling on the canal brought the disease six days after Montreal's outbreak. Away from the river, the disease was spread by people fleeing from the cities, by residents returning from visits to infected locations, and on the Craig Road by immigrants passing on their way to the United States. By the end of the summer nearly all parts of the province had seen some cholera cases.

The communities of Lower Canada tried to protect themselves against the disease. At Trois-Rivières the board of health, established by a public meeting held when news of cholera at Quebec reached the town, set up an elaborate local quarantine. Boats could land only those passengers bound for Trois-Rivières itself and they had to be examined by the health commissioner. The quays were fenced off and local residents barred from them. Health wardens were appointed to enforce the regulations and to keep the quays clean. The board proposed appointing two resident physicians and a health commissioner and planned to set up a cholera hospital. These preparations were on too grand a scale for the government at Quebec to approve and it insisted that they be reduced before granting the board £200. Despite its efforts, the town had an outbreak of cholera with 32 cases, 16 of them fatal, between 13 June and 10 July. Yet for years afterwards it was widely believed that Trois-Rivières had saved itself from the disease. The provincial government itself seemed to be ignorant of the epidemic when it complained, late in August, of the level of expenditure by the board.[41]

Some villages tried to isolate themselves from any contact with infected towns. At Baie St Paul, unarmed pickets were posted to turn back river craft that had visited Quebec or Grosse Isle. At Murray Bay, the health committee shut a man out of church and ordered the villagers to have no contact with him after he had visited Quebec. The Reverend Mr Alexander, of Leeds on the Craig Road, wrote to the Quebec Board of Health to explain the fears of residents along the road. The people of Leeds saw immigrants and the poor from Quebec flocking 'to their settlements with the hope of being enabled to live in idleness by preying upon the industrious. [Their] life and conversation spread around them a moral contagion more fatal to society than that which endangers the bodily health of those within their influence.' Alexander admitted, however, that it would 'border upon inhumanity' to

bar immigrants from sheltering in the villages. The board of
health could do nothing to protect Leeds from moral contagion
but it did send medicine for 50 people.[42]

The boards at Quebec and Montreal gave help to nearby communities. As the summer passed, the government became increasingly concerned with the cost of fighting the epidemic.
Most of the money appropriated by the house went to pay the
costs of Grosse Isle and the Quebec board. It seemed obvious that
some limit had to be put on the expenditure in the smaller
centres. As the epidemic spread, it was met by setting up subsidiary boards of health, supervised by the Quebec or Montreal
boards, and forbidden to spend more than £300. The main
boards tried hard to keep the subsidiary boards' expenses within
the limit.[43]

Cholera had appeared in June. On 1 October, Montreal again
issued clean bills of health to departing vessels. In the main
centres it had disappeared about mid-October, but it was still
present in some areas in November.

The human cost of the epidemic is difficult to calculate as all
records were incomplete and inaccurate. Returns to the Quebec
Board of Health give a figure of 3,451 dead. Robert Nelson estimated that 4,000 died in Montreal and district alone. A petition to
the House of Assembly claimed that the disease had 'slain about
TWELVE THOUSAND victims in Lower Canada!!' A.C. Buchanan,
on the other hand, declared that 'the total extent of deaths
among the Emigrant Population of this year in both Provinces
did not exceed 2350.'[44]

Recent studies by social historians of Lower Canada suggest
the impact that the epidemic had in the province. The death
rate rose to 45.7 per thousand in the province, and to 74 per
thousand in Montreal and 82 per thousand in Quebec. This
compared with an average annual mortality of 37 per thousand.
Contemporaries were right when they said that these rates exceeded those of any European city. The surviving evidence,
however, suggests that contemporaries were wrong when they
assumed that the most severely affected group were the most

destitute. The group which appears to have been hardest hit is artisans living above the level of absolute want. French Canadians were severely affected and suffered more than did the Irish Catholics. Outside the towns, the districts hardest hit were those near Montreal and on the route to the United States.[45]

A disaster on this scale was bound to provoke a political reaction. This was especially true in Lower Canada where the year had opened in political controversy and the violence of the Montreal by-election. Lord Aylmer had noted how quickly political activity resumed once the first cholera panic declined. He soon found himself criticized for failing to call the assembly into session to ask for funds for the boards of health. The work actually done was criticized and the boards denounced as sources of executive patronage. J. Guthrie Scott, secretary of the Montreal Board of Health, had been paid thirty shillings per day. The chairman of the board was his father-in-law and the *Vindicator* denounced the board's actions as 'part and parcel of that jobbing system by which places are obtained by a few important characters ... We would, however, advise the Hon. Gentleman to find some other method of portioning his daughters than by making such encroachments on the funds allotted to the poor and distressed.' In November 1832, Speaker L.-J. Papineau supported a motion that T.A. Young be denied his seat in the House of Assembly. It was charged that Young, as secretary of the Quebec Board of Health, had taken money from the executive. The motion was lost. One of Aylmer's critics took the opportunity to praise the work of the voluntary associations which 'we hope will convince the advocates of "Authority" that it is best administered when in the hands of citizens who will take pains in giving inhabitants proper information on the object in view.'[46]

Despite the political rhetoric of the year Lower Canada was spared some of the troubles which followed epidemics in Europe. After the first panic people adjusted to living amidst cholera. They did not accuse the doctors of plotting to kill them, they did not riot against the health authorities although individuals might ignore the regulations or resist efforts to enforce them. The reason for their restraint, perhaps, lies in the nature of government in Lower Canada. In Europe, the communities which were most prone to riot and disorder during the cholera epidemics were those where a strong government supported a well-developed bureaucracy in its drive to enforce regulations. In some towns in Russia and in Paris, for example, disorder and riot accompanied the epidemics. There was no developed bureaucracy in Lower Canada in 1832 and government did not attempt to apply public health rules with ruthless force. Aylmer, as we have seen, actually insisted that all the usual procedures be followed in bringing prosecutions against offenders. Those procedures were slow, cumbersome, expensive, and easily evaded.

Lower Canada escaped riot and major disorder, but cholera played a large part in the highly charged political atmosphere. Emigration had been a political issue before 1832 but the horrors of that summer made the question more urgent. Petitions were circulated in Montreal criticizing Alymer for failing to protect the people by regulating the immigrant traffic. The governor's supporters dismissed the charge as one raised by anti-British factions 'blinded by the madness of party.' There was, however, real fear behind the savage rhetoric. A correspondent, writing in the *Montreal Gazette* in August, said 'when I see my country in mourning and my native land nothing but a vast cemetery, I ask what has been the cause of all these disasters? and the voice of my father, my brother and my beloved mother, the voice of thousands of my fellow citizens responds from their tombs. It is emigration.'[47]

The first cholera epidemic struck a community already under enormous strain.[48] The growing population had imposed heavy demands on the limited resources and had produced what Fernand Ouellet has called a demographic crisis amongst French Canadians. Many sons of farmers found themselves landless labourers. Tenants found their seigneurs more demanding just when the crops they grew were less competitive on world markets. Those men who went to the towns felt the competition of anglophone immigrants, those who stayed in the countryside believed that English settlers were favoured over French residents. With the whole structure of their society menaced, French

Canadians grew more conscious of the threat to their position. French-Canadian politics grew more radical and the election disturbances of May 1832 were one sign of that change. The immigration question helped to focus the political debate and cholera helped to sharpen it and make the question more ideological and more urgent. The horror of cholera played a part in pushing the province along the path which soon led to rebellion.

3

'Nothing is to be heard but the "Cholera"': Upper Canada 1832

On Saturday 16 June 1832 the readers of the *Kingston Chronicle* found a story dated at 8:30 that morning

Dreadful Cholera at Quebec and Montreal –

By the arrival of William the IV this morning the apprehensions we entertained of the progress of this awful pestilence have been too faithfully realised in the accounts communicated by several respectable gentlemen passengers on board this vessel. The Quebec papers of Wednesday (which have not yet reached Kingston) report the deaths, amounting to forty four in forty-eight hours ... We cannot too urgently entreat our fellow townsmen to unite as one man, and use every human power within their reach to resist, if possible, the further progress of this desolating scourge ... Without every energy and every moral exertion, there will be nothing under Providence, to save this already over-populated town from the contagion that so furiously rages within *forty eight hours reach of the place!*[1]

In fact, cholera was closer than that. The first recognized cases in Upper Canada were seen in Prescott on the same day. Even before the disease was acknowledged in Montreal, some infected travellers must have reached Upper Canada. When the disease broke out on the boats, they were abandoned all along the route from Lachine to Prescott, tied up to the shore with the sick and well huddled in them. Governor Sir John Colborne ordered the local magistrates to see that the sick were brought into hospital. The Montreal Emigrant Society hired waggons to move the stranded passengers on to Upper Canada.[2]

Neither the panic among boatmen nor the blockades set up by Upper Canadian magistrates brought the movement of immigrants to a complete halt. Colborne was eager to see the immigrants dispersed and as they moved along the rivers and around the lake the cholera moved with them. Prescott, Brockville, Kingston, York, Cobourg, and Brantford had outbreaks in June. Early July saw the disease in Bytown and London and, by the third week of the month, in Hamilton. In August there was an outbreak on the Welland Canal.[3] With immigrants on the move, a number of communities tried to protect themselves by inspecting vessels arriving at their quays. At Kingston, York, Amherstburg, Bytown, and other towns vessels were ordered to heave to before docking for inspection by a health officer. The general board of health for the Western District regulated craft from Michigan and fined residents who visited Detroit against regulations. The regulations were often breached. At Brockville the crew of a vessel were allowed ashore while the immigrants were being examined. One of the crew developed cholera and nearly died. There were a number of complaints that boat captains landed sick passengers and crewmen near towns before sailing on to meet the health officer.[4]

Mutual resentments could flare into violence. The regulations, though inadequate, did help to reassure the residents of the towns that something was being done to protect them; but the boat owners and captains quickly grew resentful of the delays and expense caused by inspections at every port. They questioned the right of towns to impose regulations in the absence of any public health legislation. On 25 June, the Niagara magistrates adopted regulations ordering all craft to wait 50 yards from shore for a medical inspection. The magistrates remained firm despite the captains' protests. On 29 June, the *Niagara* arrived with a sick passenger and a sick sailor. The boat was ordered to anchor offshore and was fumigated. The crew were ordered to remain on board and the officers were allowed ashore only under the escort of special constables. The captain was enraged at the loss of a week, denied that there was cholera on board, and protested that his interests had been badly damaged.

The boat captains continued to protest but the Niagara magistrates remained adamant. When the cholera epidemic broke out at York, vessels from that port were required to heave to at the mouth of the Niagara River for inspection. This new regulation was especially offensive to the boatmen because, as one of them complained, it held them up 'most conspicuously in the face of the Americans (already too troublesome) as an infected vessel.' Boats from Canada were liable to run into difficulties when they sailed to the United States. Captain Hugh Richardson of the *Canada* had been refused permission to land passengers at Youngstown, New York, and he protested to Sir John Colborne that he was losing money every day. He appealed for an end to the 'futility and inhumanity of the proceeding.'

Sir John asked the captains to co-operate with the people of Niagara. Convinced that the board of health had no legal power to make regulations, the boatmen preferred to defy public opinion and land their passengers at the wharf. Richardson's lawyer advised him he need not 'submit to every arbitrary regulation they may think proper to make' but should tie up at the wharf and await inspection. The attorney-general agreed that the board did not have the legal power to do what it was doing. In the circumstances he urged the operators to show forbearance and co-operation. These qualities were not commonly found in lake boat captains.

On 3 July, the *Canada* sailed past a special constable sent to stop it in the river. On 4 and 5 July, Richardson allowed a medical officer to board for an inspection while the boat steamed to the wharf. He did so reluctantly and the board of health, somewhat rankled by his attitude, again ordered that he must heave to for inspection. Matters came to a head on 7 July. That evening, Dr Porter, the medical officer, hailed the *Canada* as she approached Niagara. He was told to meet the vessel at the wharf. When the *Canada* arrived at the wharf she was met by a mob yelling 'we are not going to be infected.' A running fight broke out as the mob used bludgeons to prevent the *Canada* from tying up. The fight spread as the crew of the *Great Britain* poured ashore to help the *Canada*. Dr Porter stood, apparently unchallenged, on the wheel-house of the *Great Britain* and cheered on what Richardson said were 'the lowest orders of Niagara.' The fight lasted some time and order was restored with difficulty. Here was a case in which men from various levels of Niagara society co-operated in violence to defend the public health.

Sir John Colborne came close to endorsing the mob action. The lesson he drew from the incident was that it should show steam-boat operators 'the necessity of cooperating cheerfully with the board in carrying into execution arrangements which have created confidence among the inhabitants of the adjoining town-ships.' If boat captains would not co-operate, the governor was prepared to support legislation to force them to comply with regulations. Not all boat captains were as unco-operative as Richardson, however, and the *Shannon* was allowed to land at Bytown without inspection when the captain agreed to report any cases of sickness on board.[5]

With the cholera upon them, the people of Upper Canada now began to take the precautions which they had previously neglected. The towns of Upper Canada, like those of Lower Canada, were dirty and lacked facilities. Most were small but they usually had districts where the poorer residents lived in conditions similar to those found in Quebec and Montreal. The health wardens of Bytown visited lower Bytown in June and reported many places where filth, rubbish, pools of stagnant water, and blocked drains could be found. There were many houses jammed with immigrants living in filthy conditions. The *Canadian Freeman* described the state of York: 'Stagnant pools of water, green as a leek and emitting deadly exhalations are to be met with in every corner of the town – yards and cellars send forth a stench already from rotten vegetables sufficient almost of itself to produce a plague – and the state of the bay, from which a large proportion of the inhabitants are supplied with water, is horrible.'[6]

The boards of health, created by local initiative or in response to Colborne's circular letter of 20 June, set out to enforce sanitary regulations similar to those made in Lower Canada. The civil authorities were not able to enforce them effectively and only in the military forts could the full range of sanitary rules be administered. At Fort George, Niagara, for example, drains were repaired, pools drained, and all the buildings cleaned and whitewashed. Military garrisons tried to isolate themselves from neighbouring towns when cholera broke out. As a result of these efforts most of the troops in Upper Canada were kept healthy but the demands on the military surgeons were heavy. Colborne tried to ease their load by ordering officers living outside the garrison at York to use civilian doctors.[7]

York was one of the few places in Upper Canada where such an order could reasonably be made. There were 15 doctors practising in the town, which had a resident population of about 6,000. Outside York, medical help was harder to find. One immigrant wrote that 'Physicians are much wanted here, and apothecaries still more. Ignorant persons act in that capacity, while scarcely knowing the names of the drugs they sell. At Niagara, that most necessary branch is solely conducted by a female who compounds medicines and puddings with equal confidence but not with equal skill ... Nurse tenders are in great demand. They might make their own terms.' In these circumstances, the boards of health did what they could to provide doctors for the residents. In the Ottawa district, doctors were asked to prevent neglect of local people by answering only calls from within the district. Boards in districts with few or no doctors appealed to other boards for help, sometimes successfully, sometimes not. The board at Gravelly Bay, for example, could persuade no one to come to their aid from York for less than $8 a day, which the board could not afford. Everywhere in Upper Canada people had to look after themselves, their relatives, and their neighbours.[8]

York suffered the worst epidemic of any Upper Canadian town. On 18 June, the magistrates who governed the unincorporated town laid down sanitary regulations. The town was divided into nine districts and a superintendent and four inspectors appointed for each. The inspectors were to make weekly visits to all premises and report dirty ones to the superintendent. He could recommend cleaning and supply lime and whitewash. Orders were given to clean and gravel the streets and householders were required to sweep the footpath and scrape the gutter in front of their houses. Lodging-houses were to be 'especially cleanly' and bars were ordered to close at 10 pm. On the same day, the medical board of York agreed to use the existing hospital for cholera cases and to move the ordinary patients into a shed on the grounds. On 18 June a suspected cholera victim was admitted to the hospital and by 20 June clear cases were seen.[9]

Cholera was present in York from mid-June until mid-September. Unlike Quebec and Montreal, York did not suffer from an explosive epidemic. The number of cases reported did not exceed 10 on any day in June and rarely exceeded that number in July. In August, the epidemic showed some increase, with a peak of 27 cases on 9 August. Later in the month the incidence declined and by September the number of cases was below five a day. The garrison was affected in August and 12 soldiers died. The board of health recorded 273 deaths during the epidemic. This figure is probably an underestimate. Isaac Wilson, a resident of the town, wrote to his brother: 'sometimes the Doctors made no report and when they did, not one half was stated. But it was estimated that the deaths were over 500.' John Strachan, writing to his bishop about the widows and orphans left by the epidemic, estimated there had been over 1,000 cases and 400 deaths, many of them amongst immigrants.[10]

In the first days of the epidemic, sick immigrants were arriving in York on the steamers. The *Great Britain*, for example, had landed victims on its stops at Kingston and Cobourg before reaching York on 22 June with more passengers fallen sick. Both the magistrates and the board of health took responsibility for dealing with the outbreak. The magistrates made regulations and administered the money given to the board by Sir John Colborne. Vessels calling at York had to be inspected, the cleaning of the town was speeded up, and a matron and servants were hired for the hospital. Those who died of cholera at the hospital were to be buried in potter's field outside the town on Yonge Street.[11]

The board of health dealt with the daily administration of the regulations. It made the superintendents and inspectors, appointed earlier by the magistrates, into health wardens. Their duties were similar to those of the wardens in Quebec and Montreal and they were authorized to spend public money to take people to hospital. The board doled out lime to the poor to help them clean and disinfect their houses and arranged for some of the residents to be housed in the emigrant sheds while their houses were cleaned. The board employed carters to carry away the dead and these must have met with some opposition, for at the end of June they were sworn in as special constables. As in Lower Canada, the burial of the dead was one of the greatest sources of anger against the health regulations. People deeply resented it when their relatives were carried away to be buried in the unconsecrated ground at potter's field. On a number of occasions bodies were dug up by friends or relatives of the dead. Colborne asked Bishop McDowell to persuade his flock to accept the burial regulations which they did only after the ground was consecrated.[12]

One of the most common rumours in the epidemics was that people were being buried alive. Mrs Perry's experience suggests that some might have been. In York, one rumour of a premature burial was so persistent that the grand jury ordered a hearing into the case. The story was that a young woman taken from the hospital had been found alive by her husband when he broke into the dead house. The jury heard a number of witnesses including a man named Carl who coffined the dead at the hospital, and concluded that the rumour was baseless and probably grew out of the case of Catherine McCan. Her father had broken into the dead house and taken her body but had 'expatiated his temerity on the following day by falling a victim to the same disease.' The jury tracked down one man who had been spreading the story and it ordered its report to be printed in the newspapers in the hope of ending the rumours.[13]

The link between the hospital and the rumours of premature burial is striking. The poor resented the burial regulations and they hated the hospital. Mr John Carey, who was raising money for a dispensary to help the sick poor, wrote to Sir John Colborne about the hospital. He pointed out that 'a strong prejudice' existed against it. Some people were so frightened of being forced to go there that they refused to send for help if they fell sick. Carey suggested that a number of small receiving houses be opened around the town. He thought that they would not carry the same stigma as the hospital and that they would spare the patients a long and dangerous journey through the town. The board said Carey's letter was 'undeserving of attention' and denied that it had ever 'sanctioned the use of force' when sending people to the hospital. Dr John Rolph, however, confirmed Carey's statements. His patients refused to go to the hospital until they were in the last stages of the disease. Then they would agree 'to go there and die.'[14]

Early in August, the board of health decided that Carey's letter did deserve attention. As the number of cases began to increase it decided to open some receiving houses. It asked Colborne to allow the old Royal Grammar School to be used for the sick. In doing so, it acknowledged that there was prejudice against the hospital. The government was reluctant to agree. It argued that the hospital was a better building in a healthier location than the old wooden school building standing in the notoriously dirty area known as Stuart's half-acre. In any case, it argued, prejudice would be as great against a temporary hospital as it was against the permanent one. For these reasons, it urged the board to continue its efforts to get people to use the hospital. Late in August, John Carey did manage to open his dispensary. It was in the lower part of town and gave medicine to patients before they began the journey to hospital. The dispensary stayed open for a time after the epidemic to help the sick poor. It was forced to close after eight months in operation when the doctors in charge found themselves overworked, without funds, and unable to win support for the work from their colleagues.[15]

Panic in York did not reach the same level it had in Lower Canada early in the epidemic. There were, however, a number of residents who fled from the town and the local farmers tended to stay away. The debtors in York jail begged Colborne to release them after cholera broke out there. He felt able only to ask the sheriff to make sure that they were well fed and had quick medical attention. The debtors' panic was understandable. Experience of the disease could unnerve free men. John Strachan's assistant collapsed with anxiety after seeing his first cholera victim and Strachan barred him from any further pastoral work with cholera cases. Some residents of York were said to have sealed themselves into their houses to sit out the epidemic.[16]

Despite their fear of the disease people seemed unwilling to do much to improve the condition of York. The magistrates' powers over public health were unclear and the board had no legal power to enforce its regulations. Its efforts to persuade people to observe the rules met little response. By the first week of August money was running out with only £100 remaining of the executive's grant and little hope of raising money by public subscription. The board requested Sir John to summon the assembly and ask it to vote legal powers to magistrates and boards of health. Sir John replied that he would consider the idea. He urged them in the mean time to buck up and show some initiative. He suggested that they appeal for voluntary help to clean the streets and he pointed out that they could take comfort from the facts that the hospital was open and the doctors were ready to serve. The immigrants were now moving rapidly into the countryside, and Colborne believed that the affliction had fallen 'comparatively lightly on the Province.'[17]

The members of the board did not respond positively to Colborne's remarks. Instead, it seems to have slipped deeper into the gloom which had marked its discussions. On 11 August, the board announced that 'being at length, fully convinced from their want of legal Enactment, as well as from the want of funds of their total inability to be of any further service to their fellow Townsmen, have this day dissolved themselves as a public body.' Perhaps it hoped by this gesture to force the executive into the action it had suggested, although its motives are not clear. The town soon had a new board of health which did appeal for help in cleaning the streets and reporting nuisances to the board.[18] No voluntary movement was created, however, and York remained dirty long after the epidemic was over.

In Kingston, the citizens showed more public spirit. A couple of days before cholera reached Upper Canada, a public meeting had resolved to build a temporary hospital and to open a public sub-scription for the work. The chairman of the meeting reported the resolution to Sir John Colborne and asked him for funds. The committee appointed at this meeting became the board of health and administered regulations made by the local magistrates. The magistrates laid down regulations for vessels visiting the town, formed a medical board, and set up temporary hospitals. They ordered carters to carry the sick to hospital when requested to do so by a doctor or member of the board of health. Any carter who refused would lose his licence. Immediately after cholera appeared in town, the magistrates made sanitary regulations, re-quired that the dead be buried within twelve hours, and asked the army for tents to house people near the cholera hospital. Dr Evans, who had been present in Sunderland during the first Brit-ish epidemic of 1831, was put in charge of the hospital. Dr Walter Henry, a military surgeon, offered to help and his offer was accepted.[19]

Here, too, the epidemic did not show the explosive pattern which it had in Lower Canada. Through June, between five and nine people died each day. By 2 July the magistrates believed that the epidemic had eased as the deaths dropped below five per day. By 11 July there had been 155 cases and 48 deaths. For most of July and August, the daily death rate ranged between one and three and only rarely went as high as five. By the end of August 95 people had died, half of them in the first three weeks of the epidemic.[20]

Those first three weeks brought some tension and fear to Kingston. Business slowed and, as one correspondent remarked, if one were to 'go to a merchants shop in this Town and other places, nothing is to be heard but the "cholera" ... Brandy is recommended for it ... I have no hesitation in saying that some of the cases are "Brandy cases" ... You cannot turn a corner of the street you will see some old fool thinking to save ther lives by ther own doings even young men cheapen therselves by holding Doctor's Drugs to ther nose.' The board tried to calm fears by pointing out that the few cases had mostly come from the boats 'and that no death had occurred, where proper medical, and other attention has been early, and promptly applied: that several have been discharged cured; and that this Committee possess the fullest evidence that the Town at this moment is in other respects unusually healthy.' The costs of meeting the epidemic proved to be heavy. The funds raised by public subscription to open and operate the cholera hospital were exhausted by early August. The additional costs of helping immigrants and those widowed or orphaned by the epidemic made it impossible to raise more for the hospital. The government, 'under the afflicting circumstances in which the Province is placed,' met the problem by allowing the Emigrant Society to spend £200, originally given to employ immigrants on road-work, on maintaining the hospital.[21]

Everywhere in the province the epidemic stretched resources to the limit. Early in July, the magistrates of the Midland District formed a general board of health. In each division, the magistrates and 'a reasonable number of mature and discreet persons' formed a local board advised by the local doctors acting as a medical board. The general board tried to restrain the expenditure of the local boards while meeting their appeals for help. They were soon short of money. The board at Belleville had spent £135 building a cholera hospital and that charge, combined with other expenses, reduced the general board's funds to £100 by early July. When the disease broke out at that time in Hallowell, the board had to find money to send a doctor to help at the settlement. Without legal power to enforce the regulations they made, magistrates all over the province did what they could to meet the disease when it broke out in their districts.[22]

Between mid-June and late September a dozen places in Upper Canada reported cholera. One of the worst epidemics was at St Regis where nearly one-tenth of the Indian population died. The province as a whole saw at least 550 die of the disease out of its population of less than 300,000.[23] No community experienced an explosive epidemic of the type which had horrified the residents of Quebec and Montreal. A resident of Quebec, watching the progress of the disease through Upper Canada, wrote to a correspondent in York that 'it is evident that it abates in its malignancy as it works to the West' and that it was likely to 'operate lightly in the scattered settlements of Upper Canada.' Even so, it was a calamity which caught the public imagination and lingered in the memory. The memories quickly assumed a conventional form and an account published thirty years later of the epidemic in York dwelled on its 'deserted streets, traversed continually by cholera carts conveying the dead to the grave and the dying to hospital.' As Godfrey remarks, 'it would be difficult for the streets to be deserted considering that some 40,000 emigrants came to York in the summer of 1832.'[24] What is significant, however, is that people chose to remember the first epidemic in this way.

The epidemic did create widespread fear and apprehension. One measure of that was the increase in religious activity. The Reverend Mr Anson Green, who was himself to survive an attack of cholera in 1834, noted that 'the excitement created by the cholera had induced many careless ones to think of their latter end, and to pray for pardon.' As a result, 3,652 joined the Methodists which was a three-fold increase over the previous year's admissions. The tension affected the doctors in Upper Canada and there were some squabbles among them. In York, Dr John Rolph complained that the hospital doctors were jealous of their authority and reluctant to admit their colleagues.[25] In general, however, the profession was freer of feuds and had better relations with laymen than was true in Lower Canada.

In Upper Canada, the measures taken against cholera could provoke hostility and anger. In York both the burial regulations and the efforts to send people to the hospital were resisted; yet

Niagara saw a riot in support of regulations directed against the steamboats. There were no efforts to create voluntary organizations of the kind set up in Quebec and Montreal, perhaps because in the smaller towns of Upper Canada individual efforts and the measures taken by the magistrates seemed to be sufficient. Cholera did not have the same political impact here as it had in Lower Canada. Some people in York may have felt that the government was inadequate; but in the province generally it had acted remarkably well. Although lacking legal powers, Colborne had some success in providing funds and stimulating those local governments which had been slow to act. In Upper Canada, immigration was not seen as a threat to national identity as it was by many French Canadians. Consequently, cholera did not act to intensify political feelings concerning immigration. Colborne was criticized by some for not calling the assembly into session in the summer of 1832; but when it did meet it approved what he had done without political bitterness. It also looked to the future and provided statutory powers for boards of health[26] – any new epidemic would be met by bodies with some legal authority.

4

'The ravages ... has been kept hid': Canada 1834

The year 1833 saw the political tension rise in Lower Canada. Against a background of rumours that cholera had returned, the opposition launched a series of assaults on the executive. The bishop of Quebec might declare 16 February a day of thanksgiving and say that the epidemic had been an inspiration to virtue, a source of grace, and a warning of what God could do to a community which forgot His commands, but for many politicians, the epidemic was the direct result of governmental policies which threatened the province. They challenged the executive over money bills and defeated a new quarantine bill (providing for expenditures) to replace the expired act of 1832. If a new epidemic broke out, the only legal basis for action would be the Quarantine Act of 1795.[1]

The immigrants began to arrive as navigation reopened for a new season. Aylmer appointed a council of health to advise him on what measures to take to protect the public. Because of the 'ungrateful and illiberal animadversions which the Board of Health of last year were doomed to suffer' the council was to be purely advisory. Aylmer himself would be responsible for executing their suggestions. Even so, T.A. Young refused a seat on the council.

The council recommended changes in the operation of Grosse Isle and suggested some shelter be provided for immigrants closer to Quebec than the Plains of Abraham. They urged the mayor and corporation of the city to make regulations for boarding-houses and tenements which would provide each resident with twenty square feet of space. Turning to the problem of hospital accommodation, the council accepted Aylmer's suggestion that the Emigrant Hospital be used again along with a building in the lower town. To avoid 'unpleasant altercations with neighbours' the building should be hired before an epidemic began and the council suggested the hospital commissioners immediately rent the blue store next to the customs house. When news of that plan leaked out, however, the customs officers immediately protested.

Experience in 1832 had shown that the first news of cholera created panic. Many doctors believed that panic predisposed people to the disease. The government therefore considered the question of how the news could be managed if there was another epidemic. The main problem it saw was that all news of ships arriving at Grosse Isle was sent by semaphoric telegraph to the exchange at Quebec. News spread quickly from there 'tending to alarm the inhabitants of the Town.' The government thought it should be the first to receive any news of the state of health at the island 'in order that if necessary further inquiry may be made before it is announced to the Public.'[2] In fact, it was impossible to stop news from Grosse Isle reaching Quebec. The government could not control the news, but in 1834 the newspapers of Lower Canada themselves put off mentioning cholera until long after the disease had broken out in the province.

The year 1833 passed without cholera but brought no improvement in the political climate. In 1834 the assembly and Aylmer did agree on an act to tax immigrants. The act was expected to raise £4,000 for the relief of the indigent sick at Quebec and Montreal. It did not go into force, however, as the imperial government reserved the bill.[3] There was no agreement on other provisions for the public health and Lower Canada again faced the new season's navigation protected only by the existing quarantine act. The act did not provide for boards of health and the work of executing its provisions fell on the executive council. In March 1834 the executive council recommended that quarantine be proclaimed, and ordered Grosse Isle reopened.

Throughout the summer, ships arriving from abroad would be required to stop at Grosse Isle for 40 days or until discharged. Ships with fewer than 15 steerage passengers could proceed immediately if the inspecting physician found them clean and healthy. Those with more than 15 steerage passengers had to land them all to clean themselves and their baggage while their ship was cleaned. When all passengers were declared clean and healthy the ship could proceed to Quebec. Ships arriving at Quebec without a discharge from Grosse Isle had to wait for inspection at the mouth of the St Charles River. Those with more than 15 passengers had to return to the island, those with fewer could be cleared at Quebec. No contact was allowed between uncleared ships and the shore.[4] Those regulations were clearly based on lessons learned in 1832. They continued the requirement, first made in July 1832, that all steerage passengers land from the larger vessels, and they required certain vessels to return to Grosse Isle.

Captain Reid was again given command at Grosse Isle. He asked for extra staff to deal with the immigrants but was refused. He suggested that he be appointed a justice of the peace to help him 'suppress riot and disturbances among the passengers on shore' or among mutinous crews. The council thought it a good idea but could not act as Reid owned no property in the province and was, therefore, ineligible to be a justice of the peace. In an effort to keep down one of the main causes of complaints on the island, the council ordered all traders, grocers, and sutlers at Grosse Isle not to charge more than the Quebec prices for their goods and not to sell liquor.[5]

As the number of passengers arriving at the island increased the problems which had become familiar in 1832 re-emerged. Landing passengers and cleaning the ship might be done in a day but could take much longer if the weather were poor or the island crowded. Some ships spent nine days at Grosse Isle. On the island, conditions quickly deteriorated. One leader of a party of immigrants complained that they had been crowded into a shed barely big enough for the women and children. The place set aside for washing was filthy with accumulated dirt and on the island his 'cleanly and healthy people mixed ... in the dust and filth of thousands.' It was a familiar, and dangerous, state of affairs. The passengers of the *Hebron*, for example, arrived at Grosse Isle healthy, spent three days at the island, and when they returned to the ship had an outbreak of cholera which kept them almost a month in quarantine.[6]

Human failings increased the difficulties at the station. Dr Francis Fortier, now the inspecting officer, was accused by Captain Reid of neglecting his duties. The problem arose because Fortier was expected to treat patients as well as inspect the ships. Reid complained that Fortier in one case 'did not show that immediate desire to attend the sick man which the occasion appeared to require.' The doctor argued that it was dangerous for him to visit the sick and to inspect all the ships. He thought it would be better not to board vessels with sickness on board. Aylmer ordered him to board every ship. In July, the *Orelia* was sent back from Quebec with cholera on board and Fortier was ordered to board her and to treat her captain. He did neither, but merely sailed by and hailed the ship, later arguing that he did not wish to risk spreading the disease to other vessels. As Captain Reid said, it was 'a manner of performing his duty little calculated to insure public confidence in him but rather to increase alarm on the subject of the disease.' In September, Dr Fortier was dismissed from his post.[7]

The immigrants proved sickly as the spring and summer passed. The seriously ill were taken from their ships and put in the care of the medical superintendent and his staff at the hospital. Early in the season there were many cases of measles and fever. In June, the hospital was filled with typhus cases and many of the attendants were ill. When cholera appeared among the immigrants at that time, the doctors asked for volunteers from the army to serve in the hospital but none came forward. The overworked medical staff fell out among themselves. Mr Ormsby Bourke, the assistant at the hospital, complained of Dr Charles Poole's 'repeated acts of mock tyranny ... every day adding insults to insults.' Poole responded by accusing Bourke of being drunk on duty. Bourke resigned.[8]

Quarantine was no more effective in 1834 than it had been in 1832. Almost from the start of the season, there were rumours of cholera at Grosse Isle. In May, a case was landed from the *Ocean* out of Waterford; on 11 June, the *Constantia* from Limerick landed a passenger but the diagnosis of cholera was not certain. Ten days later, a passenger from the *Mary*, out of Cork, died and in July the *Amelia* anchored off Grosse Isle and sent for a priest to attend one of its crew. The residents of Quebec were badly frightened when the *Orelia* reached the city with cholera aboard and, early in August, the *Conference* was also ordered back following an outbreak of cholera. Between 1 May and 31 October, the hospital at Grosse Isle admitted 844 patients: 290 were cholera cases, of whom 158 died.[9]

In Quebec, responsibility for public health had passed to the city council under the charter of 1833. There was no board of health at work in 1834. The most immediate threat to the city's health, it was generally agreed, came from the immigrants. The Quebec Emigrant Society was particularly concerned with helping the poorest immigrants. The poor health of many of them increased the usual distress which each season brought and the emigrant society began to hear that immigrants were dying in the streets. The Emigrant Hospital was short of money and there were no other facilities for those with fever or contagious diseases. In this crisis, the citizens turned to Lord Aylmer. Late in May, a group of merchants and inhabitants wrote to him to ask for a grant for the emigrant society. At the beginning of June, the mayor claimed there was little hope of raising money privately and asked for funds from the government.

While the mayor tried to tap provincial funds, the emigrant society launched an appeal in the city. It managed to raise £200 by subscription and used the money to open the blue store as a hospital early in June apparently without difficulty from the neighbours. The furniture for the hospital came from the old cholera hospital in the suburb of St John. On 29 June Dr William Lyons reported that he had a case of cholera at the Emigrant Hospital. The case puzzled him as the patient was from the *Elea-*

nor from Dublin which had reported no sickness on the voyage. He thought it was possible that the man was suffering only from common cholera, a term applied to the intestinal diseases seen in most summers in Canada. Soon, however, patients began to die and Lyons became increasingly certain that he was dealing with 'real cholera.' By 5 July he had no doubts. On 6 July, a patient died within fifteen minutes of being admitted. In the town, there were more and more reports of sudden deaths among lodgers in taverns and in houses on Paul Street. In this same period, the blue store was admitting patients with cholera and six of them died between 26 June and 5 July. Soon the number of cases was rising and, on 20 July, the Marine Hospital was opened to cholera victims.[10]

The second epidemic followed a different pattern to that of the first. On no day in 1834 were there more than 100 deaths and in the worst weeks, the daily rate ranged between 20 and 50 dead. The first week for which records were kept, starting on 7 July, saw 87 die. More than 200 people died in each of the next four weeks, with the peak coming in the third week, when 270 died. Not until the sixth week of the epidemic did the toll drop below 200 and by mid-August 1,169 had died. After the peak had passed, cases continued to be reported until early November and at least 1,500 people died in Quebec.[11]

A disaster on this scale was a challenge to the new city government. Its first decision was to make no statement about the disease until the number of cases was clearly dropping. Like the provincial government in 1833, the Quebec city councillors argued that news of the epidemic would create panic and predispose people to the disease. The press also kept quiet in the early days of the epidemic, later arguing that it was justified in doing so because with no board of health there were no official figures available. As a result, the full extent of the epidemic was at first hidden from the residents. Even after bulletins were issued one correspondent complained that 'the ravages of the scourge has been kept hid from the people in this city.' Lack of detailed information, familiarity with the disease, and the less violent pattern of the epidemic helped to ensure that there was no panic equal to that of the first weeks of the 1832 epidemic. One paper did later claim that cholera produced 'almost a stagnation of all business' but its opinion was not widely shared. Experience in 1832, of course, suggested that a cholera epidemic hurt trade. That was one reason for the press silence. Some people did leave Quebec and one newspaper estimated that a thousand people, including 'many working people who had friends and relatives in country parishes' left the town.[12]

The councils of Quebec and Montreal asked for the 1795 quarantine act to be extended to their cities. They hoped that this would give them some control over the immigrants passing up river. Quebec council suggested that Captain Reid be given the power to issue only conditional discharges. Quebec would then establish a quarantine ground at the St Charles River and subject passengers to a fresh medical examination. The Montreal Sanitary Committee suggested a similar plan for Montreal. Aylmer refused to extend the quarantine because it was expensive. He also argued that if he extended the quarantine to Quebec and Montreal he would soon face requests from other ports and travel would become very difficult.[13]

The Quebec council felt its ability to tackle the epidemic lessened by the assembly's failure to pass public health laws. The city's powers over public health matters were unclear. The sanitary committee believed existing legislation did not permit it to adopt certain measures it thought necessary. When the city asked Aylmer for funds to help the immigrants he refused. He did agree, however, to a request to open the Marine Hospital to cholera cases but added that he had no money to make it fit for use. In 1834 the governor apparently decided to do only what he felt the law allowed him to do. In 1833 he had spent money on the public health and had been reimbursed by the assembly. Now, he would spend only on Grosse Isle. He refused to spend on public health measures in the expectation that the assembly would approve his actions retroactively.[14] It was one sign of how much the political situation had deteriorated.

The epidemic quickly spread through the same parts of town which had been most affected in 1832. Nothing had been done to improve conditions there and some people wondered if the disease had been lingering in those parts of the town since the first epidemic. The first cases were seen among the poorer immigrants but by late July it was reported to be falling 'more heavily on residents in respectable life than on strangers and wayfarers.' With little active support from Aylmer, the Quebec city council and its sanitary committee had to cope with the epidemic with uncertain legal powers and little money. The committee could do little to clean the city or to provide for the public health. Most of its efforts were given over to finding hospital space for the sick poor. Aylmer gave a building at King's Wharf to hold the sick while they waited for transport to the hospitals. Ambulances were placed in different parts of town and were ordered to carry their patients through the quieter streets. When the Marine Hospital began to take cholera cases it was possible to classify the victims according to the seriousness of the case. This, it was hoped, would reduce prejudice against hospitals. The hospitals operated into the fall and it was mid-November before the last patient was released.[15]

In Montreal, the epidemic of 1832 had stimulated efforts to meet the city's public health needs. A public meeting in May 1833 elected a sanitary committee to replace the board of health which had been dissolved in January 1833. The health commissioner, Dr Robert Nelson, allowed the committee £500. In June 1833, the common council adopted rules and regulations to replace those which had been administered by the magistrates before the city was incorporated. Among these were public health by-laws enforcing action to keep the city clean and well drained and allowing the mayor to order premises to be inspected and cleaned.

Some efforts to clean Montreal were made in 1833 and the sanitary committee continued to work in 1834 even though its legal authority was not clear. With cholera approaching, these efforts continued but were of little effect. The jail was cleaned and whitewashed. When the residents of St Lawrence suburb complained of the danger from blocked drains and pools of stagnant water, however, the council replied that it had no control over such matters. Little had been done to clean Montreal before the epidemic appeared and little was done during the epidemic itself. The grand jury presentment at the beginning of September complained that many yards and premises were filthy and that the corporation had allowed public places and the streets to be 'encumbered with filth' and filled with stagnant water. These conditions could be improved, the jurors said, only by 'the enactment of severe municipal regulations and the appointment of officers to carry them into effect.'[16]

Summer brought the familiar scenes of suffering. Many of the immigrants passing through the city seemed to those who dealt with them generally to be of a 'better class' than in previous years, but those who were in distress were more wretched than in the past. The Montreal Emigrant Society found 300 in the sheds toward the end of June in 'a situation far more wretched and destitute than has been witnessed in these sheds in former years.' The society appealed to Aylmer for money and said that little could be raised in the city. Aylmer made it clear that the corporation must provide for the public health.[17]

Cholera was first recognized in the city on 11 July. At Dr Robert Nelson's request the council met in secret session on 12 July. Nelson reported that the victims had arrived on the *Lady of the Lake* and that two patients had died in the past twenty-four hours. A third victim was now in Montreal General Hospital. The council responded to this news by putting the emigrant sheds into the charge of a committee of the council. One of the sheds was to serve as a cholera hospital and two doctors were appointed to look after the patients. The street committee was ordered to drain the streets. The council made a request to Aylmer for an extension of quarantine and asked him for money. They also decided not to publish news of the outbreak.

The epidemic quickly took hold, with deaths rising from one on 12 July to 17 on 17 July. In the second week the daily rate was between 15 and 20. At the beginning of the third week, deaths passed 40 per day before dropping into the 30s at the end of the week and through the next. The fifth week saw the rate drop below 30 and the sixth brought a quick drop with only six deaths on 18 August. By 29 August, the epidemic was nearly over. In its seven weeks, the epidemic had killed at least 882 people.[18]

Despite the official silence, it was obvious that something unusual was happening in Montreal. Rumours spread around the town that a hundred people were being buried each day. The newspapers there, as in Quebec, kept as quiet as they could on the matter. A week after the epidemic began, the *Montreal Gazette* admitted that some cases of 'severe sickness and sudden death have been noticed in this city, which from their resemblance to the cholera of 1832, have created some uneasiness.' The editor claimed that the number of deaths had dropped and that 'the town and neighbourhood have not enjoyed such a healthy season for the last twenty years, as has been experienced by us since the opening of spring.' Ten days after that, the *Vindicator* excused the Canadian press's action in keeping quiet in the hope that the cholera would quickly fade away without harming trade and causing public alarm.[19]

With cholera on the increase, and no aid available from Aylmer, the council had to deal with the epidemic. On 16 July, the sanitary committee appointed a special committee to deal with the crisis. It was responsible for the emigrant sheds and the cholera hospital. As the epidemic grew, a second shed had to be used for convalescent patients. This committee inspected boarding-houses and tried to have the worst ones closed, and it forwarded 1,000 immigrants to Upper Canada in mid-July. The members of the committee found little money available. Aylmer still said that he had none. The corporation 'either did not, or conceived it did not possess authority to employ the city revenues for sanitary purposes.' The emigrant society had no funds to forward immigrants. With the death toll mounting daily, some money had to be found, and the council therefore borrowed from banks on the personal security of the councillors to clean and drain the streets.

A health committee of the council met the sanitary committee to plan money-raising efforts. Another approach to Aylmer was suggested but Robert Nelson spoke with passion against the idea. He argued that no further contact should be made with the governor but that his conduct in the crisis should be reported to the colonial secretary in London. The sanitary committee decided to run the emigrant sheds and forward immigrants with funds raised from the banks on the personal security of the members. During the summer, 4,000 immigrants were helped on their way to Upper Canada. The committee also established sub-committees to oversee the Cascades, Cedars, and Coteau-du-Lac and kept in touch with a committee established at Lachine. In Montreal, the Ladies Benevolent Society continued to help the widows and orphans created by the epidemic. It, as always, was short of funds but raised money by subscriptions and from other sources which allowed it to help 54 widows and over 260 children.[20]

The epidemic of 1834 in Lower Canada did not re-create the panic of 1832, but the thousands of deaths had a great political impact. The radicalization of French-Canadian politics, given a boost by the epidemic of 1832, was pushed further by the events of 1834. That year 30,000 immigrants passed through Lower Canada and the immigration question was more bitterly debated than ever. At one public meeting in Quebec, Mayor E. Caron said that the epidemic was directly attributable to immigration. He called on the imperial government to regulate emigration and contribute to the needs of sick and poor immigrants. Caron saw some benefit in a well-regulated immigration with an effective quarantine, but many did not. Now, some of the French-language papers began to suggest that the British government was involved in a plot to destroy the Canadians by unleashing cholera among them. The anger against Aylmer was intense. On 30 September, *La Minerve* appeared in mourning in memory of the victims of 21 May 1832 and the thousands of cholera victims of 1834. All were dead, it said, as a consequence of Aylmer's actions or of his failure to act.

Aylmer, in his turn, was becoming bitter over the state of politics in Lower Canada and was convinced that the opposition wanted an end to any connection with Great Britain. He may have wearied of the personal attacks on him such as those of the Central and Permanent Committee of the District of Montreal which held a rally early in September and condemned him for refusing to extend the quarantine or to provide funds. When the House of Assembly met early in 1835, some members sent a petition to Westminster accusing Aylmer of 'culpable indifference to the frightful ravages committed by the Asiatic cholera during the last summer' and saying that 'the conduct of His Excellency was one of the principle causes of their sufferings and bereavements.' Aylmer dismissed these remarks as the 'grossest calumnies.'

The governor-general had made it very difficult for his supporters to defend him in 1834. Many of them found much to criticize in his actions that summer. At the height of the epidemic, Aylmer had left Quebec and retired to Sorel. Most of the executive council also went to the country. Aylmer had approved of people leaving the cities in 1832 but it was impolitic for him to do so himself. Not only did it give an impression of personal fear or of indifference to the suffering of thousands, but it also made communication with him difficult at the height of the crisis. His supporters also criticized his refusal to advance needed funds as he had in 1833. Aylmer wrote with feeling, early in 1835, in his own defence. He dismissed the request for a quarantine at Montreal as the work of a 'branch' of the House of Assembly. He pointed out that funds he had advanced for Grosse Isle had not yet been reimbursed. He said that the people who had requested funds knew that none were available because the House of Assembly had failed to act and, in any case, both Quebec and Montreal could raise money by public subscription.[21] There was some truth in what Aylmer said and the city governments obviously would have preferred someone else to meet the costs of cleaning the streets and dealing with the immigrants. Aylmer, however, had failed to show any of the energy that he had in 1832 and the arid exchanges between the governor and his opponents pointed to the troubles soon to come.

The situation in Upper Canada stood in sharp contrast to that in Lower Canada. The House of Assembly had passed a bill in 1833 which provided for boards of health and allowed them to operate permanently in the larger towns. The province would not have to meet future epidemics in the legal confusion of 1832. The population of Upper Canada had grown by 60,000 since 1832 and people generally continued to welcome immigration. They saw the danger to public health posed by immigration and hoped that the British government would regulate the traffic and help meet the costs of caring for the sick. The House of Assembly asked the British Parliament for land grants to endow hospitals at Toronto and Kingston. In 1834, in the newly incorporated city of Toronto, the hospital was operating, and it was hoped that the Kingston one would be open before the end of the year. As both hospitals would be helping immigrants, Sir John Colborne supported the request for public lands for them but the British government was reluctant to agree.[22]

Before the news of cholera reached Upper Canada, the boards of health were set up or re-established in the communities most likely to be attacked should it return. Sir John made funds available to the boards through the Bank of Upper Canada. The boards found that the problems of urban dirt and filth were unchanged from earlier years. In May, Toronto was described by the board of health as being in 'a most deplorable state of filth and uncleanliness – so much so that the Board of Health cannot dwell upon the prospect of the ensuing summer without the most serious apprehensions.' A correspondence opened between the executive and Mayor William Lyon Mackenzie on the subject of the huts and shanties on the waterfront. The mayor wanted them removed because they were the 'haunts of the worthless and dissipated, and places for corrupting the morals of the youth of the city.' The mayor said 'I never saw anything in Europe to exceed the loathsome sights to be met with in Toronto.' Mackenzie was advised to follow the course of law and not to attempt to remove the shacks directly.[23] If other towns lacked the nest of grogshops and gambling houses that lined the lakeshore at Toronto, they resembled the capital in their dirt and limited facilities.

In the early days of July rumours that cholera had broken out in Lower Canada reached Upper Canada. It was difficult to substantiate the stories because of the decisions taken in Quebec and

Montreal to conceal the news. The wife of a minister in Kingston complained that when cholera did break out there it came suddenly and unexpectedly 'for so much concealment had prevailed elsewhere, we were scarcely aware of its existence in this country.' The *Kingston Chronicle* saw with 'astonishment the constant silence of the Lower Canada press on the subject of Cholera. There is no good to be gained from it. It is a participation in deceit that no prudential motives can justify: an abandonment of the sacred principle of truth, when truth ought most to be known.' The *Chronicle* thought that silence was 'criminal and shameful, and the consequences of such conduct must be, that they will not be believed, when they assert that their fellow citizens are free from danger.'[24]

Some communities in Upper Canada were reluctant to admit that cholera had returned. It began to appear about 15 July. On that day, Dr E. Van Cortlandt reported a case in Bytown, and a second case was reported by one of his colleagues on 16 July. Van Cortlandt was incensed when the Bytown Board of Health denied that cholera was in town when it issued its report on 18 July. By then, the disease was well established in the province. The first cases were at Bytown and Prescott. On 18 July the disease was in Brockville, on the 21st in Cornwall, and on the 26th in the garrison at Kingston. The next day, cases were reported in Toronto, Hamilton, Galt, Dumfries, Waterloo, and Leeds, and on the 31st it was in Peterborough and Ancaster. In nearly all the towns, the disease came by the lake and river boats with their crowded loads of immigrants. That was the usual way in which the disease spread. Hamilton, Galt, Ancaster, and Brantford, however, all had cases in the inns where a travelling menagerie of 'wild beasts' had stopped to put on their show. The disease continued to spread during August and by the end of the month Colborne reported that most towns on the St Lawrence and Lake Ontario had been affected along with some inland villages. He had offered boards of health the money 'indispensably necessary to enable Medical Attendance to be offered to persons who have no means of procuring it and to Towns and

Villages in which disease may appear to render the aid of the Board requisite.'[25]

In the first days of the epidemic, the disease seemed to be more virulent than it had been in 1832. Some people thought that might be because of the heat, others that it was because no precautions had been taken. Some doctors thought the disease showed a different pattern in 1834: 'not ... so uniform in its ravages' with days elapsing between one case and the next in different parts of town. Others reported that the disease was acting more rapidly, often progressing so quickly that the patient was in a state of collapse before help could arrive. The virulence of the disease caused widespread alarm. Work on the Kingston hospital and the penitentiary slowed as men fled from the town. In some small communities the inhabitants fled at the approach of cholera, leaving the stores and even the taverns closed. It became difficult to find men to bury the dead or women to wash the bedding and clothes of the sick. The price of medicine rose 'almost beyond credibility.' Trade slowed down. Benjamin Tett wrote from Kingston that 'business is in a very stagnant state ... the prevailing sickness has been so bad in Kingston that I could not obtain five pounds reddy Cash for lumber.' From Bytown, William Stewart complained 'there is nothing doing in the place from the effect of the Sickness.'

There was more alarm in Upper Canada than in Lower Canada, perhaps because many towns were experiencing the disease for the first time and it seemed more virulent than in 1832. As the epidemic spread, communities in Upper Canada began to deal with some of the problems it had created. Sir John Colborne's offer of funds encouraged towns to establish boards of health and renew the precautions taken in 1832. Temporary cholera hospitals were opened in the largest available buildings but Sir John rejected suggestions that the emergency funds be used to provide permanent hospitals.[26] The epidemic had to be fought with economy. The measures taken at Bytown, Kingston, and Toronto can be seen as examples of what was done that summer.

In Bytown, rumours of cholera were supported by Dr Van Cortlandt's insistence that he had seen cases. Consequently, a meeting of the board of health was called for 16 July. The board asked
for information from Drs Cortlandt, J.D. Gellie, and D. Scanlon.
Cortlandt and Scanlon said that they had been treating victims
but Gellie said that he had not met with a case. Van Cortlandt
was a military surgeon, just beginning what was to prove a long
civilian career in Bytown and he was young and confident. He
had seen cholera in London and felt insulted when a member of
the board dismissed his medical opinion. The board met again
that evening and after disagreements Van Cortlandt and Scanlon
resigned. The board, recognizing that some action was necessary, divided the town into wards and appointed inspectors. On
the basis of their reports the board issued on 18 July its denial
that there was cholera in Bytown.

The board was preparing for cholera even as it denied its presence in town. A cholera hospital was prepared and thought
given to regulations over traffic on the canal and the rivers. The
regulations were to be framed in a reasonable mood; there was
no attempt this year to block the traffic or to encourage people to
prevent boats landing or leaving town. Thomas Rains, master of
the *Shannon*, again offered his co-operation in meeting 'the views
of the provisional Board in all reasonable things, so that their
commands shall not induce unnecessary delay in the regular
trips of the steamers or the vexation of the Emigrants entrusted
to my charge.'[27] This spirit of reasonableness seems to have prevailed in the province and there were no incidents to match that
seen in 1832 at Niagara.

Dr Van Cortlandt appears to have been correct, for when a
report of cases was returned by Drs Gellie and Scanlon in mid-
August it covered patients treated since 16 July. The doctors remarked on the variety of illnesses which existed in town and
noted of the cholera that 'it was not so uniform in its ravages as
upon former visitation.' Although there were still some cholera
cases in town in the third week of July, the board of health resolved to close the cholera hospital on 25 July. It claimed to be
justified in doing so because the town was healthy and it had no

money. The decision was clearly not one it wholeheartedly supported – it asked the clergy to appeal for funds for the hospital and approached Sir John to ask for funds. On 2 August, the board heard that £100 would be given to the town to help immigrants and victims of cholera and a week later it reopened the hospital. The Bytown Board of Health tried to finance the operations of the hospital by requiring those who could afford it to pay 2 shillings per day which was about the daily pay of a labourer. The employers of patients were to be held responsible for their expenses and were to give guarantees for their employees when they were admitted. In addition those admitted were to be held responsible for 'their funeral expenses in case of death.' Given the prejudice which existed against hospitals it seems unlikely that many would have paid to go and it is doubtful that the board could have enforced its regulation on employers. Once reopened, the hospital continued to operate until 25 September.[28]

The board of health appointed additional inspectors early in August. They visited all parts of the town and reported on the conditions of the houses. Conditions were as bad as ever. In one case, the inspectors found a building so filthy that the residents preferred to move out rather than try to clean it. The reports of the inspectors indicated by mid-August that the disease was largely confined to the lower town. That suggested a local cause, which the board concluded to be the 'stagnant and fetid state of the waste weir of the Rideau canal.' It therefore asked the officer in charge to clean the weir. He refused, claiming that it was dirty because the inhabitants of Lower Bytown dumped their rubbish in it and he had no funds available to clean it. He did offer to open the sluices for a couple of hours each day to flush the channel. The board itself had to have the weir and basin cleaned, and suggested the weir be covered over as nothing would stop people dumping rubbish in an open stream.[29] The residents of Craig Street in Montreal had come to a similar conclusion two years earlier. In both cases, the solutions were too expensive at the time.

The epidemic killed between three and five people a day while it ran its course between 16 July and 7 September. In that time

there were 96 cases and 52 deaths. Had Sir John Colborne not
acted as he did, the town would have been without a cholera
hospital at the peak of the epidemic. Dr Van Cortlandt was critical of the work the board had done and of the appointments
which it had made to the hospital and to the secretaryship of the
board. He thought that he had been a victim of 'party feeling'
arising from the fact that he was 'not ... a Scotchman and in this
lies "the head and front of my offending."'' He felt that he was
being treated with lack of professional respect and in a vindictive
way, a feeling reinforced when the board paid only one-half of
his bill for treating cholera patients. The board replied that Van
Cortlandt's complaints were the consequence of 'unguarded
jealousy and intemperate feelings of youth which the Board
hope a more mature age and a better knowledge of the world
will correct.'[30] The board might condescendingly dismiss Van
Cortlandt's complaints, but he was not the only medical man to
feel himself a victim of political 'cronyism' and contempt for his
professional skill.

In Kingston preparations against cholera began with an increase
in the size of the board of health to cope with the extra work. The
board asked Sir John to allow it to make the regulations for vessels arriving at Kingston. The executive council agreed that if
cholera did break out some regulation might be necessary but it
advised against action before an epidemic began. An announcement, it said 'would ... excite apprehension and interrupt intercourse through the Country without a corresponding advantage
as experience has proved no precaution can prevent the extension of the disease if once introduced into the Province.'[31] 1832
had convinced men already doubtful about the value of internal
quarantines that the disruption of travel was not worthwhile.
Little more was done before cholera broke out in Kingston.
    The disease appeared in the garrison on 26 July and two days
later the troops were confined to their barracks and communication with the town cut to a minimum. Married soldiers were
moved out of their lodgings in town and sent into a camp at Fort
Henry. They were joined a few days later by companies of the

Royal Artillery after five men had fallen ill. The 66th Regiment remained in the barracks. Many of them fell ill but the surgeon thought only eight were cholera cases and none of them died. The garrison was scrubbed and cleaned and the men kept under strict medical supervision and relieved of heavy duties and parades. By 23 August, the troops were reported to be in good health.

The day after the outbreak at the barracks the first cases were reported in town. Between 27 and 30 July 20 people died and on 29 July 13 victims were buried. The outbreak took the town by surprise and some residents now blamed Kingston's lack of preparations on the fact that the disease had been concealed in Lower Canada. Once it had broken out, the residents were warned against fear and panic. One person suggested that people might be cheered if bands were hired to go about the streets playing 'merry and heart stirring tunes.' The *Upper Canada Herald* agreed that music was cheering, but dismissed this suggested excursion into psychological medicine as 'treating the matter with too great levity.' The usual sober remedies of moderation and calm were recommended as preventatives against the disease.

The board of health opened a cholera hospital with £100 borrowed by its members in the hope that the governor would reimburse them. The board was uncertain how far their authority extended into the neighbourhood about Kingston. This created difficulties when the disease broke out on 5 August at Barriefield, a town near Kingston but lying outside the township. The labourers on the public works there, at Fort Henry, were affected by an epidemic which lasted for two weeks. The Kingston board had to deal with the epidemic and asked Sir John Colborne to open a burial ground at Fort Henry to avoid the expense of bringing the bodies of the poor from Barriefield to Kingston. Sir John agreed to extend the authority of the Kingston board to cover the neighbouring township of Pittsburg and he ordered ground to be provided for the burials.[32]

Most of the board's work lay closer to home than Barriefield. The first week of the epidemic saw 33 deaths reported by the board of health in Kingston. In the second and third weeks 22 and 28 people died. There were no deaths on 17 and 18 August and about 20 August the daily number of cases began to decline. Between 20 and 26 August there were 12 deaths. This reported total of 95 deaths is far below the figure of 265 which the *Kingston Chronicle* stated was the true toll of the epidemic. Sir John Colborne himself believed that a more accurate death toll was 150. Yet the number of cases and deaths in a town with a resident population of about 4,800 was enough to cause considerable fear. The board of health called for 14 August to be a day of fasting and prayer and it was widely observed. Farmers were reluctant to come into town while cholera was there. The board asked that the news that cholera was easing be widely published early in September to persuade them to resume their trade.[33]

No distinction was made in the records between resident and immigrant victims. The problem of providing for sick immigrants, however, put a strain on the town's resources. The provincial government provided £100 in August and a further £160 in November to help to meet the costs. It seemed increasingly clear to many that cholera was brought to the town by infected persons coming from infected places. While the epidemic might be God's will, which fasting and prayer might influence, it could be ameliorated by the acts of intelligent men. Residents of Kingston agreed with the moderates in Lower Canada that the British government must regulate the immigrant traffic and end the inhumane conditions of the trade. Closer to home, life would be made safer by improving the town's facilities. One suggestion was that the local water supply be improved by finding a source other than the lake where it was affected by the discharge from the Rideau Canal.

The town had to turn to helping those most hurt by the epidemic. In early September, a public meeting elected a committee to help widows and orphans. A public appeal raised £200 which was spent on monthly cash allowances. That provoked the usual criticism that handing out cash 'may lead a certain description of the poor to squander their portion of it improvidently.' The mood of Kingston was sombre in the early winter. The town's economy had been hurt by a bank failure which involved most of the town's merchants. That had been followed, perhaps coincidentally, by a rash of fires. The two cholera epidemics had 'struck at once a blow at life and the business of life.' One newspaper editor reflected that it was not only the number of dead which hurt the town but the kind of people who had died. These included a number of skilled artisans and 'several of our most active, wealthy, intelligent and influential inhabitants ... the enterprises in which they had embarked were as suddenly stopped, causing delay and derangement.'[34] Cholera was obviously not just something which happened to the poor and its effects could sometimes be greater than raw numbers suggested.

The worst outbreak of the season occurred in Toronto, and it showed up weaknesses in the new city's government. After years at the centre of Reform agitation in provincial politics Toronto was the scene of factional struggle not only between Tory and Reformer, but between Reform factions. After an early burst of organizing activity to launch the new city government little was done after mid-June by the council under Mayor Mackenzie. His attention turned increasingly to provincial politics as factionalism affected all the operations of the city council including those of the board of health.[35]

The board, and Mackenzie, had recognized that Toronto was dirty and crowded but nothing was done about these problems in the spring. The council, with the help of funds from the government, built a shed for immigrants which was ready in the second week of June. The council asked Sir John Colborne to allow them to use the building 'erected two years ago as a Cholera Hospital.' They resolved that Drs C. Widmer, John Rolph, Thomas D. Morrison, and John E. Tims should act as visitors to the hospital. Sir John agreed to the request on 24 July, the day after it was made.[36] This was the extent of the preparations made before the epidemic struck.

The first cases were recognized on 27 July. Within two days there were 12 cases and 8 deaths. Here, as elsewhere in Upper Canada, the first reports suggested that the disease was more

virulent than it had been in 1832. On 31 July there was a case at
the jail and the jailer asked the council to 'use all *your powers* in
liberating as many from the place as is *anyway* possible ... The
place is so full, that it will be the greatest act of justice in doing as
I now recommend.' The prisoners remained in their cells. One
institution which did release its inmates was the central school.
It was so crowded that 'it bends the foundation of the building'
and it was thought safest to allow the students to start their
summer vacations on 1 August. By then, the epidemic was taking a heavy toll. The board of health reported 315 deaths by 15
August with 72 dying in the period between 11 and 14 August.
The doctors found it impossible to report all the cases and deaths
which they saw and the board turned to the burial registers for
their information. Between 15 and 31 August, 167 burials of
cholera dead were recorded. The number of cases and deaths
declined at the end of August with 7 deaths reported in the first
week of September. By 22 September cholera was thought to
have gone and the cholera hospital was closed at the beginning
of October.[37]

At least 500 people died of cholera in Toronto in 1834. Mackenzie now had a chance to see that cholera was not just an anti-
Reform fraud but a disease which affected hundreds. The crisis,
however, did not bring unity to the city this year any more than
it had in 1832. The board of health was riddled by disputes and
was divided between Thomas Carfrae and George Gurnett who
had voted against Mackenzie for mayor, and his supporters Drs
T.D. Morrison and John E. Tims. Their quarrels reflected the
divisions in the city council. Charges were made that the mayor
had interfered in the work of the health officers although the
charges were never clearly detailed. The quarrelling led Dr Morrison and Carfrae to refuse to continue in office and the board of
health was dissolved on 31 July and reconstituted under the
chairmanship of J. Lesslie with Dr Tims, Mr Jacks, John Doel,
and the mayor as members.[38] The fact that the new board was
composed entirely of Reformers did not necessarily guarantee
harmony.

There were critics of the new board who contrasted the work being done in 1834 with that done in 1832. Then, the board had published bills with advice 'and left one at every house in the place beside putting hundreds up on the streets – the effect was good – the prejudice against Hospitals gave way, people used the precautions recommended ... the cases decreased at least in violence, deaths were fewer and the public *mind* became more eased.' It was, perhaps, a flattering assessment of what had been achieved in 1832 but it suggests the failures which the board's critics saw in 1834. Neither council nor board undertook an extensive program of cleaning houses or streets, and no efforts were made to supply medicines and aid to the sick poor. The city was short of funds and found it difficult to borrow £1000 for long-term improvements. Now, the action of Sir John Colborne proved vital for the city's response to the cholera. He agreed on 24 July that the old cholera hospital could be reopened – but the council did nothing to prepare it before 29 July. With the cholera already in the city, Colborne offered the council £50 and said it was 'incumbent' upon it to prepare the hospital. With the money, the council was able to open the hospital, hire staff, and admit patients, all on 29 July.[39]

Charles E. Sheward was appointed surgeon to the hospital which was soon struck by the full force of the epidemic. Within days, 19 people had died there. Sheward complained that he was not getting supplies and Colborne asked the board if it could supply them, reminding it to act 'to render the Hospital fit in every respect for the reception of patients.' Two days later, on 9 August, Colborne indicated that he was willing to accept all the expenses of the hospital if it was put under the charge of the doctors named as visitors on 24 July. This offer led to a meeting of the board of health on the evening of 9 August to prepare a reply to the governor's offer.

It was a fire-breathing reply. The board objected to Colonel Rowan's letter which had outlined the governor's terms. Rowan, it said, had implied that the board of health 'is unfit and unworthy to exercise the Trust reposed in it by the City.' It had interviewed the surgeon and he had denied complaining of a shortage of supplies – who, it wondered, was 'the busy person ... that carried the tale?' The board complained that Colborne had once said no funds were available but now said they were – although on conditions unacceptable to the board. The conditions were 'that unless the Board shall admit its own inefficiency and consent that a part of the public Revenue should be placed under the control of another Board not of the people's but of his Excellency's nomination he will not assist the Citizens.' That, the board felt, was the true meaning of Rowan's 'ambiguous communication.' The board resolved that the medical control of the hospital – 'not the funds' – be put under the four doctors, and demanded that Colborne give aid 'without any condition save that of rendering a full and satisfactory account.' Alderman Lesslie, more moderately, wrote to Rowan to say that the hospital had supplies, attendants, and money but that the city was short of funds and needed £500 for the expenses of the hospital and the health needs of the city.

Two days later, Rowan replied to this political broadside. He pointed out that Sheward had complained to both Archdeacon Strachan and Sir John Colborne about the lack of supplies and the fact that the nurses at the hospital 'were so unfit in every respect to assist him that unless others were hired, his health must be sacrificed in endeavouring to perform his duty.' Sir John had suggested that appointment of four medical men with experience of the 1832 epidemic to superintend the hospital 'without the interference of any Civil Authority.' He was asking the Bank of Upper Canada to make available £250 or whatever sum the four doctors thought necessary to keep the hospital open. On 14 August, Colborne asked the four men to take charge at the hospital and assist Sheward. The board accepted the money, noting that £250 was 'much less than will be adequate to meet its expenditure.' It applied for funds only 'to mitigate the sufferings of the distressed, and to afford *the poor of the Community* especially the only hope of Relief.' It regretted the appearance of unnecessary economy in giving Toronto aid and offered to co-operate in the relief of widows and orphans.

This particularly graceless reply was quickly followed by trouble at the hospital. Sheward objected to suggestions made by the visitors about the management of the patients and they therefore resigned their positions. Sir John called Sheward in to see him and in the course of the interview the surgeon agreed that he would accept the visitors' suggestions. Sir John then asked them to resume their duties and to prepare a report for guidance should a cholera hospital again be needed in the future. The visitors refused to return to the hospital while Sheward was in charge and Sir John asked him to stop attending there. Dr George Parke was appointed by the board of health to replace Sheward, who made off with the hospital records and returned them, when ordered to, with the entries from his period there torn out. He then spent many months trying to get the balance of his pay under an agreement which Mackenzie had made to pay him £1.10.0 a day 'cholera or no cholera.' In the end, he settled for a total of £100.[40]

The cholera hospital had been largely financed by Sir John Colborne's initiative and it was by his prompting that it opened when it did. He had an immediate interest in what was going on as he was living in Toronto throughout the epidemic. The board of health, composed of council members, was sometimes more concerned with striking political attitudes than with the job at hand. Mackenzie's term as mayor was not marked by any noticeable vigour in tackling the major crisis of his year in office. What was done to help the city was largely done by Sir John Colborne. He proved again in 1834, as he had in 1832, to be decisive in tackling the crisis within the limits of the funds available to him. He had a clearer legal position in the second epidemic and he stood in sharper contrast than before to Lord Aylmer.

The epidemic of 1834, it is clear, did not produce a panic as severe as that of 1832. In towns experiencing their second epidemics people had some idea of what to expect and they tended to act as they had toward the end of the first epidemic. The pattern of the epidemics also helped to reduce panic for in most towns the course was not violently explosive and the peaks were lower than in 1832. If individual cases seemed to be more virulent than before the danger to the community was less. The demands made on governments were fewer in 1834 than in 1832. In both Canadas there was support for a proper regulation of the immigrant traffic by the British government. Doctors might debate whether cholera was contagious, but to laymen a link between cholera and the immigrants seemed obvious. For this reason, the cities of Lower Canada asked for quarantine to be extended beyond Grosse Isle. In contrast, however, there was less demand in Upper Canada for regulations over river and lake traffic than there had been in 1832, because the measures taken then had not checked the spread of the disease. In both Canadas, efforts were made to provide hospitals and to help the immigrants but sanitary measures were pursued less vigorously than earlier. There was no surge of volunteers as there had been in some cities in 1832. The new city governments lacked the legal authority to enforce sanitary regulations. In many communities, there was no money available for such basic work as draining the streets. However, many people were untroubled by these failures as they were not convinced that there was any necessary connection between dirt and disease. They were not inclined to demand expensive action by their local governments.

The 1834 epidemic did not produce the same levels of fear as had the earlier one but it had important political effects. In Upper Canada, Sir John Colborne had shown a great deal of vigour and by his own initiative had ensured that Kingston and Toronto had hospitals for the cholera victims. The Toronto city council had attempted to attack the governor over his actions but the epidemic largely served to point up their own incompetence. The contrast with Lower Canada was very strong. There, where immigration was an emotional question, Lord Aylmer's actions and refusal to act had provoked intense bitterness. He chose to act within the narrowest interpretations of the existing law and seemed indifferent to the enormous suffering around him as he retired to his country seat. The second epidemic, coming so quickly after the first, speeded the radicalization of politics in Lower Canada which would soon bring the province to a crisis.

5

'Distance is no security': The Maritimes 1832–4

The Maritimes region lived off the sea. Its prosperity depended on international shipping and an extensive coastal trade. Although few immigrants, compared with the number entering Lower Canada, came to the region, each year in the early 1830s brought between 1,000 and 3,000 to Nova Scotia. The ports of Nova Scotia offered refuges to immigrant-laden ships caught in storms on their way to North America. Every year, a number of immigrant ships were wrecked on the rocky shores of the province and the survivors cast onto her beaches. Nova Scotia knew the dangers of the immigrant traffic. In 1827, 800 people died of typhus in Halifax and in 1831 a smallpox hospital was built on Melville Island for diseased immigrants.[1] Nova Scotians had reason to fear cholera.

The disease would find a fertile breeding ground in Halifax. The 14,000 residents lived in wooden houses crowded together in a narrow strip below the bare slopes of Citadel Hill. The Citadel, with its large garrison, the churches, the Masonic Hall, Government House, and the empty building of Dalhousie College were the only large buildings in the town. The narrow, hilly streets were dirty and many of the houses filthy. The city water-supply was inadequate. Many of the residents were poor and each winter they were driven close to destitution. Spring of 1832 found nearly 300 of the most desperate crammed into the poor house which had become a slum. A single garret housed 47 paupers, and 48 lived in the one next door; 20 patients were housed in the room set aside for the sick. The poor house, according to a committee of the House of Assembly, threatened the whole town. 'If the cholera should find its way thither, it would sweep away the inmates and form a *nidus* of Disease sufficient to depopulate the neighbourhood.'[2]

Quarantine offered the most obvious first line of defence for the community. Early in 1832, the House of Assembly responded to a request from the lieutenant-governor, Sir Colin Campbell, and quickly debated and passed bills to regulate quarantine and to prevent the spread of infectious diseases. A grant of £1,000 from the British government helped to meet the cost of quarantine and hospitals. The acts gave Campbell the power to proclaim quarantine, provide for its enforcement, and appoint boards of health in the counties and towns of Nova Scotia. As soon as the acts came into force, in April 1832, Campbell proclaimed the quarantine.[3]

The news that cholera had broken out in Quebec brought immediate action. The quarantine was strengthened and a central board of health set up in Halifax to co-ordinate the work of nine district boards. The magistrates were instructed to nominate members for these but by the time the instructions went out many communities had already named local boards. They were accepted and confirmed by the council. The central board was expanded to admit a number of doctors elected at a meeting of Halifax physicians. It began the work of cleaning Halifax and soon had to consider the danger posed by the conditions in which many of the poor were living. The board, noting the 'extremely crowded ... habitations of the lower classes,' debated removing 'some of the inmates of the most crowded Houses to places of temporary accomodation' and considered a scheme to erect a building near the town to house some of the 'poorer labourers and their families' during the summer. Nothing came of the debate.

The board did provide hospitals for Halifax and did so on a scale generous for the times. Three were set up, one near the dockyard at the north end of town, one at Dalhousie College in the town centre, and one at the southern end of town in the levee room of Government House. Each hospital had two physicians, an assistant physician, and male and female attendants. The doctors were assured that they would be adequately paid for giving up their private practice. The hospitals were equipped with beds and supplies, and arrangements were made to provide medicines if cholera should break out. The equipment included 'Hot Air Baths and specimens of different apparatus for applying internal warmth to the body – and one waggon with a heater and covered litters for the removal of the sick to Hospital.'[4]

The board's regulations show how a well-run cholera hospital should have operated in 1832. The physicians were to work eight-hour shifts but were always on call. They were to treat patients as they thought best and send the records to the board of health when the patient died or was discharged. The board would provide medicines and other supplies needed at the hospitals. The physicians were to keep close control over the nurses. One nurse was allowed for every five acute cases and one for every ten convalescent patients and the board promised to hire them as they were needed. The nurses were to 'behave with the greatest tenderness and attention' toward the patients. They were not to leave the hospital without the doctor's permission. The doctors had to 'prevent either the nurses, patients or attendants from falling into any species of intemperance.' The patients were to be given hospital clothing when admitted and their own clothes were to be cleaned. The hospitals were to be kept clean and well ventilated with the beds at least two feet apart. When a patient gave up his bed the bedding was to be washed before being used again 'to prevent the possibility of retaining or communicating infection.'[5] All this was far removed from the filth and chaos of the cholera hospitals then operating in the Canadas.

The central board gave much of its time to enforcing the quarantine. The act provided that ships coming from specified parts of the world would be visited by a health officer. He could allow the ship to dock or require it to enter quarantine. Vessels bound elsewhere would be allowed to proceed but passengers who landed could be required to stay in quarantine. This was done in

April with the brig *Wellington* which arrived with smallpox on board. In July, the brig *William* arrived en route for New Brunswick. She had been at sea for 48 days and some of the immigrants on board had used up all their food and were almost destitute. They were desperate to land in Halifax but as eight passengers had died at sea 'of what the Master called a Bowel Complaint' the survivors were ordered to stay on board. Campbell gave them supplies and the master and the solvent passengers bought enough food to feed the destitute on the trip to New Brunswick. The *William* was closely guarded throughout her stay and sailed 'without having any communication with Halifax whatsoever.'[6]

It was difficult to regulate ships reaching Nova Scotia and plying between her ports. In the outports it was very easy, especially at night, for a small vessel to slip into harbour unseen and for its crew to make contact with the shore before being inspected. The local boards of health tried to prevent this by hiring boats and crews to patrol the harbour entrances. Some used decked vessels with large crews and insisted on inspecting ships in the coastal trade. These inspections were not required under the law; shipowners and masters were angered by the delays and objected to the dangerous anchorages chosen by some boards. The council protested at the scale of the quarantine being operated in the ports pointing out that it cost far more than was raised by the fees charged. The quarantine continued to operate until December 1832.[7]

Nova Scotia survived 1832 without an outbreak of cholera. The brig *William* had brought the closest brush with anything resembling the disease. The province had made great efforts to prevent an epidemic and to be ready if it came, and the cost of the precautions was high. The boards of health had spent nearly £3,000 of which little more than £400 was covered by fees from shipowners. The central board of health did have in hand supplies of medicines, disinfectants, and bedding and had supplied similar stores to the local boards of health. Health boards had bought five boats during the summer at what now seemed to be inflated prices. The only income generated by public health measures was the £40 Halifax raised by selling manure scraped from the streets. Public health obviously did not pay for itself. When the Legislative Assembly met, it agreed to pay the balance outstanding after the lieutenant-governor's contribution of slightly more than £1,000. The assembly, however, thought the account 'large and some cases extravagant' but accepted it as the payments had been authorized by the boards of health 'under the great excitement from the alarms which generally prevailed.'

Now that calm had returned lessons could be learned for the future. Quarantine must be operated economically, and a careful eye kept on the earnings of medical men. A committee recommended that 'in no case shall any Health Officer receive more than £25 out of the funds of the Province.' After the summer of 1833 had passed without medical incident, a house committee, eager for economy, recommended early in 1834 that the cholera medicines and boats bought in 1832 be sold. That recommendation reflected the straitened economic circumstances of the province, but was nevertheless remarkable given the widespread expectation in Nova Scotia of a cholera epidemic in 1834. There had been some efforts to improve the conditions of Halifax during 1833 but the board of health and the health wardens had little authority and few funds. The street-levelling and drain-laying which had been done were inadequate to the needs.

In the spring and early summer of 1834, Halifax suffered from the effects of an economic collapse in the United States. In August there were over 200 in the poor house. The streets were filled with hundreds of destitute labourers who had no hope of work, and no money with which to move on in search of work. Those same streets were filthy, but no efforts were made to employ the labourers in cleaning them. Not until August, when disease was in the city, were any efforts made to clean Halifax. The water-supply was as inadequate as it had been during the earlier cholera scare and the shortage was made more acute by the oppressive heat which marked the summer of 1834. A local newspaper campaigned for improved water supplies saying 'it is sometimes difficult to get any, often to get it of a pure description. If ardent spirits slays its millions, may not bad water boast of being the pioneer to some deaths?'[9]

News of cholera in Europe had led to the proclamation of quarantine and the council required that all vessels arriving with immigrants or a large number of passengers anchor at the quarantine grounds for inspection. When the news that cholera had again attacked Quebec reached Nova Scotia, in July, the central board of health recommended a quarantine against vessels from Canada. The council, however, merely required health officers to visit such vessels and detain those with disease on board. The danger from Canada was made plain in a tragedy in July. A Halifax ship, homeward-bound from Quebec, was wrecked on Prince Edward Island after four of her crew died of cholera. There were many shipwrecks that summer and a number of vessels broke up on the shores of Nova Scotia. Sir Colin Campbell was sure that cholera came to the colony with a party of shipwrecked immigrants.[10]

There is no clear date for the first appearance of cholera in Halifax. It began about the third week of July among the troops in the Citadel and about the beginning of August in the poor house where some shipwrecked emigrants had been housed. By mid-August, the military were taking extra precautions against the cholera. The barracks were cleaned, ventilated, fumigated, and whitewashed. Soldiers were ordered to wear flannel belts and shirts, keep dry and sober, and avoid the night air. Any vomiting or bowel complaints were to be reported at once. Despite these efforts, cholera made great inroads, especially in the Rifle Brigade, which lost 29 men in three weeks in August. As the cholera could not be checked in the barracks, the Rifle Brigade was marched out to camp on 23 August, to be followed by the 33rd and 96th regiments early in September. After they had left, the barracks were again cleaned and fumigated. The troops remained in camp until they were free of disease in early October.[11]

The army did not warn the city that cholera had broken out in the Citadel. Soldiers were allowed to leave the garrison and visit their friends in town. When news did reach town of the heavy losses in the Rifle Brigade it caused great alarm. 'The military are supposed to be kept clean, well clothed, and regularly fed. The particulars are acknowledged preventatives of cholera, why then ... should those enjoying them be selected as victims.' It was suggested that the explanation could be found in failings of hygiene, contamination from new uniforms, and excessive drilling in the heat followed, naturally, by excessive beer drinking or by the effects of guard duty at a wharf where the air was particularly noxious. The cholera soon appeared in Albermarle Street, just below Citadel Hill, where many soldiers spent their time off duty and one of the civilian groups hardest hit was the 'military pensioners and discharged soldiers (and their families) who had commuted their pensions, and come out here as Settlers ... They were generally of the most dissipated habits and destitute of the ordinary necessaries of life.'

Both military and civilian authorities were slow to acknowledge that they were dealing with an epidemic. Cholera had been ravaging the poor house for a week before the commissioners announced the fact. At their regular meeting on 7 August they learned that four men had died of cholera on the 6th and that five were ill. On 9 August the visiting physician reported that there were now so many cases that the hospital room was overcrowded. Not until 11 August did the poor house commissioners send a letter to the board of health. The commissioners had tried to protect the public health by arranging for the dead to be buried in the poor house burial ground and ordering a stone wall built around it. They had agreed to pay liberal wages for nurses during the emergency. By 11 August, however, it was impossible to keep the sick and well separate in the house, and the commissioners suggested that the healthy paupers be moved out and the lunatics housed in sheds in the grounds to free their cells for a cholera hospital.

With troops from the Citadel visiting town and a flurry of activity in the poor house rumours spread quickly in Halifax that cholera was in the city. Excitement mounted as the rumours intensified but the board of health on 12 August flatly denied that there was malignant cholera in any part of the town. The board did urge people to be clean, sober, and attentive to their diet. As late as 16 August the newspapers had no official word that cholera existed in Halifax. The board obviously hoped to calm the public by its denials as the boards in Lower Canada had tried to do by their silence. They could not succeed, for by 15 August cases from town were being taken to the hospital at the poor house. The lunatics' cells housed 26 patients and space had been made by pitching a marquee in the yard. Within a few days it was obvious that the poor house could not hold the growing number of the sick and the nurses and attendants were refusing to handle newly admitted cases. The commissioners asked the board of health to find a suitable hospital building.[12]

No preparations had been made before the epidemic broke out. With cholera actually present, the board of health provided for one hospital rather than the three it had set up in 1832. Despite some misgivings about its suitability, the board again took over the building of Dalhousie College and by 4 September the poor house was no longer in use as a cholera hospital. The board abandoned secrecy and began to issue daily reports from 27 August. These were combined with exhortations to the citizens and a reinvigorated program of cleaning the city. The health wardens set scavengers to work, arranged to whitewash the houses of the poor, burned tar in the streets every day, and kept a large fire burning before the doors of Dalhousie College to keep the air in motion. For years there had been a debate in the city over the need for a new cemetery and this now became a more urgent need. Public and poor house cemeteries were crowded and the church yards were filled. Cholera victims, therefore, were ordered to be buried within twelve hours of death in a plot of land south of the city at Fort Massey.

As the cholera gripped Halifax, board of health reports listed the growing toll. The board noted 46 deaths between 28 and 31 August and 302 from 31 August until 27 September. In addition, the military lost 'upward of sixty men besides women and children.' At least 8 people, but probably more, died in the poor house before 4 September. The poor house records show that 285 large and 28 small coffins were made for delivery in the town and to Dalhousie hospital during August and September. Over 400 people died in Halifax during the epidemic, which reached its peak between 10 and 15 September and lingered on into October. It was 11 October before the board of health was able to issue clean bills for the port of Halifax.[13]

Dr John Adamson, who ran a drugstore, kept a list of the patients he treated for what he said was cholera. It shows that cases were heavily concentrated in the central part of the city, particularly in the small streets and alleys in its heart. The victims were labourers, masons, painters, carpenters, poor women, and blacks. They included Adamson's own apprentice. The concentration of the disease in the heart of town is emphasized in the burial records of two churches. St Paul's Church stood on Barrington Street, at the opposite end of the Grand Parade from Dalhousie College. In 1833, the parish had a population of 11,105, and Archdeacon Willis recorded 210 baptisms, 72 marriages, and 131 burials. A change of boundaries reduced the population to 8,000 in 1834, but that year Willis recorded 152 baptisms, 56 marriages, and 251 burials. There were 28 burials in August and 62 in September. The Reverend Mr F. Uniacke of St George's Church on Brunswick Street, in the north end of town, reported that cholera visited his parish and that he was at 'many' deathbeds, but he buried only 37 that year as compared to 30 in 1833.[14]

The poor were the hardest hit in Halifax. At first, this was some comfort to the better off but the disease soon found victims in their ranks. Some of them were as disturbed by that as they had been by the outbreak in the barracks. As one of them wrote early in September 'We were at first in hopes that it would confine itself to the lower orders and that it would touch none but the starved, drunken and filthy wretches with which Halifax abounds. Having, however, carried off numbers of *them* it has acquired strength and confidence enough to attack more respectable people, and lately the majority of cases has been among the latter classes.'[15]

If the disease was such a threat to the respectable people, it followed that they might have to take note of the conditions of the poor. Sir Colin Campbell again suggested, as he had in 1832, that some of the poor be evacuated from their houses to a place outside the town, but the board of health did not think that necessary. They preferred to provide relief for the poor in their own homes. Much of their aid consisted of urging the poor, crowded into the packed streets between the waterfront and the Citadel, to be aware of the value of space, air, and cleanliness. There were those however, who recognized that the epidemic 'loudly tells the man of comfort and respectability ... that the filth and immorality which he allows to grow up around him may become his own fearful scourge.'

There was an obvious ambivalence in this attitude as philanthropy and self-interest merged. In their turn, the poor of Halifax were not especially eager to respond to the new interest in them shown by the 'better sort.' In normal times, the sick poor of Halifax relied for their medical aid on the Halifax Dispensary. Supported by a small public grant and operated voluntarily by two doctors who found it useful experience for their apprentices, the dispensary handled 1,400 to 1,500 patients per year. Those who could afford to pay for treatment usually went to one of the city's three drugstores. Now, in the epidemic, doctors and a hospital were made available to, and even forced on, the poor. When Dalhousie began to operate as a hospital many refused to go or to allow their relatives to be moved there despite assurances that the hospital offered 'well ventilated apartments and constant medical attendance' unavailable to them at home. Not only did people refuse to give up their sick, they also refused to give up their dead. In some cases, they wanted to keep the body while holding a wake; in others, there was fear of premature burial which was widely rumoured in Halifax as in Canada. The authorities turned to punitive measures. 'Magistrates, Police Officers, Constables and others' were empowered to enforce the removal of the sick. A £10 fine was imposed on those who reisted removal of the dead. Some practical help was available to the poor as the citizens of Halifax subscribed £400 for poor relief, to which the lieutenant-governor added £250. A further £250 was raised by subscription to meet the needs of the sick at Dalhousie hospital.[16]

Outside Halifax, the only Nova Scotia community attacked by
cholera in 1834 was Preston. Established after the War of 1812 to
house blacks escaped from the United States, the town had fallen
on hard times. In 1833, the distress was so great that the province had distributed Indian meal to over 800 of the 1,000 residents. The general economic slump hurt Preston, and the central
board of health asked the treasury for £50 to relieve the distress
in the town. It appointed a medical attendant, who was not a
physician, to reside there, paid him 20 shillings per day, and
provided him with a supply of medicine. During the epidemic,
Sir Colin Campbell wrote: 'the Free Negroes ... have also suffered from Cholera, but in a much less degree than could have
been expected considering their poverty, great distress and indolent habits.' In the same letter, he mentioned the fate of another
of Nova Scotia's minorities. The Indian population had escaped
the disease and fled to the interior where, he hoped, 'they may
continue free from it.'[17] There are no fuller details of the effect of
the epidemic on these communities.

In the outports, 1834 was a reprise of 1832. The local boards of
health again took on the task of keeping the disease out of their
communities. They seem to have been more conscious of the
need for economy than they had been during the hectic summer
of 1832. However, the smaller communities were aware that in
1834, with cholera in the province, they were in immediate
danger. Some of them, therefore, tried to invoke quarantine
against domestic traffic. The lieutenant-governor received a
number of requests for internal quarantines. The Hants County
board suggested that travellers and baggage from Halifax be subject to 'some proper restrictions' to prevent the introduction of
the disease into the western parts. Without proper restrictions
'ill advised persons, under the influence of fear and from a
regard to personal safety, will be induced to adopt forcible and
unlawful measures to stop or impede ... traffic.' Guyesborough
board of health obliged all vessels, passengers, and goods from
Halifax to perform quarantine. Other health boards made similar requests. The interest of these communities in internal quarantine suggests that there was some flight from Halifax during
the epidemic.

If quarantine was used to defend the province against the epidemic, logic suggested that it could save the separate communities. Sir Colin Campbell had doubts that quarantine was, in fact, effective, but he was sure that internal quarantine raised delicate political problems. He therefore stood firm against all the requests for quarantine. Such schemes did more harm than good, he said; European experience showed that cholera vaulted such barriers and they merely aggravated the situation. England had never considered internal quarantine 'and his Excellency thinks we cannot do wrong in following the example of the Mother Country.' When a 'forcible and unlawful measure' was adopted by anonymous evil-doers who felled trees to block the road between Halifax and Pictou, the lieutenant-governor stated his opinions publicly in a proclamation offering a £50 reward for their capture.[18]

Late in November, it seemed safe to proclaim a day of thanksgiving to celebrate the end of the cholera and the fact that it had been confined to Halifax. Now was the time to count the financial cost of the epidemic. Fighting cholera in 1834 proved to be cheaper than preparing for it in 1832. The central board of health spent about £1,200 of which the British government paid about £300. The House of Assembly agreed to pay the balance and some further small sums for enforcing quarantine and setting up cholera hospitals in some of the outports. The house questioned some items in the accounts but had less reason for indignation than in 1832, given the obvious efforts at economy.

'We tremble at cholera, and feel inclined to fly from its influence, let us not trifle then, with childish and criminal indecision over the acknowledged sources of such plagues.'[19] With these words, a newspaper challenged the citizens of Halifax to learn from their experience. The epidemic had made the poor, and the conditions in which they lived, more visible to the wealthier citizens for a while, but did not change their attitudes toward them. The lessons drawn were practical ones. The aftermath of the epidemic did encourage debate in Halifax about how to improve the sewerage and drainage of the town and the water-supply. Schemes were considered for condemning and destroying the more offensive tenements, banning the slaughter of cattle within the city limits, and providing a regular and efficient street-cleaning and scavenging system. The debates came to nothing, however, in the face of the expense of such improvements for a shaky economy. As a result, the sewerage remained inadequate, the water impure, the tenements filthy, the slaughterhouses in operation, and the streets offensive in the cities and towns of Nova Scotia.

New Brunswick, like Nova Scotia, was a province with an extensive maritime trade and some immigrant traffic. The residents were conscious of the danger they were exposed to and in the early 1830s took legal measures to regulate sea traffic and provide against the introduction and spread of infectious diseases. In addition, the major ports of Saint John and Miramichi designated Partridge Island and Sheldrake Island respectively to serve as quarantine stations. The pattern of preparation in the early months of 1832 was similar to that in Canada and Nova Scotia. An act against infectious diseases permitted the local magistrates to order the communities cleaned. The towns needed to be cleaned; a grand jury reported on the condition of Saint John in March 1832, and noted that while the jail was clean, the poor house was filthy and some of the streets in a disgusting condition. Quarantine was to be the first line of defence, and the lieutenant-governor, Sir Archibald Campbell, suggested that all vessels spend twenty-four hours in quarantine in order to allow the health officer in the port to inspect them. He was so committed to this that he offered the magistrates at Saint John the use of a military detachment to help enforce regulations.[20]

June brought some fears. Early in the month panic briefly swept Miramichi when a vessel arrived from Dublin with cholera on board. Later in the same month, the steamer *Royal William* arrived at Miramichi from Quebec. When the health officer visited the vessel, he learned that a carpenter had died on the voyage and that four of the crew were sick. The steerage passengers were therefore landed at Sheldrake Island and housed in the newly erected lazar-house. There a mother and child fell ill and the child died. The steamer stayed at the island for more than a week. No cases appeared among the local community and the medical officer was able to claim that the rigid quarantine had been justified.[21]

The news from Quebec stimulated action in New Brunswick. In Saint John, the mayor summoned the common council late in June to consider action. In the course of the next month, boards of health were established or revived in Saint John, Miramichi, and St Andrews. The executive council allowed £1,000 from the provincial treasury to meet the cost of setting up cholera hospitals. The money was to be used 'for buildings only, and not for other expenses and [familiar refrain] His Excellency relies on the strictest economy being used in this regard.' Hospitals were set up by boards of health or magistrates in Portland, Saint John, Northumberland, Charlotte, and Fredericton and the costs quickly exceeded the sum provided. This expenditure left the boards of health and the magistrates in difficulties as they attempted to clean the towns or provide medical assistance for the remoter parts of the province, and they appealed for further help to the lieutenant-governor.

In Saint John, the council and the board of health came into conflict. The board laid down quarantine regulations for vessels arriving at the port. In some cases, their requirements were set aside by the council, and it was not clear who had the final legal authority over the question. As a result, some members of the board resigned and it was virtually dissolved. This helped to prompt the founding of a voluntary health association. Its members visited various parts of the town to report on the general state of cleanliness and health. The association also provided lime and whitewash for the poor. The members acted as a pressure group, asking the council for information on the progress of the cholera.[22]

The cost of preparing the defences of New Brunswick amounted to nearly £3,000, including the cost of buying Sheldrake Island, preparing hospitals in the province, enforcing the laws of quarantine, and meeting the costs of sick emigrants. The lessons learned from the experiences of 1832 were incorporated in a number of acts passed in 1833. An act to prevent the importation and spreading of infectious distempers in the city of Saint John laid down stricter regulations for vessels reaching the ports and empowered the physicians to order them to stay at anchor and out of contact with the shore. The act made clearer the nature of quarantine to be performed. Masters were made liable to fines for concealing illness on board. The act also provided that should disease break out among passengers landed from the vessels they could be removed from the city. A further act dealt with the boards of health in New Brunswick. It allowed the governor to appoint them in the various counties and the city of Saint John. The boards were to enforce the quarantine acts and make regulations for the public health. They were given the power to enter houses and remove nuisances, close up foul streets, regulate travel by land and water, and order vessels to the quarantine grounds. The boards could build or hire hospitals and equip and man them. The total expenditure of the boards was limited to £500 per board each year. The boards could remove those who were sick and unable to provide for themselves to a public hospital. Failure to obey the board's orders would be punished by fines ranging from £5 to £100.

A major concern of the acts of 1833 was to regulate the large maritime traffic and to lay down strict regulations to prevent vessels from approaching the shore. The stations at Sheldrake and Partridge islands had prevented contact between sick immigrants and the residents during the summer. The health officer on Partridge Island himself spent the summer isolated from the resident population, communicating only by speaking trumpet. Captains were not to be allowed to undermine that success by ignoring the regulations. The boards of health received clearer legal powers, to force the sick poor into hospitals and allowing officers to enter private buildings in the interest of public health. Nevertheless, the boards of health in 1833 were not noticeably active or efficient. Little had changed in the towns of New Brunswick before 1834.

Early in 1834 a grand jury reported on the state of Saint John. It concluded that the city was 'generally in very good order' but they singled out parts of it – St John Street, York Point, Drury

Lane, and Nelson Street – as 'very filthy' or 'uncommonly filthy.' In June, the grand jury called the attention of the board of
health to continuing failures of public hygiene in the city. By
then, the need for action was beginning to be felt. News of the
spread of cholera in Europe was catching the public attention
and the board reflected that anxiety by reinforcing the quarantine. Late in June, it prohibited contact between the city and its
neighbourhood and Partridge Island 'further than is absolutely
necessary' and required that all who came or went there did so
only by order of the board or a medical officer. With nearly 3,000
immigrants arriving in Saint John by early June, this was a sens-
ible precaution.

When news of cholera at Quebec and in Nova Scotia reached
New Brunswick it intensified the general anxiety. The board of
health asked for the city to be cleaned and distributed lime to the
poor who could not afford to buy it. A cholera hospital was prepared and the Kent Marine Hospital was also ready to admit
patients in case of an epidemic. The board's work during the
summer was commended by the press and in the presentments
of the grand jury. They reported in September that the city was
generally clean, thanks especially to the efforts of the board of
health, but some places still needed attention. With cholera so
near, the lieutenant-governor agreed to dispense with militia
drill at Saint John, as the board of health had requested, to avoid
the crowds and drunkenness that the drill would produce.[24] The
anxious watch continued in the early weeks of September and it
began to seem that quarantine and sanitary measures would
again save New Brunswick.

It was not to be. About 23 September, doctors in Saint John
began to see cases marked by severe vomiting and purging
among residents of York Point. This notoriously dirty part of
town was the place of residence of some of the more intemperate
citizens of Saint John. The board of health considered the reports
but felt able to say on 25 September that clean bills of health
could continue to be issued at the port 'until they are fully satisfied some case has broken out in this city or County of Asiatic or
malignant Cholera.' It was not possible to deny the facts much

longer and 25 September came to be recognized as the first day of an epidemic which was to last into November. The board of health established a cholera hospital and adopted a policy of isolating houses where cases occurred to prevent the disease from spreading.

In the first week, there were 11 cases and 5 deaths. The next four days, however, produced only one new case. During October, there were 2 or 3 cases per day, and by the beginning of November the epidemic had killed 32 people out of 68 reported cases. The disease was at first confined to York Point and Portland, two of the poorest and most crowded parts of town, and not until the peak was passed did it begin to spread elsewhere. The cholera continued to claim victims during November and the cholera hospital did not close until the last week of that month. About 50 people died in the Saint John epidemic.[25]

The boards of health had power under the act to 'prohibit or regulate the internal Intercourse by land or water between the Counties and Districts for which they are respectively appointed and any other Part of Place within the Province.' Acting on this clear legal authority, the boards of Saint John, Fredericton, and St Andrews set up road-blocks and established quarantines. At Fredericton, all mail from down river was fumigated. The unfortunate travellers who arrived at the town from Nova Scotia were also fumigated. Saint John felt able to lift travel restrictions on 4 October, but Fredericton kept them in force through the epidemic despite objections from the press.

As the epidemic spread in the poorest parts of Saint John the needs of the poor attracted attention. The board of health set up soup houses in Portland and in Saint John where soup would be given to those who held tickets from members of the board of health, physicians, or members of 'the Soup Committee.' In addition, the board provided bath-tubs and blankets for the poor to be used 'under the direction of several members of the Medical profession.' Within a week, the press could report that the soup houses were proving very effective 'and many families who were suffering the pangs of hunger, unnoticed and unknown' were now better nourished. That, and the fine weather of early November 'have tended most materially to diminish the number of Cholera cases during the past week.'[26] The epidemic did not spread beyond Saint John and the attempts to isolate the houses of victims may have helped to confine it. The residents of New Brunswick could be satisfied with the work done by the boards of health.

Prince Edward Island was a small community and Charlottetown itself little more than a village in 1832. Like the other Maritime provinces, it had a foreign and domestic trade which exposed it to the danger of infection and early in 1832 the legislature passed an infectious diseases act. This provided for the inspection of vessels – whether carrying immigrants, having on board infectious diseases, coming from infected places, or having had deaths on board – before they entered the harbour at Charlottetown or travelled up river from there. The health officer could hold a vessel for three days, the lieutenant-governor could order it into quarantine for up to 40 days. Penalities were laid down for those who established contact between ship and shore before the vessel was cleared. The pilots were warned not to board vessels with infectious diseases on board. The sick were to be landed and held at the quarantine ground. The same limits on entering harbour were extended to all the ports of the island. Health officers were to be appointed at the out harbours. Under the terms of the act, Dr B. de St Croix was appointed health officer at Charlottetown and a boat and crew hired for his use at the harbour. He was ordered to treat all vessels arriving from Europe as though they were arriving from places where cholera prevailed. In May, the citizens of Charlottetown nominated a board of health and commissioners, who began to clean the town. The board of health had plenty to do for even in a community as small as this, there was filth enough to worry the residents. Printed instructions were issued and provisions made for a hospital and a supply of medicine for the poor. The board asked the medical men to provide a statement of the best precautions against the disease and they responded with the customary suggestions of cleanliness, moderation, and fresh air which they had drawn 'from the best authorities.'[27]

The board followed the news of cholera at Quebec and Montreal closely but it was the report of cholera aboard a ship at Miramichi which produced further action. A ship from Miramichi was put into quarantine and the board of health at Charlottetown held a special meeting on 1 July under Lieutenant-Governor Arctas William Young's chairmanship. The board resolved to establish a dispensary for the poor and to send medicine to the country villages. The lieutenant-governor pointed out that the house had not voted funds for the public health but he offered to do what he could to find the money. The board also heard that no building suitable for a hospital had yet been found and resolved to search harder. The summer was marked by frequent meetings of the board of health 'on every alarm' and the general fear was so great that the chairman reported that meetings of the board were 'the only public meeting in this place at which the people are at all on the alert – they are too indolent to attend on any occasion when they do not particularly consider their lives in jeopardy.' The lieutenant-governor approved a number of cases of quarantine and on one occasion reprimanded St Croix for not holding a vessel for the full period of three days. The quarantine boat was withdrawn at the end of October but a vessel arriving from Dublin in November was required to anchor for three days. Prince Edward Island escaped the cholera and at a more modest cost than many provinces – barely £200 of public funds were spent on quarantine, medical attendance, and medicines.[28]

After the experience of 1832 it was agreed that there should be some legal basis for the boards of health. This was provided in an act of 1833 which permitted the lieutenant-governor to appoint a central board of health at Charlottetown, and district boards where necessary. The boards were given the power to enter premises and order them cleaned. The district boards were to make monthly returns to the central board. If cholera should break out the lieutenant-governor was given the power, with the advice and consent of the council, to make what rules he thought necessary. The lieutenant-governor appointed a central board and 18 district boards in May 1833.[29]

The experience gained with boards of health and quarantine regulations was put to good use in 1834. News of the epidemic at Halifax caused general alarm in the island, which had frequent contacts with Nova Scotia by large and small craft. The central board of health recommended that all passengers from Halifax should have been at least 15 days out before landing in the island. The lieutenant-governor ordered a 10-day interval between sailing and landing, but extended that to 15 days for passengers with baggage. Vessels from Halifax, Canada, and Ireland were ordered quarantined and a schooner and military force were stationed in the harbour at Charlottetown to enforce the regulations. Men and boats were also provided to enforce quarantine in the outports. The central board of health again provided supplies of medicine for the country districts. The rigorous quarantine continued until the third week of October, and there were a number of complaints against the inconvenience and disruption they caused, especially on the steamer traffic to Halifax and Pictou. The health officer was paid no salary, but charged the ship's master £1 sterling for his inspection, which was an added irritation to shipowners.[30]

The summer saw occasional shipwrecks, such as that of the *John Wallace* in July, of vessels whose crews were perhaps victims of cholera. The lieutenant-governor thought that some passengers on wrecked vessels might have the disease and he warned doctors in the outports to be especially vigilant. All suspected visitors, he said, were to be kept in quarantine before coming into contact with residents. Charlottetown did have one death that summer which was, in a peculiar way, connected with cholera, and it illustrates the power thoughts of cholera had on the minds of laymen and doctors. Eliza Good, aged 18½, dreamed that 'she was in a large Hospital, where Patients were dying in crowds around her and expiring in all manner of agonies with Pestilential Cholera' and she woke 'much alarmed.' Over the next hours she brooded on her dream and took to her bed, where she developed a headache and fever and a variety of other symptoms, dying a couple of days later to her doctor's great surprise. He marked her death down to 'Hysteria? or Phrenzy?'[31]

Newfoundlanders followed the progress of cholera in Europe as reported in the newspapers and in August 1831 the governor laid down quarantine regulations for vessels arriving from Europe. In March 1832, the quarantine was extended to vessels from the United Kingdom but no quarantine ground was named – the choice being left until the necessity arose. The *Public Ledger* in St John's printed a number of articles from European newspapers about the disease and urged that the recommendations about cleanliness be followed. Not until news of the epidemic at Quebec broke was anything done about the cleanliness of St John's, 'this far too dirty town.' On 2 July a public meeting resolved to establish a board of health to be appointed by the high sheriff, and to name a committee of 40 to oversee the cleaning of the city. The high sheriff was asked to find a building for a cholera hospital. The costs of running the hospital and cleaning the town would be met by public subscription and, it was hoped, government funds. The citizens were urged to keep clean and sober. The acting governor, R.A. Tucker, issued a proclamation requiring all to avoid communication with vessels arriving from anywhere other than Newfoundland ports until the vessels had performed quarantine. The health officer of St John's was to report daily to the cholera prevention committee of the board of health and similar precautions were to be followed where possible in the outports. At Harbour Grace, a boat and crew were hired to operate the quarantine. A later proclamation urged the citizens of Newfoundland to keep themselves clean and authorized constables to remove heaps of uncovered fish manure. Newfoundlanders did what they could to protect themselves against the disease and 1832 passed with no incidents.

All the precautions in 1832 had been effected by proclamation or through public action, for there was no framework of law for public health in Newfoundland. The experience of 1832 encouraged debate on filling that gap. When the Legislative Assembly met in January 1833, it considered a message from the governor. He pointed out that the fixed population of Newfoundland was growing and the security which Newfoundland had enjoyed in past years by its distance from Europe was no longer as sure. The past year had shown 'that diseases do exist, against the attacks of which distance is no security.' Newfoundland had defended itself by a quarantine which was not enforceable in law but operated only because most people accepted it. There had, however, been violations of the regulations and Newfoundland should now consider adopting a quarantine act modelled on that of Nova Scotia. By the end of March, a quarantine bill had been passed and received assent.

In the spring of 1833, a public meeting invited the St John's Cholera Prevention Committee to resume its work of cleaning the town and recommended a further public subscription for the work. The need to help the poor, hard hit by the crop failure of 1832, was sharpened in many minds by the idea that poverty, weakness, dirt, and insobriety were linked and posed a threat to public health. Relief of distress was more necessary than ever. The community had to be protected from attack and the chamber of commerce of St John's urged its members to forget any misgivings and ensure that the quarantine laws were obeyed.

News of cholera in Ireland in 1834 brought a proclamation requiring vessels from there to perform a period of quarantine to make up a period of 30 days from their sailing. Quarantine was extended to vessels from Canadian ports when news of the epidemics there reached the island. In September, the Legislative Assembly debated what measures should be taken, given the presence of cholera in Nova Scotia. The debate ranged over the operation of the existing quarantine act. In the course of the debate there were accusations that the heavy fees collected under it were being applied for patronage and speakers demanded a full accounting of the use of the money. The debate was not fruitful but Newfoundland escaped cholera, despite the fact that it was only three days away, in Nova Scotia. The mercantile community, in the annual report of the chamber of commerce, congratulated its members for co-operating despite the expense and inconvenience of quarantine and welcomed the abolition of the quarantine establishment on the 'total disappearance of the Asiatic Cholera from every port of North America.'[32]

Nowhere in the Maritimes did cholera have the political impact it had in Lower Canada. The threat of cholera was met by action, however, in all the Maritime colonies, and led directly to public health legislation. The legislation in New Brunswick was unique in providing internal quarantines which elsewhere were being abandoned by 1834. The Maritime colonies had a level of immigration high enough to encourage action but not so high that it overwhelmed the resources of the communities. As a result, it was possible to operate quarantine which did not threaten the health of immigrants as Grosse Isle did. In the Maritimes, the authorities were often dealing with one set of sick people at a time and it was less likely that sick and well would be mixed. The relatively small number of victims made it possible for some boards to isolate the homes of the sick and try to contain the spread of disease.

The Maritimers showed the same range of response to sanitary regulations as Canadians. Some were willing to take illegal action, such as blocking roads, to protect their communities. Where the established boards did not seem to be working efficiently, voluntary associations were created. There was some resentment against public health regulations, especially those connected with hospitals and burials, but indifference and inertia were the more common responses to the recommendations. Each winter brought chronic unemployment and want to Maritime communities and the cholera epidemics emphasized once again the need to provide for the poor. The better off at first tried to find comfort in the belief that the poor and intemperate brought the disease on themselves. It was a belief hard to maintain as cholera killed its victims at all levels of society. Some efforts were made to improve the conditions of the poor but they had little impact. Events showed that while cholera brought changes in the framework of law in the provinces it, alone, could not change attitudes on public health or the treatment of the poor.

6

'Ample room ... for further improvements': Later Epidemics

Cholera continued to provoke fear whenever it appeared. In 1849, the Toronto *Globe* said that it must be 'regarded by every reflecting mind, as a scourge sent from the Almighty, and having in it a voice calling loudly for humiliation and deep thought.' Over twenty years later, at the time of Canada's last outbreak, the Halifax *Morning Chronicle* wrote under the headline 'The Alarm of Cholera': 'It is not necessary by any description to add to the horror of this fatal word. It should rather be the business of the press to assuage its horrors ... this grisly plague has been near us. It has thrust its terrible visage inside the city doors, and it is still hanging on the outskirts ... Should providence now permit us to escape unscathed, it behoves us to be in a position to use all the wise precautions which science and experience have elaborated to ward off a like danger in the future.'[1]

The disease returned with major outbreaks in 1849 and 1854 and minor ones in 1851 and 1852. There were local incidents in 1866 and 1871, and considerable alarm when the United Stated suffered a major epidemic in 1873. As experience with the disease grew, it seemed possible to take precautions to limit the spread of the disease by isolating the victims and disinfecting their houses as had been done in the Maritimes in the 1830s. These precautions were only effective in minor outbreaks. The few advances which were made in public health during mid-century were stimulated by cholera's power to shock, and J.J.

Heagerty has said that 'the story of public health in Canada, as in England, might well be written around the occurrences of the epidemics of cholera.'[2] Only one other event in this period had impact on public health provisions comparable to that of cholera. The typhus epidemic of 1847 which killed immigrants by the thousands and threatened all the cities through which they passed brought action in both Britain and Canada.

The British government acted, after that epidemic, to improve the conditions of the emigrant traffic as Canadians had been demanding since the 1830s. Regulations laid down more stringent provisions for accommodation and rations. These well-meant regulations, and others made in the 1850s, were often hampered by the fact that the poorest passengers, especially those from Ireland, could not afford the extra cost involved. Many could not pay for the full food ration laid down by legislation. After the epidemic of 1847, the Canadian government imposed a tax on immigrants to raise money for the relief of paupers. The combined effect of British and Canadian legislation was to divert immigrants to the United States which could be reached more cheaply.

Recognizing that the tax was discouraging immigrants, the Canadian government reduced it in 1849. Passengers who were detained in quarantine and those arriving late in the year were exempted entirely. The year 1849 brought 38,000 immigrants to Canada, one of the largest totals since 1832. The immigrants ranged from paupers brought out by their relatives already settled in Canada to substantial yeoman farmers who were leaving Ireland in large numbers. The immigrants appeared to observers to be 'of higher social standing and greater solvency than in previous years.' This increased immigration coincided with a renewed outbreak of cholera which was seen in England in 1848. Once again, the immigrant was at the centre of the question of public health.

In March 1849, the assembly of the united province of Canada, meeting in Montreal, began to debate a public health bill in anticipation of the new navigation season. The act provided that the governor could proclaim the bill as law when there was a threat of contagious disease. While the act was in force, a central board of health would be appointed with power to make regulations which superseded local regulations. The central board's expenses would be met from government funds. Each local authority was required to appoint a local board and if it failed to do so the governor could appoint one on petition from 10 ratepayers in the community. The local boards' costs were to be met from local taxes.[3]

The central board of health, constituted on 9 June, was widely criticized. Some doctors complained that the board, dominated by laymen, had the power to control the medical profession. One medical journal saw in this a sign that laymen would soon be thought knowledgeable enough to suggest 'immediate legislation for the profession and the public, on some of the most subtle and intricate questions which can possibly engage the attention of men.' The editor warned that the profession would not submit to the board especially as, he hinted, it was composed not of the best men but of the politically complaisant. There were laymen who agreed that doctors alone should be appointed to the board. The *Montreal Gazette*, for example, argued that lay membership of local boards was necessary but that the central board, because it was advisory, ought to be exclusively professional. Local boards were executive rather than advisory and their members were drawn from local government.

The supervisory power of the central board was denounced and its composition seen as a political issue. The *Hamilton Spectator* complained that the board had been given power 'to control and dictate to the volunteer Boards throughout the country ... The principle is most objectionable – monstrous.' No central board could know the local conditions in Hamilton. City council sent a delegation to Montreal to protest against the dictatorial power of the central board. The Kingston *British Whig* was incensed at the composition of the board: 'a great job' to give favours to seven creatures of the administration, two of them to be paid 'for labours the most useless and unsatisfactory, because no two opinions are in unison.' For many people, the hardest thing to accept about the board was the alleged fact that it was

mostly French and the certain truth that it was chaired by Wolfred Nelson, a former rebel now placed in charge of the health of
her majesty's subjects.[4] This was a cause of intense anger in a
year when the debate over the Rebellion Losses Bill, with its
compensation for some rebels, was inflaming Canada.

The central board set to work against this chorus of professional and political criticism. Its actions provoked further criticism and some ridicule. It issued directions for cleaning towns
and houses. It recommended personal cleanliness and warm feet
as protections against the disease. It advised that people follow a
'light and nourishing' diet sparing of vegetables and cautious
with fish. It advised those used to alcohol not to cut themselves
off but to confine their drinking to 'good Port or old Sherry ... or
very weak Brandy and water.' Excess was to be avoided. Quick
action should be taken against premonitory symptoms. The
board urged 'the more wealthy parts of the community' to help
doctors aid the poor: 'Were it from no nobler motive than self
preservation, the pressing wants of the unfortunate should meet
with prompt relief for where starvation exists during the epidemic, there will cholera prevail, and from such a focus its pestilential breath may reach the affluent and voluptuous.'

The board then gave advice on treating and disinfecting the
sick. It required that all by-laws on public health be rigorously
enforced unless superseded by its own regulations. These regulations covered the sale of meat, the cleaning of houses, and the
draining of stagnant water, and required that pigs be removed
from residential areas. Cholera dead were to be put into a coffin
as soon as possible and 25 pounds of lime strewn over the
corpse. If victims were buried in a churchyard, 20 pounds of
slaked lime were to be put in the bottom of the coffin and 20
pounds of chloride of lime under the winding sheet. Local
boards were to report to the central board at least once a week on
the state of the public health.[5]

It became clear, as the summer passed, that the central board
was not going to become the dictatorial monster its critics had
feared. It could not even enforce the reporting provisions of its
own regulations. The Quebec board of health, for example, did

not make its first report until late July. As an agency for co-ordinating news of the epidemic the central board was almost useless. It reported, incorrectly, that cholera broke out in Quebec before it was seen in Kingston. Fear of the board's powers soon turned into criticism of its performance. So general did the latter become that the board issued a circular in August defending its activities. The fault, it said, lay with local boards which had not enforced health regulations from 'the paltry consideration of fifty or a hundred pounds ... With the fell destroyer at our doors' people did nothing to implement the sanitary laws. Only in Quebec and Berthier had local boards been 'efficient, judicious and humane ... in providing relief, medicine and a liberal supply of lime for the indigent.'[6] The local boards would have to do the work, for they alone had the power to spend money on the public health.

In 1849, as before, quarantine was the first line of defence. In April, the governor-general, Lord Elgin, proclaimed a quarantine for the season and on 19 April he requested that a military detachment be sent to Grosse Isle to man the battery and open the station. By early May, vessels were arriving at the St Charles River and there were complaints that the quarantine station was inefficient. Vessels arrived uninspected after having deaths on their voyages. While these were not cholera deaths the *Quebec Mercury* was concerned enough to write that 'it appears to us, that since 1832, never has there been such urgent necessity for having an efficient Grosse Isle establishment.'

The Quebec board of health called for an increased staff at the island and demanded that all passengers land and clean themselves before travelling up river. Questions were asked in the assembly about Grosse Isle. The pilots on the St Lawrence had contributed to the confusion by claiming that vessels with fewer than 15 passengers and no record of deaths on the voyage could go directly to Quebec. That had been the case in 1848 but was no longer so. The regulations for 1849 required all vessels to stop at Grosse Isle for inspection. Those granted a clean bill of health could proceed to Quebec where they had to wait without communication with the shore until discharged by the inspecting physician. The doctors at Quebec were told to ensure that the regulations were obeyed and to return to the island any vessels which had broken them.

When, at last, the quarantine station was functioning properly, it did so with the typhus epidemic of 1847 as a guide. There was a greater effort than had been made in the 1830s to keep sick and well apart. Ships which had had sickness on board were confined to the western part of the island where the passengers cleaned themselves before proceeding up river. Captains who did not want to be detained could leave passengers by paying a fee for their keep and proceed on their voyage after the vessel was purified. The island did shelter some cholera sufferers and 60 people died of the disease in the hospital there that summer.[7] The precautions at the island lessened the chance of passengers coming into contact with the sick but the station could still only separate the clearly sick from the apparently well. Quarantine remained a permeable and uncertain defence.

Immigration may have been a national question but it was a local problem. There were many complaints in 1849 that the expense of dealing with indigent immigrants was thrown onto local communities. Cities and towns through which they passed complained constantly. The Montreal board of health tried to make a distinction between residents and immigrants but was told that it could not do so. The city was legally obliged to provide for the indigent at its own cost. Residents of Canada West now objected strongly against the burden of immigrants. Toronto city council argued that if cholera reached the city it would be by the immigrant traffic. Immigrants would be pushed quickly up the St Lawrence to land 'diseased, destitute and sometimes dying on our wharves.' The city, therefore, sent a protest to Elgin and resolved to keep a record of what it spent on immigrants in the hope that Parliament would accept the cost. Hamilton, too, protested at the burden of coping with transient immigrants. In that town, immigrants forwarded from elsewhere in Canada accumulated in large numbers as they waited for waggons to transport them to their new homes. The city council sent a delegation to Montreal to ask for funds for immi-

grant relief. In the meantime, it would provide relief 'economically' and, to its credit, the council rejected a suggestion that no
relief be given to healthy immigrants. Complaints were heard in
smaller centres, too, such as Prescott and Brockville. At Prescott,
the police board resolved to prevent the landing of the indigent
sick unless the government provided a place for their accommodation. At Brockville, the board of health resigned when it
learned it would receive no funds to relieve the immigrants passing through the town. The most that the government could offer
was a chance to share in the distribution of any surplus in the
emigrant fund at the end of the season.[8]

Many communities established local boards of health or began to
consider the problems of cleaning their neighbourhoods well
before the central board of health began to operate in June. Little
had changed in the fifteen years since cholera had last drawn
people's attention to the state of their streets and houses. In
Quebec, Montreal, Toronto, Kingston, and the smaller centres of
Canada East and West the catalogue of horrors was the same. A
medical writer claimed that Montreal 'for cleanliness ... is ... now
probably without a parallel on the continent. Still, there is a
great deal yet to be done in the way of drainage.' Writing some
weeks later, the same correspondent gave a glimpse of what the
best on the continent offered: 'The filth of yards is scattered about
in all directions to become, with the heat of our vernal or summer sun, pestilential foci.' In Toronto, the city council received
many complaints, early in 1849, of stagnant water, poor drainage, and filth in the streets. In Hamilton, a journalist revealed
how private benefit could lead to public difficulty when he criticized the growing use of water-closets. They were a danger in
inland towns, he said, because the sewage was discharged into
lakes and not into flowing water.

The larger towns had trouble providing their residents, and
particularly their poor residents, with adequate supplies of water.
The Quebec board of health reported that people were forced to
use foul river water and often had trouble getting an adequate
amount even of that. In Montreal, the *Gazette* protested when the

city demanded six months water rent in advance. It was a 'most arbitrary and outrageous demand' in the face of cholera. Toronto had a private water company, founded in 1841, but it served very few people. Two weeks after the epidemic broke out the company did agree to open seven water-plugs for the poor. In return, the council agreed to employ men to watch the plugs to check waste and prevent their use by those who could provide for themselves[9] There is no need to continue the catalogue. Canada's cities were larger and more populous than in 1834 but they were little more successful at providing sanitary services for their inhabitants.

A number of communites had boards of health in operation before the act of 1849 was passed. In Quebec a board named by the city council was at work late in 1848 and when, in May 1849, the assembly passed an act for the public health of Quebec the board operated under the provisions of that act. The council adopted measures allowing the board to appoint officers and to take sanitary precautions and voted £150 for its expenses. Some communities learned with surprise that they had a board of health. At Guelph, the chairman of the board appointed in 1847 was told that his commission had never been cancelled and that the board could resume its functions at once. Many communities set up boards of health early in the year as fear of a cholera epidemic spread, and Lord Elgin always responded positively to applications to establish a board. The public health act recognized this local initiative when it provided for the appointment of boards of health on the petition of 10 ratepayers.

There were, however, some towns which took half a year to debate the need for a board or to act to establish one. Toronto did not appoint a board until nearly a month after the public health act was proclaimed. Its board went into operation on 2 July. At Niagara, the magistrates considered setting up a board in February but did not do so until July. Once the central board was in existence it did apply pressure to communities reluctant to meet their responsibilities. The magistrates of the Newcastle District were reminded of their obligations when, in June, they refused to call a meeting to appoint a board of health. For the most part, boards were local creations and the central board was not able to dictate the pattern of public health administration in the country as a whole. In nearly all cases, the boards were temporary bodies set up to deal with what was thought to be an immediate crisis.[10]

The work of the Quebec board serves as an example of the best that was done to meet the epidemic. In its final report, the board noted that the ravages of cholera could be reduced by public and private actions which promoted cleanliness. The board had tried to clean the city. It had provided visiting physicians for the poor and set up medicine depots open day and night. The free medicine had saved 'many a man [who] if he had been required to pay for relief thus furnished, would have delayed to procure it, until it was unavailable.' Shortage of funds, however, had made it impossible to appoint enough physicians to visit every family in the town. A subcommittee had investigated the reasons why Quebec suffered so badly from cholera. It recommended better drainage and a pure water-supply. The poor, in particular, needed access to clean water and better housing. The transient population lived in overcrowded and ill-ventilated houses where scenes of 'excess, riot, drunkenness and debauchery of every kind' were common. The best protection for the city's health was not the hasty calling together of a board at the threat of an epidemic but 'continuous well-directed persevering effort in time of health.' Improvements in the conditions of the lower classes through better housing, pure water, sewerage, clean streets, and English-style baths and wash-houses were vital for the public health.

The implications of this kind of thinking were extensive. Middle-class observers still believed the poor to be inclined to debauchery amid squalor but they accepted that something needed to be done beyond exhorting them to change their ways. The *Quebec Gazette*, commenting on the report, agreed that some permanent provision was needed for the public health. The city had allowed ten days to pass at the start of the epidemic before appointing the visiting physicians. The city ought to be able to meet future epidemics with physicians and hospitals as soon as they began. This would cost money, but Quebec had the necessary wealth and could afford much more than the £600 it had spent to help its 70,000 people in 1849. To make these provisions, however, would require 'changes in the powers and constitution of the Corporation.'[11]

Other towns reached the same kind of conclusions. The Dundas board of health recommended that as 'providence and prompt measures to clean the town' had saved it from an epidemic in 1849, the measures should be taken again in 1850 whether or not cholera was feared. They would 'promote the health and well being of the Town.' The mayor of Toronto, too, endorsed the idea that public health measures rendered cities safer. Just how difficult it was to supply them under existing interpretations of city charters was shown by the fact that he had to appeal for volunteers to clean the city. Toronto had no funds in 1849 and no powers to raise a special tax for the work. Any attempt to provide permanent public health services would meet great financial and political opposition.

Not only spending aroused opposition to public health provisions. Any such schemes called for special powers for inspectors. Many householders had strong objections to laws which allowed inspectors to enter their homes in search of dirt. Butchers resented the regulation of slaughterhouses and the poor resented the impounding of their pigs. A general invasion of privacy was likely to provoke opposition. When Quebec appointed a health officer, the city provided a police sergeant to be his assistant. A newspaper there appealed for all levels of society to support the scheme of house visits by a doctor put into effect in July. 'These visits by paid officers are meant to apply principally to our poorer citizens' it assured its readers' 'but *the Board trust that all classes will not only countenance, but aid these officers in the discharge of their duty.*' It urged heads of households to carry out their own daily inspections of their families and to get medical aid in case of sickness.[12] Here was a delicate political problem. The 'better sort' might accept the need to keep an eye on the poor but resented an eye being turned on them. In their turn, the poor resented arbitrary and intrusive public health provisions now as they had 15 years earlier.

Hospitals were the institution which aroused the most overt popular resistance. Most boards of health set aside a building to serve as a hospital for the sick poor and immigrants. The hospital was still regarded by the sick as the last resort. The Toronto *Globe* reported that 'there is no intention to remove any patient from his house to the Cholera hospital against the desire of his friends.' The *British Colonist* reassured its readers that the Toronto board of health had no intention of sending people to the hospital if they had their own doctor. Where the board was supplying medical aid 'the patients are sent to the hospital and placed under the care of medical and other officers of the Board of Health. This would only occur with poor persons, who cannot employ medical men, and who, but for the existence of the Board of Health and the regulations under which they are acting would be deprived entirely of the benefit of medical attendance.' Just how poor the patients admitted to the hospital were can be judged from the fact that the board appealed for gifts of clothing. The clothes of those admitted were usually burned as a safety precaution and few could replace them from their own resources. The sick poor resisted being sent to hospital and there were complaints that the board was endangering public health by not overriding their refusals and forcing them into hospital.[13]

Hospitals tended to refuse to admit cholera patients. The Montreal General Hospital refused on the grounds that to do so would be 'ruinous to the usefulness of the Institution as a General Hospital.' The committee of management refused to discuss with the board of health a request that cholera patients be admitted 'for a short time at least.' A hospital therefore was opened in the emigrant sheds near the Wellington Barracks. The Kingston hospital and the Toronto hospital were reminded that as they received government grants they were expected to receive immigrants without charge. They were warned that the grants would be reconsidered if they refused. Consequently, they admitted cholera patients. The emigrant agent, A.B. Hawke, had operated hospitals at Toronto, Kingston, and Hamilton before 1849 and these now became the responsibility of the local corporations under the public health act. Few communities had permanent hospitals and none with space enough to accommodate victims in a major epidemic. Temporary shelter had to be built or rented for cholera patients.

The cholera hospitals were no more welcome to their neighbours than they had been earlier. In 1849, opposition to the hospitals took both peaceful and violent forms. The residents of the west end of Toronto petitioned city council when they learned that a hospital was to be built near the market reserve. They complained that it would be 'a dangerous nuisance both as to the health and cleanliness of the neighbourhood' and would endanger 'the lives of themselves and families.' They asked that it be put near the lunatic asylum (where, presumably, they had no relatives). In London, a hospital had been erected in the fever year of 1847. Its neighbours became increasingly anxious as A.B. Hawke's efforts to sell it to the corporation or to individuals failed. The corporation called for tenders to have it removed but before they came in the building was 'wilfully destroyed by fire.' In Prince Edward Island, which like other Maritimes colonies was preparing for cholera, an emigrant hospital on the banks of the Hillsborough River was also burned that summer.[14]

The most violent action against a proposed cholera hospital occurred in Quebec. Life on the waterfront was turbulent that year as seamen attempted to organize a strike, and tempers were high. The board of health considered for some time the question of where to put the cholera hospital. The members preferred to put it where the greatest number of cases were likely to be found. They reasoned that this would save the patients long journeys. It would also avoid the dangers that arose from carrying victims through the busy streets. The residents of the closely packed parts of town where the board wanted to open hospitals were unhappy. They did not want large numbers of cholera patients concentrated in their neighbourhoods. In July, the board of health asked the mayor to allow it to use the Old Customs House at Cul-de-Sac as a cholera hospital. This was an area which had been badly affected in the earlier epidemics and the mayor agreed to the request. The customs house was ordered to be cleaned and a doctor appointed to serve the hospital.

At that time, the building was being used as a police station, which may have influenced the course of events which followed. The decision to open a cholera hospital provoked widespread anger among the residents of the district. On the night of 11 July, a mob estimated at 2,000 gathered in front of the building. After some hesitation, part of the mob burst in and drove out the police. Robert Symes, who was both the health officer and a justice of the peace, tried to stop them and had his face cut in the fracas. Once inside the building, the mob pulled down everything, destroyed the interior, and disappeared before troops could be called. No one was ever identified or punished for the attack on the customs house, as a result, some said, of political manipulation.

The customs house was left unfit for use as a hospital or police station. The board resolved to have it repaired and protected against future assaults, but it could not be prepared in time. Patients had to be treated at the maritime hospital where sheds were built to house them – the neighbours petitioned in protest, but were ignored. The board of health claimed that the assault had cost the lives of some patients who could not stand the longer journey to the marine hospital. It was, said the board, 'deplorable that in the nineteenth century and in a city having any pretensions to civilization, such profound ignorance should have prevailed.'[15]

In the early summer of 1849 rumours of cholera began to circulate. As early as May there were rumours of sudden deaths. In Quebec, the rumour that Captain Townshend of the *Joseph* had died of cholera was so strong that the coroner asked the newspapers to publish the fact that he had died of drink. Summer brought the usual digestive troubles and raised the possibility that doctors were treating premonitory symptoms of Asiatic cholera. In Kingston, some doctors thought as early as 30 April that they were treating cholera cases, but the disease then disappeared until late May. In earlier epidemics the disease had first appeared at Quebec or Grosse Isle but in 1849 the first confirmed cases developed in Kingston.

On 2 June, the emigrant agent was asked by the government to investigate rumours of cholera at Kingston. Hawke replied that a number of doctors in the town were treating cases similar to those they had dealt with in the 1830s. The first deaths had occurred on 26 May, and by 5 June there had been 15 cases. On 6 June, the public health act was proclaimed and the pace of preparation in the country intensified. In Kingston, the disease spread to the penitentiary and consolidated its hold on the notoriously dirty Lot 24 which was 'fearfully suffering from its long accustomed habits of filthiness and uncleanliness.'

The acting mayor appealed to the government for funds for the hospital but was refused. Private charity had to supplement the hospital's resources. The disease continued in Kingston until late August and killed at least 130 people.[16] The outbreak of the disease some time before it developed elsewhere suggests it may have entered Kingston from the United States. A.B. Hawke reported that immigrants arriving from the St Lawrence at the time of the first outbreaks were healthy.

Before the end of June, cholera had broken out in Montreal. The garrison there reported that some cases were seen as early as 20 June. After an initial decline, the epidemic among the troops increased to an extent which led the surgeon of the 19th Regiment to recommend that they move to camp on St Helen's Island. This had been done with good results in the earlier epidemics. There were doctors who believed that they had treated civilian cases as early as 15 June, and unconfirmed rumours that the disease was in town circulated on 20 June. It was not until the week of 2 to 9 July that cholera deaths were officially recorded. In the first week 18 deaths were noted and the epidemic rose quickly to a peak with 50 deaths between 14 and 16 July and 31 in the next twenty-four hours. 439 people had died by 2 August when the daily toll dropped below 10 a day. By the beginning of September, the epidemic was virtually ended and the board of health recorded a total of 527 deaths during its course.[17]

The disease was officially reported in Quebec a couple of days after it had been recognized in Montreal. The first cases were admitted to the emigrant hospital on 4 July. Not until a week had passed did the daily toll pass 10 and then climbed rapidly to peak at 53 deaths on 16 July. Through July and up to 3 August, the daily death toll ranged between the mid-20s and the mid-30s with more than 50 deaths on some days. From 4 August, the rate dropped below 20 a day and in the second week it dropped below 10 a day. The epidemic ended in mid-September after at least 1,066 had died. Cholera did not appear at Grosse Isle until late in the summer when, in a two-week epidemic, 60 people died.[18]

The epidemic began in Toronto on 5 July, when Dr John King reported the first case. When he reported a second to the mayor on 9 July the council appointed a board of health. These first cases were found among the poor residents of the dirtiest part of town and, for a time, Torontonians hoped that they would prove not to be cholera. Some doctors denied that they were but the board of health reported 31 deaths by 16 July and a total of 126 for the month. In August the epidemic intensified. The temporary lunatic asylum was attacked and had to be closed to new admissions. During the month, the death toll was about 10 per day and the worst week was that ending 25 August, with 77 deaths. By the end of August, 399 had died and by the end of the epidemic in late September the official toll was 464.[19] In the three major cities of Quebec, Montreal, and Toronto, more than 2,000 people died in the 1849 epidemics. There were smaller outbreaks in Kingston and Hamilton. In the first epidemics, the disease had followed the immigrants along the rivers and lakes from the St Lawrence into Upper Canada. In 1849, the pattern was not so clear: cholera entered at Kingston and may have entered also through Quebec, and the more sophisticated and rapid network of transportation spread it more rapidly than before to the major centres. As society became more complex public health measures became more urgent.

The appearance of cholera encouraged more acitivity to clean the towns and their inhabitants. In Montreal, a paper reported that 'it is very certain that the dread of the ravages of Cholera has caused our city authorities to display an unwonted, but very necessary energy, and a marked improvement is visible in the cleanliness of the city.' Entrepreneurs began to build public baths. In Quebec, a number of doctors including J. Painchaud and William Marsden endorsed bathing as a useful public health measure. A bath was opened on the river but it provoked some suspicion. On the night that the customs house was destroyed, a mob gathered to destroy the baths. They left it undisturbed only after being convinced that it was not intended for hospital purposes but was a 'private undertaking for public benefit.' The proprietor of a bath-house at Hamilton does not seem to have had any similar trouble. He advertised 'the greatest luxury of the Season! BATHS!!' and offered hot baths at 1/10½d, cold at 1/3 and a season ticket for £5: these baths were obviously not intended as a service to the poor. The drive to clean the streets did not carry everyone along. The Quebec *Morning Chronicle*, for example, wondered if the link between dirt and disease had been convincingly demonstrated. The fact that larger numbers of people died in the dirty parts of town might be explained by the fact that more people lived there. It was also possible that the poor, because of their deprivations, were less able to stand the changes in the atmosphere which the *Chronicle* believed to be the cause of cholera.[20]

Responses to the cholera in this epidemic varied greatly. Some people could be as business-like as Mr Sword, proprietor of Sword's Hotel in Quebec. When one of his guests fell ill, the staff fled and Sword tried to put the man out of the hotel. Dr James Douglas threatened to have Sword charged with manslaughter if the guest died after being evicted. Sword let him stay but went off to buy a coffin. That proved to be premature as the man recovered. Undaunted, Sword put the charge for the coffin on the man's bill. Some could be as indifferent as the nursemaids who were said to be letting the children in their charge play among the coffins stacked up for burial at the Saint Antoine cemetery in Montreal. Anger, however, was never far below the surface. In Quebec, there were threats of mob action against the drivers of hearses who were plying for hire in the streets. The residents of Champlain Street were ready to assault 'the hearse, ready horsed on the carter's stand in that street, the animal munching his oats and the hearse awaiting a call.' The board of health forestalled trouble by ordering any hearse on the stands or wandering the streets to be seized and impounded by the police.

There were signs that tension was not as high as it had been in the first epidemics. There were fewer tales of premature burials, little boycotting of immigrants, and no panic on the scale of the first weeks of 1832. No figure like Stephen Ayres appeared in this epidemic to comfort a desperate population. People seem to have found comfort enough in the advice of their local druggists and chemists. The college of physicians of Lower Canada used its recently acquired powers to prosecute a number of them for 'practising without a licence.' The public reaction was similar to that which had greeted Robert Nelson's efforts years before. The Montreal *Transcript* attacked the prosecutions, saying that it would as soon trust a good druggist as half the doctors turned out by the college. It hoped to hear 'no more of respectable parties being harassed by prosecutions got up in the name of the medical faculty calculated to restrain the rights of the public under the pretence of providing for their safety.'

During the epidemic there were a number of religious observances. The churches held days of prayer and humiliation. The citizens of the Faubourg St Laurent in Montreal held a religious procession with the statue of St Jacques in the hope of ending the epidemic in their district. After the epidemic the churches gave thanks and the council appointed 3 January 1850 'a day of general Thanksgiving to Almighty God for His great mercy in the removal of the Cholera.' Some looked for the moral lesson of the epidemic. One commentator asked 'who can doubt the benevolent purpose – the great moral ends – designed to be subserved by such strange chastisements.'[21]

Conventional religious and moral sentiments were expressed, even while Canadians tried to analyse what had happened and to suggest practical remedies. The analysis was crude and unsatisfactory. The Quebec board of health made a note of the number of dead with French-Canadian names, presumably to test the contention that they were more affected than other ethnic groups. This did not appear to be true in 1849. Some observers said that the cholera had taken a heavier toll among the better off than it had in 1832. There was no solid statistical basis for this impressionistic suggestion. It did seem true that the poorer parts of towns had suffered heavily. The central board of health had failed to collect full reports of the epidemic and the figures which existed were incomplete and incompletely analysed. The advocates of particular defences against cholera and of permanent public health provisions were too feeble to win the day. The central board of health was dissolved on 26 October with the epidemic hardly ended.[22]

Minor outbreaks of cholera occurred in Canada in 1851 and 1852, but were largely confined to Quebec and Montreal where about 200 died in each epidemic. These epidemics were not reported in the press until they were almost over and they caused little panic. They did, however, add urgency to the discussions on public services which were going on at the time. Montreal investigated the problem of water-supply once more and in 1854 the water committee published an extensive report. It recommended efforts to provide water for domestic use, industrial needs, and fire protection and to feed fountains to purify the air. A supply would relieve people of the need to drink the St Lawrence water which had the same ill effects described twenty years before. The supply should come from the head of the Lachine Rapids, away from the pollution which fouled the St Lawrence. The committee did not make a direct link between dirty water and disease, saying that it could not determine 'whether dirty water is unwholesome' but it did suggest that the suspicion was too strong to ignore.[23]

Toronto held a competition for plans to improve its water-supply. One of the prizes was won by Henry Youle Hind, professor of chemistry at Trinity College and Sandford Fleming, the engineer. Their entry was based on the assumption that a plentiful supply of clean, soft water was necessary for the public health. They quoted the experiences of a Glasgow parish which escaped cholera because of the quality of its water-supply. For Hind, the danger in a water-supply lay in the 'earthy particles' present in hard water. Their absence from soft water made it safer to drink. There is no suggestion here of an analysis like that of John Snow who had published studies in England on the role of water in transmitting disease. There was, however, a recognition that clean water was probably safer, and certainly pleasanter, to drink than muddy, brackish, and dirty water. Even in villages schemes were suggested to improve the water-supply. With cholera once more in the country, the council at Galt discussed plans to pipe water from springs into tanks.[24]

The last major epidemic of the disease occurred in 1854. It raised again the question of the origin of cholera. There were rumours that cholera had been seen in Canada before the navigation season opened, which suggested it arose from conditions in Canada and was not imported from outside. The debate was as old as the disease in the country and the government appointed a commission to consider the question. They reported that the disease had appeared in Canada in mid-June after transatlantic travel had opened. The first cases arrived in Canada on board the *Glenmanna*, which had lost six passengers on her voyage from Britain. At Grosse Isle an old story was repeated. The passengers from the *Glenmanna* were allowed to mix with those of the *John Howell* which had lost no one on its passage to Canada. Both ships sailed for Quebec on 17 June and were found to be free of disease on arrival. The immigrants stayed on board the ships but were allowed to visit the town. On 20 June, cholera broke out on both vessels and the sick were sent to the marine hospital. By 22 June the disease was in Montreal, the next day in Hamilton, and on 25 June Toronto and Kingston reported cases.

The commissioners' report reinforced the idea that cholera was linked to immigration. There were some charges that the doctors in charge of quarantine had not enforced it effectively because they doubted its usefulness. While the report on the *Glenmanna* did not end the debate it did strengthen the hands of those who argued that quarantine could be made to work. After the epidemic, the central board of health recommended improvements at Grosse Isle. They said that the station was useful for 'the segregation of those infected with the disease ... that in all epidemics, the establishment will be found useful as a cleansing and purifying post, by which means the extension of epidemic disease in general will, to a certain degree, be limited.' The board made suggestions about the operation of the station which were intended to prevent the mingling of passengers which had occurred.[25] The justifications for keeping Grosse Isle in operation were thus the same as in 1832.

It was some time after the 1854 epidemic began before the governor-general established a central board of health under the act of 1849. The board was constituted on 5 July with Thomas Blatherwick as secretary and he began to gather information on which to base the board's sanitary regulations. It took some time to find a copy of the English central board of health report of 1849 which Blatherwick wished to use. Not until 14 July did the central board adopt regulations 'founded on the experience of former Boards of Health both in England and this country and also on that of the best and most recent medical and general authorities.' The regulations as adopted were essentially those of 1849. The board could not enforce them by imposing penalties as its attempt to do so was declared to be *ultra vires*.

The central board did not provoke the same hostility which its predecessor had done in 1849, but it did not go entirely without criticism. Dr William Marsden made charges of political favouritism and professional incompetence when he resigned from the board. He claimed that it was through his initiative the board had been reconstituted. While he had declined the secretaryship he had been left with the impression that he would be asked to serve as chairman. Despite his anger at the provincial secretary, who had asked him how he intended to vote at the forthcoming election, Marsden helped to organize the board. When it was organized, he learned that it would choose its own chairman and secretary. The board chose Dr Oliver Robitaille as chairman. Marsden then resigned because he could not 'without professional degradation consent to act under a head so totally incompetent and inexperienced ... to whom the members of the Central Board of Health who voted for him would not go for treatment.' Marsden was convinced that the appointment was a political one and that it was 'a slight to the whole medical profession of Canada.'[26] No body, it seemed, could be established without some charge of political interference. Experience with the board of 1849 had presumably calmed the extravagant fears expressed then, and the board of 1854 was not attacked as potentially dictatorial.

The central board asked councils and communities to set up local boards. It hoped to see 164 created but many communities failed to respond. The board was thus thwarted in its efforts to collect full statistics of the epidemic as it developed across the country. It did receive returns from 100 communities which suffered cholera in the period between 20 June and 15 August. Its published list did not include Toronto, which suggests some of the shortcomings of the reporting system. The reports received did not allow the board to make any detailed analysis of an epidemic. The closest that it came to doing so was with the figures from Quebec which were broken down into categories of resident, immigrant, or sailor, and sex. The conclusions drawn were limited: the epidemic had shown a steady pattern through its course, rather than an explosive one, and St John's ward was the worst affected part of the city.

No other community reported in such detail and the board had to be content with reporting that Quebec, Montreal, Hamilton, and Kingston were the worst hit communities in an epidemic which killed over 3,600. There were epidemics in communities which did not appear in the board's report. The village of Dundas had one between late June and late September in which 30 people died. Toronto, too, had an epidemic in which 142 died in the general hospital. The board concluded that 'the adoption of thorough drainage, sewerage, and ventilation, with a plentiful supply of pure water, attention to cleanliness, and the prevention of overcrowding' would bring health to the cities.[27]

The same conclusions were clearly drawn that year elsewhere in British North America. The Maritimes had been spared in 1849 but in 1854 the worst epidemic in the colonies took place in Saint John, New Brunswick. The city had experienced cholera in 1834 but since then the population had come to believe that geography and topography protected it from the disease, and people thought the air especially healthy and the city well situated to avoid sickness.

The residents of Saint John learned late in June that their city was not safe from cholera. An epidemic began in the heart of the town in the most crowded and dirty district. An investigation by city authorities traced the outbreak to passengers from the *Blanche*, a vessel from Liverpool. The epidemic lasted until mid-September and 1,500 died in a city of 30,000.

The Saint John board of health recommended the sanitary measures in use elsewhere, but was slow to act. Soon there were threats of mob action and the city came close to seeing riots in the streets. Action to enforce the regulations alone ended the threats. The epidemic was so savage it caused panic, with many refugees fleeing from the city including a number of poor people who camped in the woods near the town. Captains of riverboats reported they had been threatened with violence at Fredericton. A number of communities tried to set up internal quarantines but, as these were no longer allowed by law, the executive council disallowed the attempts. The epidemic shook the morale of Saint John residents badly, and for nearly fifty years afterwards people dated events from 'the year of the cholera.' More practical consequences followed: commissioners of water and sewerage were appointed and were able to make progress in providing services over the next years. The provincial legislature passed an act in 1855 to provide a board of health for Saint John and it became a permanent body with Dr William Bayard as chairman for the next thirty years.[28]

The epidemic thus had a lasting effect on public health provisions in the city. It was savage enough to shock the residents into support for services and for a permanent board of health. Its influence was not confined to New Brunswick for it created such fear in Nova Scotia that 'as a direct result a City Hospital was built' in Halifax. The province escaped the disease but Newfoundland was less fortunate. In October, an epidemic began at St John's and lasted until late December with 88 deaths. The board of health established in June made the usual recommendations about the need to clean the communities. An incident at Harbour Grace showed the fear which cholera could inspire in a community freshly exposed to it. Two victims died there in November and Robert Pretient reported from the settlement that 'you cannot conceive the excitement and alarm which prevailed here, among the great mass of the people, who have never before had a case of the disease of the kind among them. We could not get possession of the house, to which we carried the stranger, without the presence of Soldiers, and now we hold it in fear of its being burnt down in the night.' That was no idle threat; in Saint John, people had burnt the houses of victims of the disease. At Harbour Grace, the panic died when no more cases developed. During the epidemic money was collected in St John's for an asylum for widows and orphans and, after it was over, discussions began about making permanent improvements in the city's sanitary condition.[29]

The epidemics in the 1830s had produced public health laws in the Maritimes and the epidemic of 1854 saw some efforts to bring about sanitary reforms. It had the same effect in Canada, too, but expectations about acceptable government activity were limited. The tendency was to have governments do less, not more, if any doubt arose.

In 1866 the authors of the *Memorandum on Cholera* wrote that the role of central government was 'to keep the grand watch, and to defend the approaches, if they can be defended.' People should not make 'the too common error of expecting more from Government than the Government can possibly perform, and thus individuals or corporations neglect what is most needed in such circumstances.'[30] Much of the work of defending society against disease had to fall on local government but there were limits on what it could do to protect individuals who, most commentators believed, ought to be protecting themselves.

In 1866, however, there were some apparent successes against cholera, which suggested that effective action against the disease was possible. Advocates of public health reform could cite these when making their case. The year had begun with preparations inspired by the news of fresh cholera outbreaks in Europe. As early as February, sheriffs in Canada were advised to take precautions in the jails 'in view of the probable appearance of Cholera in Canada during the approaching summer.' Cleanliness, clean water, careful diet, fresh clothing, warmth, and a chance to bathe were recommended for the prisoners. Any sick were to be isolated. The advice, it was said, could be followed with benefit even if there was no cholera. The executive council recommended, in February, that a central board of health be established and in March a medical conference was held in Ottawa which produced the *Memorandum on Cholera*.[31]

Three weeks after the conference closed, the central board of health was appointed. Unlike the board of 1849, it was composed exclusively of professional men and there was some effort to give it a geographical spread. As its more than 50 meetings were held in Ottawa, the members there tended to dominate. The main content of its discussions was the progress of cholera across Europe. The board had no responsibility for the quarantine, which was under the control of the bureau of agriculture. It recommended that communities form local boards and it approved sanitary codes which were submitted to it. The board prepared a form for reporting cases but, interestingly, thought it best not to print and distribute it for fear of causing a panic. When cholera broke out in the United States, the board prepared a circular letter recommending precautions. Its relations with the local boards were so tenuous, however, that it was forced to send the letter to the mayors of the towns. In its final report, in November, the board warned that future outbreaks on the continent could affect Canada and recommended that sanitary precautions taken in 1866 should be maintained and extended as 'there is ample room still left for further improvements.'

The work of the central board had little impact in 1866. The members seem to have been unaware of incidents in Toronto during the summer. During the year the Toronto board of health reported 145 'zymotic' deaths – a category in which cholera was sometimes included. The board did say that there had been five incidents of cholera in the town but that they had been stopped before they could spread. Toronto had appointed two health officers to oversee sanitary improvements in the town. Ottawa also appointed two health officers to serve until the beginning of the winter. The doctors analysed the city's water-supply and found it contaminated by sawdust and sewage. Nevertheless, they felt able to congratulate the city, in their final report, on 'the great and general improvement in the sanitary condition of the city.'

The year 1866 seemed to promise some hope of limiting the impact of the disease. At Grosse Isle, the superintendent, Dr A. van Iffland, was able to report that although many ships had arrived from cholera ports Canada had been protected against the disease. Conditions of the voyage had improved, although it was still hard for children, and the immigrants were generally healthy. The claim to have contained outbreaks of cholera was something new in Canada. The *Memorandum* had argued that it was possible by cleanliness and sequestering the sick and those in contact with the disease. The authors still inclined to think that the atmosphere played a part in spreading the disease but they also recommended that the evacuations of victims be disinfected and buried. Dr William Marsden, making no reference to the work of Snow or others, wrote that thirty years of study had convinced him that cholera was spread by 'water, which has been contaminated by diseased ejecta from a cholera patient' and that the best protection was to boil drinking-water. A writer on the *Morning News* of Saint John was even more optimistic. Referring to Snow's work he argued that water spread the disease: 'Thus little by little the most mysterious and dreaded pestilences get robbed of their terror and become largely avoidable by human foresight and vigilance.'[32] This sort of optimism seemed to be well grounded following the events in Halifax that summer.

In Nova Scotia, the council had proclaimed a quarantine against infected ports in April. It was barely in time, for on 28 March, the steamer *England* left Liverpool for New York. She stopped at Queenstown and took on passengers. Four days later, one of the Irish passengers died, to be followed by a second the next day. The doctors on board declared the deaths to be by cholera. At that point, the *England* ran into a storm and for three days the passengers were battened below decks. The disease became virulent and as many as 15 people died on some days. Faced with disaster and with his crew beginning to fall sick, the master headed for Halifax and arrived on 9 April. Of the 1,202 passengers 49 had died and, with her engineers sick, the *England* was forced to stay in port.

The ship lay anchored off McNab's Island for nine days and in that time more than 200 of her company died. When she sailed she left behind 50 convalescent patients. Medical men, labourers, and Sisters of Charity were sent to the island to cope with the tragedy. A naval hulk was anchored near the *England* to serve as a hospital, and 25 soldiers were drafted to protect women and children from some of the male passengers who were forcing them out of the tents into which they had been moved and stealing their food.

McNab's Island became a place of horrors. A detachment of city police was sent to cut communication with the mainland but about 100 passengers escaped from the camp. The authorities did not succeed in isolating McNab's but they were more successful at sequestering on the mainland people who became sick. The pilot who had brought the *England* into harbour sickened and died. People who handled debris from the island also fell sick. The victims' houses were isolated and the disease confined to the residents. Crews were sent to search the shore and burn debris from the quarantine ground. With much luck and considerable effort, Halifax was spared an epidemic. It did seem true that even a violent outbreak of the disease could be contained. These apparent successes were not followed by mass conversion to sanitary reforms, but the need for action now received church support. A circular letter from the archdiocese of Quebec, issued 1 May 1866, pointed out that while God alone could save men from disease, they were able to take precautions suggested by prudence and science. The letter concluded with a list of sanitary recommendations no different from those issued by boards of health.[33]

After 1866, a number of communities set up permanent boards of health, usually in the form of committees of the local council. Yet even these communities were reluctant to accept the idea that medical officers should serve and be paid when there was no immediate crisis at hand. Toronto had passed a by-law which allowed it to employ health officers and health inspectors. The system could claim some success in 1866 but within a couple of years there were complaints about its cost. In 1868, the city estimates, which allowed $600 per year for each of two health officers, were attacked on the grounds that the expenditure was not needed. Despite the mayor's pleas that the officers' work had saved the city thousands of dollars, their salaries were cut to $300. The majority of councillors felt that medical officers were not needed when there was no extraordinary sickness in town. A medical journalist could only hope that the time would come 'when the public will more fully understand the importance of availing themselves of scientific knowledge to prevent disease.'[34]

In the newly formed Confederation after 1867, the responsibility for public health became more diffused. The federal government, through its department of agriculture, had charge of the quarantine stations and was responsible for preventing the introduction of infectious disease. There was no central body which could co-ordinate public health action. The new nation made no provision for a body even as temporary and feeble as that of the central boards of health which had been created under the act of 1849. Each province made its own provision, and in Ontario the first public health act was passed in 1873, the year of the last great cholera epidemic in the United States and the last major scare in Canada.[35]

In 1871 there was one more incident involving cholera in Canada. Halifax was again the scene. There, efforts had been made since 1866 to provide a more secure quarantine ground than McNab's Island but they had not succeeded. Dr J. Gossip had been made health officer at Halifax despite complaints about his performance in the summer of 1866. In April 1871, he was criticized for allowing a ship with smallpox on board to approach the wharfs with the plague flag flying. The passengers and crew made contact with the shore. There was a similar incident the next month and the citizens of Halifax became concerned about Gossip's lax administration. In November, the *Franklin* put into Halifax. Her captain reported that he had lost nine passengers to dysentery and seasickness on the voyage, but Gossip issued a clean bill of health. The *Franklin* landed a passenger and sailed for New York. She left behind many rumours that she had cholera on board and that she had put bodies over the side at night. News soon came from New York that the *Franklin* had been quarantined for cholera.

Panic and demands for Gossip's resignation swept Halifax. A man who had worked on the *Franklin* and a coal-heaver who had helped to fuel the ship were reported to be sick at Chezzetcook near the town. Both had symptoms of cholera. Doctors were sent to the settlement and a proclamation issued to establish a central board of health for Nova Scotia. At Chezzetcook the outbreaks were confined by isolating the victims' houses and burning their clothes. The community was cut off from the outside world and a doctor stayed there until it was thought safe for him to return to Halifax. Seven people were ill and two died. In Halifax, a hastily organized internal health committee set about cleaning the town and distributing disinfectant to the poor. No further cases developed and the incident closed with the dismissal of Gossip following an enquiry by the central board of health. Once more it seemed that if lax administration exposed a town to danger, vigorous action could contain the threat.[36]

For the rest of the century, cholera continued to demand care and vigilance whenever there was an outbreak elsewhere. In 1873, Canada escaped the epidemic which swept the United States. Its escape was due more to good fortune than to anything else. As public health organizations developed they kept alert to cholera. In 1888, for example, news of an outbreak of the disease in Italy found a young doctor in Toronto being sent 'to visit all the Italian boarding houses in the City, and besides reporting the sanitary conditions, to ascertain if any of the recent arrivals had come from any of the infected districts.' At the end of the tale, as at the beginning, cholera and the immigrant were linked.[37]

In the 1870s, Canadian doctors increased their pressure for public health reforms. Dr James Grant, in his presidential address to the Canadian Medical Association in 1873, urged sanitary measures against cholera. He stressed the need for public health precautions even in years when there was no scare, and suggested that Canada create something like the national sanitary bureau which the American Medical Association had proposed for the United States. Others took up the idea and called for a national organization to oversee public health. As one said, this would improve the 'present perfunctory methods of providing against the spread of contagious diseases and of enforcing sanitary laws and of registering births and deaths.' Only with dominion leadership could 'municipal and village councils ... meet the dangers often suddenly sprung upon them' – their record of failure was well known. Lord Palmerston's response to a party of clerics became a favourite with sanitary reformers. When asked to declare a fast on the approach of cholera, he had sent them away with the advice that they 'cleanse their sewers, and diligently visit the dwellings of the poor.' One writer went as far as to suggest that the provision of a 'stringent Public Health Act' was 'of greater moment to this country than even a Pacific Railway.'

That, perhaps, was too big a claim for a Canadian to make, but the drive for permanent public health provisions began to gain ground in the late 1870s. It would be some time, however, before a public health doctor could remark of the early public health efforts that 'to modern sanitarians accustomed to seeing Boards of Health permanently established and pursuing their work systematically in the field of preventive medicine the spasmodic activity in health matters developed in these early years of the century seems crude, and with results proportionately imperfect.' But even he had to admit that affairs in 1891 were not so perfect that his contemporaries could afford to relax.[38] Those early efforts at sanitary reform, crude as they were, resulted from the successive visits of the cholera. The later achievements in public health rested on that foundation.

7

'Charlatanism of every description'

Thousands of people needed help in every cholera epidemic. Those who could afford the fees turned to the regular doctors.[1] The less fortunate asked the apothecary for advice when they bought their medicines. Many preferred to ignore the conventionally trained doctor and to seek the help of the irregular practitioners. The irregular might be a man trained in eclectic or homeopathic medicine, or a herbalist, or a self-educated person with a knowledge of folk medicine, or a practitioner of a system of medicine such as the Thomsonian one, based on formulae of plants devised by the American, Samuel Thomson. The irregulars usually demanded payment, which was one reason why Ayres made such an impact when he worked for nothing in Montreal. A large number of people treated themselves or were helped by friends and neighbours.

The demand for medical help coincided with efforts by the regular doctors to organize themselves into a medical profession. Their performance during the cholera epidemics helped to shape public attitudes toward those efforts. Some doctors had been trying for many years to close the practice of medicine to 'outsiders.' They hoped to create a profession of men (with women allowed only to act as midwives) clearly distinguished from laymen and holding a special position in society. Their ambitions were financial and social and they hoped to make the practice of medicine the exclusive right of a group of gentlemen. The most obvious way to do this was to license entry into the profession and licensing could be justified as a way to protect the public from incompetents. In Lower Canada a medical board had been established late in the eighteenth century to issue licences. Its operations were resented by many laymen and by some doctors who accused members of the board of favouritism toward their own students. The board's operations helped to provoke antagonism between French and English doctors in 1831 and again in 1846.[2]

In Upper Canada, efforts to license entry into the profession met many difficulties in the early nineteenth century. A medical board was set up in 1819 to examine applicants but many men practised without licences and were welcomed in the thinly settled province. When the act was amended in 1827 it allowed for a large number of exemptions from examination. All those who held a diploma from a university in the British Empire or were licensed by the Royal College of Physicians in London and all those who held a warrant or commission as a medical officer in the Royal Navy or the British Army were exempted. Anyone practising in the colony before the War of 1812 could continue to do so if he was declared competent by three licensed physicians or surgeons. Women acting as midwives were alone allowed to practise for gain without a licence. The exemptions were allowed by the assembly because it recognized that 'during the more infant state of the Province' it was impossible to enforce a highly selective law of entry into the profession.[3] As it was, the revised law was widely ignored.

The legislation passed in Upper Canada was watched closely by the royal colleges in Britain. The act of 1827 brought complaints from the Royal College of Surgeons in Dublin that, as its members had not been exempted from examination, an invidious distinction had been made between them and those practitioners trained in England and Scotland. Dr Christopher Widmer, president of the Medical Board of Upper Canada, pointed out that the distinctions were between graduates and non-graduates, and English and other British colleges. Members of the Edinburgh colleges were no more free to practise than those of the Dublin colleges. Graduates of the university in Dublin were as free to practise as any other British graduates. The British colleges continued to keep a close eye on developments in Canada. When the College of Physicians and Surgeons was formed in Upper Canada in 1839, the legislation was disallowed by the British government for infringing the liberties of the Royal College of Surgeons.

The influence of British institutions in London and the frontier nature of Upper Canada both hampered efforts to close the profession in Upper Canada. The doctors did not win any support from the lawyers. A proposal that medical men form a corporation to regulate themselves was rejected in the early 1830s. When the British Crown lawyers, in London, objected to the 1839 legislation that allowed doctors in Upper Canada to organize as a college, they argued that it would 'have a tendency to establish a monopoly which might be found injurious to the inhabitants of the Province.' The lawyers of Upper Canada, secure within the Law Society which was one of the first institutions created in the province, agreed that medicine should be a trade open to all with the law as the remedy against error.[4]

Without a legally protected professional status regular doctors in Upper Canada were often sensitive about real or imagined professional slights. The regulars' fears about their status showed up clearly in their quarrels with lay boards of health and particularly in their protests about the central board established in 1849. In Lower Canada, the profession was shaken by sharp ethnic divisions and French resentment of British dominance. Everywhere, the regulars were challenged by the irregulars. In 1852, a medical writer complained that Upper Canada was flooded with 'a horde of root doctors, steamers and quacks' who divided 'with the regularly qualified physicians the scanty subsistence the neighbourhood is capable of affording [by] ingratiating themselves into the good opinions of the farmers and country shopkeepers, and descending to familiarities with the lower classes to which educated gentlemen cannot stoop and soon the latter finds his ignorant and low competitor is preferred to himself, or at least divides pretty equally, public confidence.' The writer scorned both the knowledge and the behaviour of the irregulars.

They did not behave in a 'professional' way, but treated medicine as a trade and cheerfully crossed the class barriers in their all too successful search for business. The public seemed to welcome them. That fact was driven home when, despite the regular's opposition, homeopaths and eclectics won legal recognition. The Ontario Medical Act of 1869 included them in the definition of medical practitioners.[5]

Canadian doctors' efforts to win the status of professional gentlemen found little popular support during the cholera years. They did win a system of registration, introduced in 1865, which gave registered doctors alone the right to sue in court for unpaid fees and to hold such official posts as medical officers or militia surgeons. These posts had always been eagerly sought. Whenever a position was created in the quarantine service, in public health, or in the cholera hospitals there were many applicants. The prospect of a salary of £1.10s to £3 a day for their services was obviously attractive. In most epidemics the assemblies complained that doctors' claims for their services were too high. The period after each epidemic saw doctors' petitions for payment in full rejected or ignored. The evidence suggests that many doctors were financially hard pressed. In these circumstances, it was galling for them to learn that medical practice was regarded as well paid. In 1852, the legislature abolished the University of Toronto medical faculty on the grounds that the public should not finance the education of men entering so lucrative a profession.

Education was the key to professional standing. The claim to special status rested on a claim to special knowledge. A university education gave the highest status and, failing that, membership of one of the royal colleges or service in the armed forces distinguished the regular doctor from the irregular. Many doctors were trained by apprenticeship in the first half of the century, but medical boards tended to recommend attendance at a course of lectures. Well-known doctors gave such courses and led their students around the wards of hospitals in the years before medical schools were established. Immigrants were more likely than native Canadians to have the higher qualifications, for only those Canadians who could afford to study abroad could go beyond apprenticeship in the early nineteenth century. Canadians objected to the fact that their sons had to study abroad and after 1812 there were a number of complaints that young Canadians were going to the United States and learning both bad medicine and 'democratical' ideas. The cholera years coincided with efforts to create medical schools in Canada. Dr William Caldwell and his colleagues began the Montreal Medical Institution in 1823. Dr Charles Jacques Fremont opened the École de médecine de Québec in 1845. There was no medical school in Upper Canada at the time of the first epidemics, but shortly afterwards John Rolph opened a school which became the Toronto School of Medicine in 1843 on his return from exile following his participation in the 1837 rebellion. The founders of Canadian medical schools usually sought a university affiliation, which would give their graduates a degree and exemption from licensing examinations, and they kept up their entry standards. By mid-century, some of the alternative medical practitioners had their own medical schools. Canada, unlike the United Schools, did not produce a flood of commercially operated schools which lowered their entry standards in pursuit of students and profits.[6] In time, however, the profession would find that its efforts to control the content of education were sometimes challenged by the universities.

The medical schools offered lectures on materia medica and therapeutics, anatomy and physiology, principles and practice of medicine, principles and practice of surgery, midwifery and the disease of women and children, and medical jurisprudence. The students dissected and, even where there was no medical school, the medical apprentices sometimes had a chance to practise anatomy. In 1834, the Toronto cholera hospital was turned into an anatomy theatre after the epidemic. One former student recalled that 'when I look back upon the scenes which were transacted in the cholera hospital during the winter, my mind almost revolts on itself – I believe there were something like a dozen bodies mangled and dissected.' Dr Widmer had to assure the governor that stories of grave-robbing and evil-doings in the theatre 'are utterly without foundation.' Students at medical school learned from lectures, demonstrations, and practice in the hospital and on the doctors' rounds. The medical students of Toronto in 1834 thought a school so much an improvement over their own training by apprenticeship that they lobbied for one and Sir John Colborne agreed that 'the establishment of a Medical School can no longer be delayed without injury to the Province.'[7]

The schools which did operate in this period had many short-comings for they were primarily concerned with producing doctors trained for the daily round of medicine. Few taught chemistry or demanded laboratory work. The microscope was little used. At Laval, after 1862, the students did some microscopic work in anatomy. McGill, by the 1870s, was said to have the best medical school north of Philadelphia and it was for that reason that William Osler went there from Toronto. Little had changed since the school opened thirty years before. Not until Osler returned from Europe to take up a chair at McGill in the mid-1870s were the students required to use the microscope and work in the laboratory. At the same time, McGill offered its students the first lectures given there on public health.[8] No medical school taught statisics at mid-century and the Canadian medical student graduated with no knowledge of the microscope or statistical analysis – two of the most useful tools developed in the period for the study of medicine and health.

Canadian life and the nature of medical practice gave doctors few opportunities for theoretical studies. Most doctors were concerned with scratching a living. The colonies, however, were not cut off from medical ideas. A steady stream of immigrant doctors brought their books and journals with them and Canadians continued to study abroad. There were always some men interested enough in medical developments and professional organization to form local medical societies. As early as 1826, Dr Joseph Morrin had set up the Quebec Medical Society and in the next decades medico-chirugical societies were established in many of the major centres of Lower and Upper Canada. Out of these societies came a movement to create a single association and in

1844, Dr Joseph Painchaud proposed that an association be formed to represent the needs of the profession and to supply governments with 'statistical and hygienic' information. This proposal ran into objections from doctors who feared the burden of offering advice to the public 'without remuneration' and the scheme failed.[9] Not until 1867 did Canadian doctors take the opportunity (offered by Confederation) to organize the Canadian Medical Association.

The same aims of spreading medical knowledge and creating a profession lay behind the founding of medical journals. A number of these appeared in the years after the first epidemic, some to die quickly and others to run for years. Most were filled with medical news from foreign journals interspersed with contributions from Canadian doctors. The journals thus acted as conduits of information and allowed local doctors to test their own experience against what they read.[10] The readership was usually small in number.

Canadian doctors could keep abreast of the long and often heated debate on cholera which continued throughout the mid–nineteenth century. At the heart of the debate was the question of whether or not cholera was a contagious disease. The question was not resolved until the profession generally accepted the germ theory of disease which postulated that each disease was a separate entity created by a specific germ. That acceptance could not come until technical developments late in the century made the theory persuasive. Robert Koch was able, in 1883, to isolate the cholera *vibrio* and grow it in culture. His experiments convinced most doctors that cholera was produced in a susceptible patient by micro-organisms usually transmitted in contaminated water. Not everyone was convinced. Max von Pettenkoffer, one of the most respected medical theorists of the time, thought the *vibrio* could produce disease only if specific conditions existed to make it poisonous. He demonstrated his faith in his theory by swallowing a tumbler of water laced with cholera *vibrios* and living to continue his criticism. In the years during which cholera visited Canada, the germ theory was one of a number which tried to explain the origin of disease. Other theories suggested that disease was produced by a process of fermentation, or by miasma, atmospheric change, or spontaneous generation.[11] No theory in mid-century had the explanatory power which the germ theory acquired in the last decades and debate over the nature of cholera was inevitably confused.

As there was no agreement on how the disease was caused, there could be none on how it spread. In the late 1840s and early 1850s, William Budd and John Snow, working separately in Great Britain, suggested that water supplies infected by victims spread the disease. In Italy, in 1854, Filippo Pacini described the cholera vibrio which he had seen through the microscope. He suggested a way in which the vibrio might develop in the victim's body and later suggested that fluid loss was the cause of death. While some medical men found this work convincing, most continued to insist that the atmosphere played a part in transmitting the disease.[12]

In addition to the theoretical reasons, there were social reasons for rejecting the germ theory. If cholera were contagious then quarantine might be effective; hence opponents of quarantine preferred non-contagion explanations. If germs, rather than effluvia from filth, caused diseases, people might lose interest in removing the filth, and sanitary reformers accordingly feared acceptance of the germ theory would reduce support for their work. If victims of the disease were throwing off germs people might abandon them to die alone, as they had in epidemics of the plague – the model of contagious disease; humanitarians were therefore unwilling to accept the idea. When Canadians thought about cholera, they showed the same range of opinions expressed in the debate elsewhere.

In dealing with cholera, as we have seen, the Canadian governments turned for advice to the regular doctors. In doing so, they recognized the regulars' claims to special knowledge. The doctors in 1832 had a number of sources on which to draw. Some doctors had experience of the disease either in India or in the first British epidemic. Military doctors had written on the disease since the early part of the century. The British government sent circulars with the latest debates and information on cholera to Canada. The Canadian press published papers on the disease taken from English and Continental papers. After 1832, Canadian doctors could add their own experiences to what they read.

In Lower Canada, the debate on contagion was coloured by the political debate. Men found convincing those theories which best fitted their attitudes toward immigration, quarantine, and the government's public health role. Before the first epidemic, Canadian doctors tended to accept that the disease was not contagious but was 'epidemic,' i.e. the product of atmospheric changes and local conditions. The New York commissioners claimed to have found general agreement that cholera 'ha[d] not been imported, but ha[d] originated in Canada under circumstances favourable to its development and increase.' Dr George Roberts, like many of his fellow Canadians, supported that conclusion. In a letter to Lord Aylmer he argued for atmospheric causes and claimed that those who said the disease was imported 'are very unwilling to admit or acknowledge that there exists materials amongst them capable of producing such a disease.' If they did admit this, he said, they would have to clean the towns and relieve the poor. He thought the disease had come with 'forty days of easterly winds.' Roberts had his own political point to make – he may have favoured sanitary reform and poor relief – but he was opposed to quarantine as 'an immense expensive system which never can be considered a preventative or a method capable of warding off disease.'

Not everyone agreed with Roberts or with the conclusions of the New York commission. Given the central role of immigration in Lower Canadian politics this is not surprising. The committee established by the medical profession during its quarrel with the Quebec board of health, and reflecting French opinion, declared itself convinced that cholera was contagious, not 'epidemic.' The impact of the immigrants on Canada made it very difficult for many doctors to maintain an absolute non-contagion stance. Dr A.F. Holmes argued that the pattern by which the disease spread, the fact that it first attacked French Canadians, and that it appeared in Quebec before it did at Grosse Isle gave 'sufficient ground to repudiate the idea of its having spread from one point, or its having been introduced by emigrants'; yet the disease did seem to follow commercial routes and that raised questions he felt could not be answered. At the start of the epidemic he had believed that the disease could not be passed from person to person, but 'from personal observation' he was forced to conclude that cholera was 'generally devoid of infective power, but subject, under circumstances favourable to it, to acquire that power.'[13]

Cholera did not fit the known pattern of a contagious disease. People with no apparent contact with a victim would fall ill, while those who handled the sick and the dead frequently escaped the disease. The idea that the disease might be non-contagious in some circumstances and contagious in others helped to explain these anomalies. If a non-contagious disease sometimes became contagious, all measures of defence should be adopted. The quarantine at least would protect residents from the dirt in which the immigrants travelled, with its danger of an 'epidemic atmosphere.' Sanitary measures in the town to reduce dirt and crowding and to increase ventilation might modify conditions which produced or spread cholera. After the second epidemic in 1834, some doctors were convinced contagionists. Dr Joseph Workman presented a thesis on cholera when he took his degree at McGill in 1835. He argued that all cases were found among people who had contact with victims and that 'its close adherence to emigrants proved still more incontestably the agency by which it is transmitted from country to country.' Thirty years later, he recalled that his thesis had not been challenged by his examiners.

Most doctors lacked Workman's youthful certainty and they joined Holmes on the road to contingent contagionism. News of the microscopic studies of Budd and F. Brittain, which suggested the presence of specific bodies in the evacuations of cholera victims, was published in the Canadian medical press in 1849. They had no more impact here than in Britain. By 1849 however, support for the idea that cholera could sometimes be contagious was growing. Dr George Douglas, for many years medical superintendent at Grosse Isle, had noticed that doctors, clergymen, and nurses who attended cholera patients were in less danger than those who helped typhus victims. His tentative conclusion was that cholera was not 'contagious in the same degree as typhus fever or smallpox.' There was, however, widespread condemnation of the Medico-Chirugical Society of Montreal in 1849 for adopting a resolution that cholera was 'essentially non-contagious.'

Dr Archibald Hall, one of the most active medical journalists in mid–nineteenth century Canada expressed the profession's confusion, writing 'when we reflect that contagious diseases frequently exhibit themselves in a form apparently epidemic and that epidemics assume many of the features of contagious diseases, it becomes a matter of exceeding difficulty to draw the line of demarcation between them.' Given this difficulty there were doctors who chose to emphasize the essentially contagious nature of the disease. Dr William Marsden, a distinguished physician and public health pioneer, began a campaign in 1849 to convince his colleagues that cholera was contagious and that it was spread, by direct or indirect contact, from person to person. He thought – taking as models smallpox and the plague – that the means by which it spread was either a virus or a miasmata from the victim.

There were doctors who saw danger in accepting the idea that cholera was to some degree contagious. Dr A. van Iffland, who had long experience in cholera hospitals from 1832 on, thought that belief in contagion increased the level of panic in a community. He also feared that widespread belief in contagion would give the profession an undeserved reputation as 'a preserver endued with courage to confront, and skill to disarm, the unseen destroyer.' Despite that danger, each epidemic increased the number of doctors who agreed that cholera could be contagious. One clear example of that was seen in Saint John in 1854. Before the epidemic of that year, most doctors in Saint John had been non-contagionists. Direct experience of a major epidemic in their city converted most of them to contagionist ideas.

By 1866, the profession was able to come close to a consensus on the question of contagion. In that year, the memorandum adopted by the participants at the cholera conference in Ottawa represented something of an official opinion on the disease. The 'unbiased and well informed minds' which gathered there agreed that cholera was 'portable' and that it was best to assume 'that it is carried by persons, effects and merchandise and even by the winds of the air and currents and streams.' Cholera could 'make a jump over distances of several hundred miles.' The practical consequence was that quarantine should be maintained to 'delay' and 'limit the spread' of a disease which it could not prevent. The conclusions remained acceptable when the memorandum was reissued unaltered in 1873. Clearly the Canadian profession had been no more convinced by Snow and his fellow thinkers than had doctors elsewhere. They still did not know how the disease was spread but they advised that it be treated as a contagious disease.[14]

Those responsible for quarantine had treated cholera as a contagious disease. Whatever the medical arguments about contagion, no government wanted to release hordes of 'filthy immigrants' onto the domestic population without some sort of inspection. By the early 1870s supporters of quarantine could claim some successes for the system. In 1873, the *Canada Medical and Surgical Journal* stated flatly that 'of the contagious character of cholera there can be no doubt' and argued that it could be stopped by quarantine. It pointed for proof to the case of the *Franklin* in 1871 at Halifax. After a stirring defence of quarantine, the editor retreated slightly to argue that 'if it does not prevent the introduction of the disease, [it] at least induces a feeling of public security which is itself beneficial.'

William Marsden by this time had no doubt that a well-designed quarantine system based on '*absolute non-intercourse* for a short period with persons from abroad suspected of being infected, and a thorough disinfection of personal effects' would prevent the entry of cholera into a country. By the 1880s quarantine had become an accepted part of public health management of cholera. The provincial board of health of Ontario, for example, laid down plans to deal with cholera should it occur in the province in 1884 among people coming from the south of Europe. Every community was to appoint medical health and quarantine officers and all cases were to be taken to isolation hospitals while their contacts were quarantined.[15] The need did not arise that year and there were no epidemics of the disease after the question of contagion had been settled.

The theory of contingent contagion gave support to sanitary reformers. Given the mysterious pattern of the disease it seemed wise to clean the city and remove nuisances which might, somehow, play a role in the spread of disease. Cholera, or the threat of its approach, prompted a flood of essays and exhortations designed to overcome widespread indifference to sanitation. In January 1849, for example, the *British American Journal* editorialized on precautions against cholera. Experience had shown, it said, 'that the disease will manifest itself with greatest virulence, and will predominate to the greatest extent, in close, ill ventilated places and wherever impurities, whether of animal or vegetable origin, exist ... it follows that the utmost solicitude should be exhibited in regard to drainage and cleanliness ... The lower orders are proverbially negligent in this respect' and their houses should be inspected by the police. Five years later, the central board of health urged 'the adoption of thorough drainage, sewerage and ventilation, with a plentiful supply of pure water, attention to cleanliness, and the prevention of overcrowding.' That year, however, Dr Wolfred Nelson had to urge Montreal to overcome years of neglect in the search for 'absolute cleanliness'; and Saint John was as filthy as it had ever been when the great epidemic struck.

As Canada's cities grew, the problem of keeping them clean increased. Dirt and rubbish accumulated in the winters and was rarely removed when spring came. The poor often kept pigs, and some kept cows in their houses, because they needed the food. The need for meat was met by slaughterhouses which operated in residential districts and supported ancillary trades, such as tallow-boiling, which were offensive. Refuse from these businesses and from households was dumped into any convenient creek or stretch of open water which offered the chance that it would be washed away. The streets of towns were often poorly drained, choked with refuse, or covered with stagnant water. Those local and provincial politicians who accepted the need for clean water, good sewers, and well-drained and sanitary streets and houses found the financial and political problems of providing them almost insurmountable. In 1866, a London, Ontario, doctor complained that 'the cities and towns of Canada are not in that condition of cleanliness which the history of the past three months loudly demanded the proper authorities to attain, and, when reached, to maintain with all the power at their command.' He had heard that 'many places in Canada West are ripe for cholera ... of Montreal, it would seem almost idle to write a word. No one blessed with good eyesight, and a good nose, could possibly fail to notice daily in his travels, the filth and decaying vegetable matter which abounds on every hand, in back lanes, and even in crowded thoroughfares.' He thought that if everyone visited districts seen by doctors in general practice 'there would be such a weight brought to bear on the city authorities that they would be compelled to act.'

Doctors did not make a case for cleanliness convincing enough to overcome inertia or political obstacles to action. Many years brought no epidemics to cities which remained filthy. The customary round of summer digestive troubles, measles, tuberculosis, and other killing diseases lacked the power to shock people into action. Cholera did have that power, and if it had come more frequently quicker progress might have been made. In the early 1850s a series of epidemics did encourage action, but at the time of the last great cholera scare in 1873 the *Canada Lancet* could complain of the lack of action on public health measures. It lamented that 'these are matters, however, that are usually unattended to, until the approach of cholera, or some other fearful epidemic arouses us from our slumbers, and then frantic efforts are put forth, and loads of money expended in cleansing the city, when it is, in all probability, too late.'[16]

Medical statistics had helped to convince many European sceptics of a link between dirt and disease. In Canada, there were few vital statistics available and very few doctors interested in their use. In 1834, William Kelly, a surgeon of the Royal Navy, read a paper on medical statistics to the Literary and Historical Society of Montreal. He complained of the difficulties he faced from inadequate statistics and 'slovenly record keeping in the hospitals.' He was able, nevertheless, to show that mortality in the towns of Lower Canada was double that in the country. He suggested that the mortality was due to the failure to keep cities clean and well supplied with water. He argued that the poor ought to be supplied with water 'as scarcity of water is perhaps the only one of the sources of disease peculiar to them, that can be met by municipal regulations.' He warned that 'when disease begins among the poor, it sooner or later spreads to the rich.' This was a lesson quickly learned in the cholera epidemics.

There were always a few doctors who were interested in medical statistics and demanded that governments keep more accurate records. Dr Painchaud's failure to persuade doctors to collect this information themselves suggests that the numbers were small. However, the central board of health argued in 1854 that 'the value of statistical information is so vast ... that the Board would earnestly advise the Government to introduce an Act to provide for the complete registration of the Province basing it on the principles of the Registration Act of England.' In 1861, Dr George Fenwick complained of the lack of statistics but used what figures he could find in cemetery records to identify the 'unhealthy localities' of Montreal. He thought that there was a connection between the disease and marshy ground, open drains, and the outlet of the Craig Street tunnel which carried half of the city's sewage. He was able to work out comparative mortality rates for different parts of the city.[17] Interest in the subject was sufficient for the Canadian Medical Association, at its founding in 1867, to set up a committee on statistics, but statistical work was rare in mid-century and no one appears to have tried to map an epidemic.

With no hard facts to work on, doctors could give no clear answer to the question of what predisposed some people to the disease. It was obvious that not everybody living in a town attacked by the disease fell ill. Any approach to a solution of this problem was necessarily impressionistic. It was clear that each town had districts, such as Champlain Street in Montreal and Cul-de-Sac in Quebec, which were more badly ravaged by the disease than other parts. Urban conditions most resembling those on immigrant ships seemed to produce the greatest concentration of disease. The disease also seemed to hit some groups harder than others. The first outbreaks were devastating to immigrants and to French Canadians, and all epidemics were hard on the poor. In asking how they were predisposed to cholera, a doctor's conscious and unconscious prejudices came into play. French Canadians were said to live on vegetables, soup, and bread, pay little attention to comfort or cleanliness, and to be intemperate. The British, on the other hand, had 'good, substantial nutriment.'

Cholera was overwhelmingly a disease of the poor and it was easy for doctors to moralize when discussing predisposing causes. If moderate diet, cleanliness, and temperance were defences against the disease perhaps those who fell ill had brought it on themselves. Cholera could be used to drive home moral points. When Robert Nelson refused to accept a connection between drunkeness and cholera in the 1830s, he had been 'remonstrated with on the ground that, even if I were correct, it was of great moral importance that the statement should go abroad.' As cholera began to claim its victims among the middle classes, doctors found it less easy to moralize about the victims and were forced to suggest a host of predisposing causes. Even though the moral explanations began to fade with the second epidemic they were not quickly abandoned, especially when doctors spoke of the poor. As late as 1854, Dr Wolfred Nelson warned Montrealers that 'there is a close affinity between moral depravity and physical degradation' and that while many conditions predisposed people to cholera it 'respects cleanliness, sobriety and decent habits. It seldom intrudes where industry and good morals prevail. Hence, in regard to this dreadful pestilence, man is, in no small degree, the arbiter of his own fate.'

The idea that moral failings predisposed the victims to cholera became perfunctory and almost ritualistic by 1866. The government committee writing the memorandum that year intended its suggestions 'to improve generally the moral, the domestic and the social habits of our population.' Cleanliness and godliness were still linked although there was a danger that cleanliness, at least, could go too far. 'Occasional use of bathing and the constant habit of daily cleanliness of person are evidently needed, but caution should be observed against too prolonged and frequent bathing.' By 1872, a medical journal thought 'novel' the 'doctrine that vice and ignorance give rise to contagious maladies. If this be the case, it is greatly to be wondered at that these diseases are so prevalent among the virtuous and educated.' After the germ theory had begun to win support in the 1880s one commentator completed the retreat from moral explanations. Drunkards were less likely to recover, he said, but 'it is notorious that during cholera epidemics drunkards in the better classes of society enjoy a certain degree of immunity from the disease, which is easy to explain on the ground that they imbibe but little water.'[18]

Doctors were no more successful in elucidating the nature of the disease than they were in explaining how it chose its victims. Its course was dramatically clear. Usually there were premonitory symptoms such as looseness of the bowels and a sense of anxiety or depression. These symptoms were similar to those of 'common cholera,' the digestive troubles common in the summer. Some doctors believed that common cholera, if untreated, could develop into Asiatic cholera – a logical belief before the germ explanation. If the premonitory stage did not end the attack the patient could begin purging and vomiting with a huge loss of liquid. Cramps, spasms, and a whole train of ghastly effects such as blue skin and low and husky 'cholera voice' followed, with collapse and death in over half the serious cases. These characteristics of the disease are now seen to be the consequence of the loss of liquid and minerals which disrupts the body's normal processes. In the nineteenth century the action of the disease caused great debate.

From the first days, Canadian doctors performed autopsies in a search for clues to the disease. They tried to combine their observation of the dying patient with the post-mortem discoveries. The result was confusion. The dying patient was suffering from a disruption of his 'gastric and intestinal functions' but the results of bleeding suggested that the disease affected the blood, which became thick and changed in character. Autopsies showed no clear reason for the change, although it was impossible to ignore the 'sudden abstraction of saline particles' in considering the disease. One writer suggested that the disease 'is caused by a deficiency of electricity in the locality where the disease prevails, causing powerful currents from the Sanguiniferous system, towards the mucuous membrane of the alimentary canal.' Dr Archibald Hall found in his autopsies 'with the exception of congestion of the internal blood vessels ... insufficient causes of death' and concluded that cholera killed by acting on the nervous system to reduce the 'vital and dynamic forces.' Dr L.F. Chaperon, however, concluded from his observations and autopsies that the disease produced an indigestible mass in the stomach which proved so irritating that the body tried to throw it off with the consequences seen in all severe cases. As contingent contagion found support in the profession, the idea that cholera was the product of a poison began to dominate. Dr Robert Nelson wrote that cholera was a poison but 'what the poison is like cannot be demonstrated, it is known only by its effects': 'a certain catalysis or liquefaction of certain elements of the body' as the poison converted 'certain constituents of the body into a special liquid, hitherto unknown.' Many doctors also came to believe that cholera had the power to drive other diseases out of the community which it invaded.[19]

Few doctors were interested in the theoretical discussions about cholera, but all were interested in trying to cure it. Faced with a sick patient, the doctor had to act and he hurled a whole battery of therapies against the disease. One historian has called the mid–nineteenth century 'a grotesque chapter' in cholera therapy, amounting to 'a form of benevolent homicide.'[20] In the 1830s some of the treatments used were bleeding, doses of calomel (a preparation of mercury) large enough to make the gums bleed, opium in various doses, and counter-irritant therapy – blistering and cautery. The prospects of treatment were grim enough that people sometimes avoided the doctor.

One example of a course of treatment in 1832 was that given to Private Patrick Mullany of the 32nd Regiment at Quebec. When he fell ill, he hid from the doctors until he was seen to be sick and taken to hospital on 17 July at 9 am. He was bled thirty ounces, given fifteen grains of calomel and two of opium, given a turpentine enema, rubbed with turpentine for his cramps, then given ginger tea and allowed to rest. At 2 pm he was given three grains of calomel and put on a course of one-eighth grain of opium every half-hour with calomel every third hour. In the evening he was dosed with castor oil. On 18 and 19 July he was given an enema and dosed with calomel, opium, castor oil, and port wine every two or three hours. On 20 July he was given a variety of drinks and had a blister applied to his stomach. The next day he was dosed with rhubarb, had twelve leeches applied to his stomach, followed by a second blister, and was allowed beef tea and arrowroot. On 22 July he was fit enough to eat porridge for breakfast, but the mercury had begun to blister his mouth and he was given bicarbonate of soda in addition to his beef tea and arrowroot. On 23 July the medicines were withdrawn and he began to improve slowly until on 11 August he was declared fit for duty.

Private Mullany was perhaps right to hide on 17 July but he received the best treatment available. The course seemed to have been based on the idea that the natural purging should be assisted by enemas and laxatives, while the circulation was stimulated and the cramps eased by bleeding. Opium calmed the stomach and the blisters were applied under the dictates of counter-irritant therapy. The bleeding, blisters, and calomel did him little good – but the opium must have been welcome. In one respect Mullany was luckier than many other survivors in this epidemic. His doctors allowed him liquids from the start of the treatment. Many did not, arguing that it was dangerous to allow fluids despite the patient's immense craving for them.

The first epidemics saw doctors try a number of approaches to treatment. The thickness of the blood when bleeding was attempted suggested that the patient might be helped by transfusions. These had been tried in Britain in 1831 and reports of them were published in the newspapers. In 1832 a number of trials were made in Canada. In one case the almost dead patient was given a transfusion of seventeen pints of rain water 'carefully filtered' and mixed with 180 grains of muriate of soda, 206 grains of carbonate of soda, and 204 grains of phosphate of soda. After ten minutes he opened his eyes and said he felt better; but ten minutes later, after he had received eight pints of fluid, 'he suddenly vomited ... and died in a few minutes.' A number of these experiments were tried, varying the liquid, the chemical additives, and the temperature of the transfusion. In 1849, Dr James Bovell tried transfusions of milk. Given the state of medical knowledge of human chemistry and aseptic procedures these efforts could not succeed. They were only attempted on patients in the state of collapse.

In the second epidemic, some doctors began to retreat from the heroic efforts of 1832. Staff surgeon Walter Henry, serving in Kingston, noted that remedies were used 'more sparingly than before.' Bleeding was less used 'for those violent tetanic spasms which it had so frequently relieved in the former year were not now so general. Calomel ... was now used less indiscriminately.' Henry modified his treatment because he believed that the cholera was less severe than it had been in 1832. All doctors insisted that part of their skill lay in knowing just what treatment was needed for a particular case.

Later epidemics saw less bleeding, because bleeding was in decline in the 1840s. One doctor in the 1880s regretted the change and wrote that 'in medicine, the furious bloodletting are gone, and well would it have been had we retained the lancet, using it moderately, instead of doing as we did about 1845, by taking up stimulants, and, like bleeding, carrying it to excess.' If the use of bleeding declined in the 1840s it was never abandoned as a treatment for cholera and it always had its enthusiastic supporters. William Marsden urged its use in 1849. He said that his practice in 1832 had been 'bleeding whenever blood could be obtained, even in collapse and I am not sure that any better practice could be adopted now in very many cases.' He bled to restore the circulation and combined venesection with massive doses of calomel 'of upwards of 200 grains within a few hours.' There were reports of success with bleeding in the later epidemics of 1849 and 1854, with one advocate claiming that 'the judicious use of the lancet ... was the key to successful treatment.'

Calomel remained the stand-by of many doctors in all the epidemics. Archibad Hall recommended large doses of calomel and morphine at the start of an attack, followed by smaller doses every half-hour or hour. Dr Ayre, of Hull, England, published a recommendation for calomel treatment in the *Lancet* in 1848, which was followed by a number of Canadian doctors including van Iffland during the Quebec epidemic of 1849. Dr George Gibb followed Ayre's recommendations in a later epidemic. He wrote: 'I have never regarded the quantity of calomel taken of any moment in such a dreadful disease, trusting to combat the ill effects by proper treatment after subduing the cholera.'

The range of therapies attempted in cholera was very wide and usually unpleasant. Regular doctors emphasized in every epidemic the need for speedy treatment of the specific case. They were critical of those who sold nostrums. A medical journal denounced Dr Seguin of Quebec who advertised 'Sachets Anticholeriques' in 1849. These were two bags, one to be worn in front and one on the middle of the back, costing five shillings cash. The editor wrote: 'The days of Amulets and Charms we thought had passed away ... Dr. Seguin must know that while filling his pockets in this unworthy manner, he has secured for himself the scorn of a profession which discountenances charlatanism of every description ... We wonder if Dr. Seguin cured his cholera patients by incantations when they were attacked.' The profession was incensed when, in 1866, the central board of health was associated with the publication of a cholera recipe to be used until the doctor came. It was denounced as 'a glaring act of official ignorance.' The editor of the *Canada Medical Journal* reflected professional pique when he wrote that people should have 'the common civility to apply to the physician if they have confidence in his faith and honesty if not [they can turn to] trash to be had at any of our drug stores for ready money.'

There were reports in the 1850s that some doctors in England were attempting to bring about cures by helping nature to do its work. One danger of this approach was that it exposed regulars to accusations that they were acting like irregulars. An English doctor, George Johnson, suggesting that purgatives be used to help nature expel the cholera poison, recognized the danger: 'I am told that there are some weak brethren who are haunted by the fear lest, in treating cholera by purgatives they be supposed to act upon the homeopathic doctrine, similia similibus curantur.' He claimed, however, that his analysis of collapse showed that purging was not the disease but the cure; 'the way, then to escape the dreaded suspicion of an alliance with homeopathy is to adopt a truly scientific pathology.' That was the base of the doctors' claims. In all their attempts to stimulate the depressed patients, calm the spasms, and restore the circulation they were guided by what they understood of the pathology of the disease. As they had little understanding of that pathology, their efforts to cure the disease were unavailing. They retained their confidence that they were the best qualified to attempt the cure. The 1866 *Memorandum* observed that 'the treatment of Cholera is one of the most difficult of all therapeutic efforts which can be required from even the most experienced medical man ... none but a professional practitioner should undertake such a task.'[21]

In conclusion, the doctors' confidence in their own abilities had not been shared by the lay population. The latter could see little evidence that regular doctors were better qualified to help them than were irregulars, and they turned to the irregulars for treatment. In the United States, the trend was very marked and in Canada it was clear enough to cause comment in the medical journals. As they could not cure cholera, the regulars could not sustain their claims to special skill. This failure was reinforced by their frequent divisions on ethnic lines or over their qualifications. The often bitter quarrels among doctors was echoed in their disagreements over the theoretical questions of whether or not cholera was contagious and just how it affected its victims. To laymen these differences were signs of confusion rather than of learning. The English profession experienced a similar lay reaction when its debates over the disease were forced into the open.[22]

The government's failings and their own educational shortcomings denied doctors the tools to do as effective a job of analysing public health needs as was possible. They did make some recommendations but their supporting arguments were not so convincing that they could overcome inertia and political obstacles. The later cholera epidemics did stimulate some public health reforms and suggested that effective action could be taken against the disease, but progress was very slow and the greatest achievements came later in the nineteenth century. By that time, the development of a scientific basis for medicine allowed Canadian doctors to consolidate their claim to special knowledge. When that claim was accepted, the doctors won the recognition and status they had sought with limited success at mid-century.

8

'Shortcomings ... exposed relentlessly'

Cholera inspired fear whenever it struck. People were terrified by the mystery and brutality of the disease, by its suddenness, and by its apparently random choice of victims. Cholera could strike at any time during an epidemic. Thomas Need was staying at a hotel in York in 1832, and 'as the waiter was bringing me some tea at Breakfast, he was suddenly seized with so violent an attack of Cholera that he was a corpse before teatime, his cries of agony were truly pitiable.'[1] Many people heard those cries in their own homes or saw their closest relatives carried off to die in an overcrowded and foul hospital. It was common to see poor immigrants dying on the wharfs and in the streets. No one could ignore the disease in a town suffering a major epidemic.

Surviving board of health reports show about 17,000 deaths in the cholera epidemics. The figure is low because some records are missing and those which exist are incomplete. The boards depended on doctors' reports and doctors were often too busy to report. The boards themselves were sometimes disorganized and unable to insist on full information. Occasionally, a board turned to interment records to get fuller figures. Between one-half and two-thirds of patients were treated privately, many without a doctor in attendance, and they were likely to escape the official count. It is probable that at least 20,000 died of the disease in Canada.

The vast majority of the victims are anonymous. They died attended by relatives, friends, a priest, and sometimes a harassed and overworked doctor. Most of the dead were from among immigrants and the poor and were more likely to be adults than children. In Quebec, in 1832, most of the victims were artisans, not paupers, and French Canadians were particularly hard hit. In later epidemics, however, contemporary investigations did not show French Canadians to be more affected than other groups. A total of 20,000 dead created a huge sum of misery. In each epidemic hundreds of families lost their wage earner and the survivors needed help. Immigrant families were left to find a new life without husbands and fathers and some immigrant children found themselves orphaned in a strange country. The suffering is obvious but the demographic impact of the deaths on Canada is less clear. The deaths were spread over a twenty-year period and some who died did not intend to settle in Canada. Immigrants brought cholera but they also built up Canada's population. Some cities doubled in size between the first and later epidemics. All the deaths by cholera amounted to less than one year's immigration and it seems reasonable to say that the demographic impact of the disease was slight.

Even so, cholera could be a heavy blow to a particular community. A Kingston newspaper editor assessed the effects of the epidemic of 1834 on his town. He pointed out that the town had been suffering from economic hardship and business failures. When cholera came, it carried off a number of the town's skilled artisans and businessmen and deepened the business slump. This kind of qualitative loss must have affected other communities, too, at a time when there were few skilled people in the country. The loss of a number of artisans, a lawyer, the doctor, the member of the assembly, or one of the more effective entrepreneurs could deal a heavy blow to a town. A major epidemic undermined morale and some communities took years to recover.

An epidemic was a highly emotional experience for those who lived through it and saw their family and friends destroyed. The disease always produced a range of emotional responses. In the first epidemics, fear and anger at the health regulations produced rumours of premature burial. In all epidemics, the psychological impact of the attack was expressed through the clichés in which it was described. A town or city suffering the disease was usually described as a place of empty streets, where nothing was to be seen but the cholera carts carrying the sick to hospital and the dead to burial. Little could be heard but the sound of footsteps echoing from the walls as the doctor or priest hurried to the bedside of the sick and dying. Sometimes, and for some places, these descriptions were accurate enough – but not for all times and places. The fact that people chose to remember an epidemic in these ways is a measure of the effect of the disease.

The response to an epidemic could vary in intensity. It was largely conditioned by the violence of the epidemic and the novelty of the experience. An epidemic which took an explosive shape, with a sudden rise in the number of deaths, striking a town for the first time, provoked the greatest reactions. A less explosive epidemic, or one in a town with earlier experience, had less impact. There are resemblances between the impact of cholera in Canada and the effect of the Second World War bombing of Britain. Before the war began, warnings of the destruction to be expected from air raids on civilian populations claimed that hundreds of thousands would die in a very short time. When the first raids began they created widespread panic and hysteria. People eagerly joined schemes to evacuate them from the cities. After experiencing a few raids, peoples' behaviour began to change. They quickly came to believe that as they had survived the first raids they would probably live through the later ones. Many of those who fled returned to their familiar homes and all settled down to endure what had been thought unendurable.[2] The population of Canada had discussed cholera for months before it came and many were tense and fearful. The first violent epidemics brought panic and flight. Governments spent more freely on more elaborate precautions than they ever would again. After a couple of weeks, it was clear that cholera was not going to kill everybody and people began to learn to work with cholera on all sides. For some, cholera inspired more scrupulous religious attendance, or stricter attention to diet and health, but others faced it with the indifference and callousness of the carter who carried off Mr Perry.

While people learned to live with cholera, they were not indifferent to it and each epidemic brought demands that governments act. In Canada, as in England and Continental Europe, cholera was regarded as a scourge which could be contained and it 'exposed relentlessly political, social and moral shortcomings.'[3] Governments had to do something when their populations were threatened by the disease and the emotions aroused by the epidemics quickly spilled over into political life. The first epidemics in Lower Canada were particularly important in this way and had a direct effect on politics.

This happened because cholera was so clearly a disease of immigration. The effect of cholera was to intensify already savage criticism of immigration among French-Canadian politicians in the 1830s. Immigration was seen to be a threat to French survival and the first epidemics brought charges that the British were plotting to destroy them by allowing disease into the country. The emotional impact of cholera was great enough to speed the radicalization of politics which was to bring the province to rebellion before the end of the decade. The charges in Lower Canada were the closest the country came to the kind of accusations made in France, where doctors were attacked as agents sent by government to destroy the people. After the 1830s, and at all times outside Lower Canada, the political impact of the disease was less intense.

The epidemic of 1832 was 'the decisive test of the efficiency of the legislation' controlling the immigrant trade.[4] The British legislation was shown to be ineffective. Schemes of emigration from the poorer parts of the British Isles, and emigration by nearly destitute labourers, filled the small ships in the Atlantic trade nearly to bursting. The immigrants lived in filth and were often thirsty and hungry. Disease was common in the crowded holds and the travellers could arrive dirty, sick, and nearly exhausted to fall on the charity of Canadians for their survival.

Only gradually during the cholera period did changed regulations, faster Atlantic crossings, and the greater prosperity of many of the later emigrants bring real improvements to the emigrant trade.

Quarantine was always the first line of defence against cholera. Despite uncertainty over its medical value and criticisms of its effects on trade, quarantine at least offered a means of segregating the sick and cleaning the dirty. It could never prevent the entry of cholera because too little was known of the disease, and in some cases the quarantine station spread the disease by mingling the sick and the healthy. Only toward the end of the period could medical officers claim some success at containing the disease by quarantining the sick. Those successes came in small outbreaks and owed something to good luck. While quarantine was acceptable at points of entry, it was rarely welcome within a province. New Brunswick alone made legal provision for internal quarantine and the legislation soon lapsed. Elsewhere, provincial authorities resisted efforts to create internal quarantine and after the first epidemic it was rarely attempted.

The major efforts to protect Canadians against cholera were made by provincial and local governments. They acted within the framework of the law and 1832 quickly showed that the laws were inadequate. Lower Canada had laws governing quarantine and allowing boards of health in the major centres. In Upper Canada and the Maritimes there were no such laws. In both these regions, public health legislation was passed directly as a consequence of experience of cholera. Political divisions between Aylmer and the assembly allowed the legislation to lapse in Lower Canada, but new legislation was passed later. Through the middle years of the nineteenth century some public health legislation was written, usually when the threat of cholera added urgency to the debate. It was generally directed to meeting what were seen to be occasional temporary needs. Each epidemic or threat of cholera inspired a scramble to bolt together a ramshackle machine which would operate for a few months before being dismantled – if it had not already collapsed. Canadians were slow to develop agreement that public health required permanent care.

The uncertain legal powers of governments, especially in the first epidemics, left room for executive initiative. The success of that initiative varied greatly. In the rancorous political atmosphere of Lower Canada in the early 1830s, Aylmer took an impolitic course. He refused to take the initiative and insisted that there was little that he could do. He thus invited criticism and made it difficult for his friends to defend him, particularly after his retreat to Sorel in 1834. The often hysterical and always bitter criticism of his performance gave a clear sign of how badly the political climate in the province had worsened. In contrast, governors such as Sir John Colborne and Sir Colin Campbell proved more effective. Sir John's actions overcame the shortcomings of a number of the city authorities in Upper Canada. In the later epidemics, provincial governments played a lesser role than they had earlier, as legislation tended to make local government responsibility for public health more explicit.

Local governments responded slowly and inadequately to the challenges posed by cholera. They resented the fact that responsibility for the immigrants was flung onto them with little or no financial help from the province. Local governments reacted to each epidemic as a separate crisis by setting up boards of health, opening hospitals, and hiring medical officers and health wardens. During the epidemic, the boards tried to clean the towns and encourage the residents to clean themselves, and this aided and encouraged the sanitary reformers. Boards varied widely in efficiency. In 1832 the Quebec board was reasonably efficient, that of Montreal was not; in 1834 the Toronto board collapsed amid party feuds and mayoral indifference. The idea that boards should operate permanently developed slowly; and without the obvious need posed by an epidemic many people were unwilling to pay for public health measures.

The repeated crises did leave a residue of support for the idea that public health required permanent measures. The support was not strong enough to overcome the restraints under which governments operated in mid–nineteenth century Canada. They were constrained by shortage of money, which made any grand schemes to meet public health needs futile. They were constrained by the lack of clear legal powers to do what sanitary reformers said should be done. City charters, for example, often did not grant cities the necessary powers to act for the public health. Governments were constrained, perhaps most effectively of all, by what was expected of them. Those people who had political influence did not expect governments to play too active a part, and certainly not too expensive a part, in the citizens' day-to-day lives. Housing for the poor was provided by private landlords who were not greatly affected by weakly enforced laws on overcrowding. Even at the end of the century, urban reformers still expected business, not government, to provide good cheap housing for the poor. The water-supply of many cities remained a private business for much of the period, with inadequate supplies in the poorer parts of town. Often the need for protection against fire, rather than the provision of drinking-water, encouraged city governments to take over the supply. Years could pass between the acceptance of the principle of municipal water-supply and its implementation.[5] Sewerage and street cleaning were municipal functions but the cost often inhibited action. In England, sanitary reformers made some advances at mid-century partly by calculating the return on an investment in public health measures and suggesting that reform paid a dividend.

Boards of health might have overcome some of the constraints if they had been able to offer a convincing rationale for what they wanted done. People could see the need for hospitals, some short-term medical help for the poor, and shelter for the immigrants. They were less easily convinced of the need for the range of regulations on cleanliness. For the forty years during which cholera attacked Canada, boards argued that clean streets, clean houses, and clean water were the keys to good health – and for forty years these were lacking in Canada. Dirt was a normal condition of urban life in Canada. It was unpleasant to walk around pools of stagnant water and to pick one's way between heaps of garbage. People preferred not to live next to tanneries and slaughterhouses and to live in houses with clean cellars and yards, but these considerations were as much aesthetic as sanitary. The link between dirt and disease was not absolutely clear and efforts to clean the towns foundered on that uncertainty.

This fact did not save boards from being attacked for not doing enough during an epidemic by people who had done nothing before the outbreak and would do nothing when it was over. Cholera did seem to affect most severely the dirtiest parts of town and its visits were terrible enough to encourage some action. Commonsense suggested that clean water was safer than unclean. Many Canadians were repelled by the idea of drinking water contaminated by sewage. A particularly bad epidemic might be followed, as it was in Saint John in 1854, by permanent efforts to improve water-supply and sewerage but, although cholera retained its power to force action reform was slow. Cholera did not return often enough to consolidate the gains made at each assault. Only when the germ theory was generally accepted in the 1880s was there convincing scientific support for sanitary reforms.

Twentieth-century Canadians may be astonished by the descriptions of the conditions in which their countrymen lived. The reforms seem to be so obvious and so clearly needed that they should have been unavoidable. In their own day, however, Canadians of today have learned that the air of their towns is often dangerously fouled by automobile and industrial exhaust. Each week brings its reports of a new hazard associated with hitherto unsuspected material in the air we breathe. The water-supplies of cities, safe by nineteenth-century standards, are shown to be contaminated by a new range of industrial wastes liable to maim and kill. Working conditions in some industries are shown to be potentially lethal. Some cities continue to pour untreated sewage into major water-ways. Despite a battery of scientific knowledge far more convincing than that available in the nineteenth century, reforms come slowly, hindered by political and economic considerations akin to those of the cholera years.

The scientific information available to nineteenth-century governments came from the regular doctors. They were consulted by governments from the provincial to the village level. The best informed Canadian doctors knew as much about the disease as doctors anywhere, drawing their information mainly from Britain and Europe. Their sources were British government circulars, newspaper reports, and medical journals, all of which helped them to learn of the latest ideas on the nature of the disease and changes in therapy. Some doctors had seen cholera elsewhere before it reached Canada and all doctors relied heavily on the experience they acquired in treating the victims of each successive outbreak. In all the epidemics, Canadian doctors performed autopsies in pursuit of understanding of the disease but there were no microscopic studies reported and few statistical studies made. As a result, Canadian doctors did not make original contributions to the study of the disease.

Although regular doctors were called on almost exclusively to offer advice and to hold government posts during the epidemics, the cholera years were not happy ones for them. The disease was ruthless in exposing their divisions and ignorance. Their claims to special standing based on special knowledge were undermined by their inability to understand the disease, and they made only slow progress. Their demands for respect were weakened by their inability to cure the disease. In the teeth of evidence to the contrary, they claimed to be able to cure cholera, and the fact that many cases remain mild, even if untreated, helped them to sustain faith in their own ability.

Theirs was not a faith widely shared among laymen. Doctors were prepared to experiment with the most radical treatments, including transfusion, but most stuck to some combination of bleeding, calomel, and opium. Over the years, efforts at treatment became a little less brutal but many sufferers must have agreed with the Reverend Mr Anson Green. When he was attacked by cholera in 1834, his friends tried a number of home remedies. Green was convinced that he survived the attack because those remedies were working before the doctor could get to the house and try his own cures.[6] Regular doctors could never treat all the sick, and many turned to the apothecaries, and to the irregulars, some of whom won an equal status with the regulars in mid-century Upper Canada. For many of the poor help came only from clergy, relatives, and friends – or a neighbour thought to have some skill with the sick.

Cholera led to a temporary rediscovery of the poor with every epidemic. The first epidemics occurred in cities and towns where poor and rich lived close together. When it became clear that the disease would not confine its attacks to the poor, the wealthier citizens often felt obliged to do something to change the conditions of the poor, if only in self-defence. In later years, patterns of urban settlement changed and the wealthier citizens withdrew to parts of town more distant from the poor. The young doctor starting his practice and the clergyman were among the few middle-class people with any regular experience of the conditions in which the poor lived. When cholera struck, it forcibly drew the attention of the richer citizens to those conditions. Their response was ambivalent, a compound of self-interest and charity. In each epidemic some people argued for the need to improve the services of the towns and raise the living standards of the poor. These were goals beyond the scope of local governments of the time. The epidemics, therefore, stimulated considerable charitable efforts in support of hospitals, aid for the destitute, food for the hungry, and shelter for widows and orphans. Some of these efforts produced permanent results in the form of hospitals, charitable societies, and orphanages which stood as monuments to cholera's power to call attention to the needs of society.

The operations of charitable institutions were shaped by middle-class attitudes to the poor. The operators had to reassure their prospective supporters that they would not be the dupes of the 'undeserving poor.' The understanding of cholera suggested that it could be the product of immoderate behaviour and intemperence. When it fell heavily on the poor it could confirm prejudices and encourage moralizing. If the Irish or the French suffered, it was perhaps because they were debauched. The poor might be responsible for the conditions in which they lived by preferring drink and sloth to good food and hard work with the scrubbing brush. The moralizing became less certain as the rich began to die, and it faded in the later epidemics – but it never completely disappeared; the rediscovery of the poor did not necessarily bring fresh attitudes.

It did, however, become clear in the course of the epidemics that the poor could not be acted on without reaction. The poor were individuals, capable of helping one another, and holding strong opinions about what governments could do to them. The operation of public health laws was restricted by the public attitude and the poor could act violently against laws which they felt to be unfeeling or intrusive. Even those who could not articulate their objections could express themselves by resisting the health wardens and forcing them to seek police protection, by ignoring regulations, reoccupying condemned buildings, and opposing efforts to remove their friends and relatives to hospitals. Some of the most insensitive regulations dealt with the customary treatment of the dead. Laws demanding quick burial in special grounds were bitterly resented. In England, the resentment sometimes flared into riot; in Canada there were a number of cases in which the dead were dug out of the unconsecrated ground in which they had been buried hastily without mourning or prayers.

The most forceful expression of popular opposition to public health measures was directed against the hospitals. Hated by the poor, who alone were sent to them, and feared by those who lived nearby, the hospitals were fought with petition, crowbar, and torch. In some towns, too, the houses of victims of the disease were burned by mobs. The mob did not turn out only in opposition however, but could sometimes be found supporting health regulations. Vessels which ignored regulations were attacked or threatened, boats were turned back if they came from infected ports, and men erected road-blocks and tried to close their villages to outsiders. In Saint John, in 1854, mob action was only narrowly avoided when authorities were slow to clean the town. There was an obvious potential for violent action in mid-century Canada but it was reduced by the feebleness of the governments and the bureaucracy. In European cities, rigid and powerful bureaucracies backed by strong governments provoked major disorders and riots. Canada's regulations were made by temporary bodies and enforced, slowly and ineffectively, through the courts. That helped to save Canada from worse violence than did occur.

The experience of cholera left its mark on Canada. The disease had little demographic effect, but it tested the various levels of government and frequently found them inadequate. The emotions aroused by the disease had a major impact on Lower Canadian politics in the 1830s. The epidemics exposed the shortcomings of the Canadian medical profession, pointed in Canadian cities to public service failures which went uncorrected for years, and made the needs of the poor visible from time to time. Cholera could force action and each epidemic left some residue in the shape of hospitals, orphanages, or health committees. In some towns, a major epidemic was followed by permanent public health provisions, but for many others cholera raised questions about public health and left the answers for the future when cholera had ceased to be a part of Canadian life.

Tables of deaths

WEEKLY FIGURES

TABLE 1
Cholera deaths in Lower Canada 1832

Quebec			
Deaths in hospital[a]		Deaths reported to board of health[b]	Montreal[c]
9 June	8	6	
16 June	189	488	261
23 June	206	630	632
30 June	72	245	166
7 July	48	146	99
14 July	23[d]	76	61
21 July	18	24	50
28 July	18	———	126
4 Aug.	12	Total 1615[e]	162
11 Aug.	29		116
18 Aug.	30		98
25 Aug.	32		77
1 Sept.	23		63
8 Sept. ⎱	30		26
15 Sept. ⎰			13
to 18 Sept.	4		

a Public Archives of Canada (PAC) RG7G18 vol 16–17. Board of Health reports show 5,820 deaths in Lower Canada.
b 14 Aug. 1834, Common Council of Quebec, PAC RG4A 1S–327 pt II 186.
c PAC RG5A1 vol 116–17 65,509 (to 14 July); PAC RG4A1 S-286 108, and *La Minerve* (to 6 Aug.); PAC RG4A1 S-287 pt II 138, S-288 63,156 (to 30 Aug.); PAC RG4A1 S-289 52, and *Gazette* (to 5 Sept.); PAC RG4A1 S-290 93,120.
d City burial register shows 1,622 dead to 18 July. *Neilson's Gazette* in *Montreal Gazette* 24 July 1832.
e *Bulletin des récherches historiques* 12 (1906) 88–92 shows 3,451 deaths at Quebec. Report of Central Board of Health for 1854 shows 2,218 deaths at Quebec in 1832.

TABLE 2
Cholera deaths in Upper Canada 1832

	York[a]	Kingston[b]
23 June	3	6
30 June	20	29
7 July	20	8[c]
14 July	12[d]	1
21 July	7[e]	3
28 July	14	9
4 Aug.	13	10
11 Aug.	37	6
18 Aug.	26	5
25 Aug.	19	8
1 Sept.	13	
8 Sept.	8	
15 Sept.	1	

a PAC RG5A1 vol 121 67,291–67,329: board of health
   reports are incomplete; at least 273 died by 8 August
   (Toronto Public Library, York Board of Health Minutes).
b PAC RG5A1 vol 121 67,035, 67,037, 67,041, 67,047, 67,054,
   67,065, 67,097, 67,126, 67,132, 67,150, 67,152, 67,162,
   67,168, 67,190, 67,192. Board of health reports show 504
   deaths in Upper Canada.
c To 5 July.
d To 12 July.
e For 17 July only.

TABLE 3
Cholera deaths 1834[a]

	Quebec[b]	Montreal[c]	Toronto[d]	Halifax[e]
13 July	87	2		
20 July	245	91		
27 July	270	176		
3 Aug.	234	231	5	
10 Aug.	240	193	29[f]	
17 Aug.	93	133	65[g]	
24 Aug.	9	33	39[h]	
31 Aug.	13	23	13	18
7 Sept.	7		7	127
14 Sept.	4			106
21 Sept.				52
28 Sept.				17

a Grosse Isle: 158 dead PAC RG7G18 vol 16–17. Board of health reports give total deaths from cholera in 1834 as 2,358 in Lower Canada and 555 in Upper Canada.
b To 14 Aug. 1834, Common Council Report, PAC RG4A1 S-327 pt II 186; PAC RG42A3 vol 23.
c Return of interments 29 Aug. 1834, PAC RG4A1 S-328 pt I 36.
d PAC RG5A1 vol 145 79,303–56.
e Board of health reports, *Nova Scotian* 3, 6, and 13 Sept. 1834; *Acadian Recorder* 23 Sept. 1834. Board of health reports show 320 dead in Nova Scotia from cholera in 1834.
f *Canadian Courant* 16 Aug. 1834 records 80 burials for this week.
g Ibid shows 72 burials to 14 Aug.
h Ibid shows 34 burials.

TABLE 4
Cholera deaths 1849[a]

	Quebec[b]	Montreal[c]	Toronto[d]
10 July	31	25	
17 July	213	127	38
24 July	191	152	48
31 July	251	119	45
7 Aug.	130	46	63
14 Aug.	38	17	61
21 Aug.	29	9	45
4 Sept.	37	1	55
11 Sept.	19		21
18 Sept.	13		

a Total deaths: Lower Canada 1,638, Upper Canada 638.

b *Central Board of Health Report* 1854, to 14 Aug.; *Quebec Mercury* to 18 Sept. 1849.

c 11 Aug. 1849 Montreal *Transcript*; *British American Journal* 1 Sept., 1 Oct. 1849.

d Board of health reports in *British Colonist*; *Annual Report Ontario Board of Health* 10 (1891) shows 464 deaths from cholera in Toronto in 1849.

Notes

ABBREVIATIONS

ANQ   Archives nationales du Québec
ANfld   Newfoundland Archives
AO   Archives of Ontario
BAJ   *British American Journal*
BH   Board of Health
PAC   Public Archives of Canada
PANB   Provincial Archives, New Brunswick
PANS   Public Archives of Nova Scotia
PAPEI   Public Archives of Prince Edward Island
PRO   Public Record Office, London, England
QBH   Quebec Board of Health
QCHA   Quebec City Hall, Archives
TPL   Toronto Public Library

INTRODUCTION

1 R. Pollitzer *Cholera* (Geneva 1959) is a standard work on the disease.
   Dhiman Barrua and William Burrows eds *Cholera* (Toronto 1976)
   discusses the nature of the disease. N. Howard-Jones 'The Scientific Background of the International Sanitary Conferences 1851–1938' *WHO Chronicle* 28 (1974) 159–71, 229–47, 369–84, 414–61 discusses the developments
   in understanding the disease during the nineteenth century.

CHAPTER 1 'Scrape, wash and cleanse'

1 'Copies or Extracts of all Information ... communicated to Government'
   27 June 1831, PAC RG 1E3 vol 16

2 PAC RG4A1 S-269, 150, 151, S-272 5
3 R. Christie *A History of the Late Province of Lower Canada, Parliamentary and Political* 3 (Quebec 1850) 386, 382–3
4 Fernand Ouellet *Le Bas-Canada 1791–1840* (Ottawa 1976) 221
5 A.C. Buchanan *Report on Emigration to the Canadas in 1832* 12 Dec. 1832, PRO CO42/241
6 5 Dec. 1831 Petition, Quebec Emigrant Society, and 23 Feb. 1832 A.C. Buchanan to Lord Aylmer, PRO CO42/236, and *Report*
7 *Quebec Gazette* 11 Nov. 1831
8 PAC RG4A1 S-272 5; 28 May 1832 Petition of Louis Bernier, PAC RG4A1 S-292 91; 20 Aug. 1832 Report on complaints of Pierre Duplain, PAC RG4A1 S-288 41; 25–31 Aug. 1832 George Robinson Diary, PAC MG24I9 M-128; 25 April 1832 Memo of instructions for Capt. Alderson, PAC RG8C vol 300 no. 30
9 *Orders and Directions Made by the Board of Health for the Regulation of Pilots* (Quebec 1832)
10 26, 29, 30 March 1832 Reports of the Quebec Board of Health, PAC RG4A1 S-279 77, 78, 111–12, 121; 12 July 1832 PAC RG4A1 S-285 124–124a
11 *Orders and Directions*
12 PAC RG7G18 vol 16, 17; 28 July 1832 Quebec BH to Sec. Craig, PAC RG4A1 S-286 141; 3 Aug. 1832 Solicitor-General's opinion PAC RG4A1 S-287 48
13 Susanna Moodie *Roughing It in the Bush* (Toronto 1916) 28–33
14 24 May, 14 July 1832 Dr G. Griffin to Sec. Craig, PAC RG4A1 S-282 3, 58; 19 May 1832 QBH resolution in ibid 32; 10 July, 17 July 1832 Capt. H. Reid to Col. Clegg, PAC RG8C vol 300 no. 117–19; PAC RG4A1 S-286 20–1
15 3, 7 May Dr. Griffin 14 July 1832 QBH to Sec. Craig, PAC RG4A1 S-281 25, 67, S-285 116–17; PAC RG4A1 S-285 116–17
16 26 June 1832 Report of a committee of the board of health, PAC RG4A1 S-284 137
17 6 July 1832 E. McMahon to John Smyth, PAC RG7G16C vol 26 103–4
18 23 June 1832 Bytown magistrates to William Graham, PAC MG24I9 vol 21 5640, 5645; 28 June 1832, AO Western District Quarter Sessions Minutes 1821–1834 vol 166; 29 June Samuel Wilmot to E. McMahon, 9 July 1832 Sandwich BH, PAC RG5A1 vol 116–17 65, 905, vol 121, 67, 103; 23 June Capt. Yale to Charles Sheriff, 29 June 1832 C.J. Forbes to Bytown magistrates, PAC MG24I9 vol 18, 4,480, 4,489–91; 11 July 1832 Lt.Col. Rowan to President, Niagara BH, PAC RG7G16C vol 26 117–18
19 There were 29 doctors in Quebec and 18 in Montreal; J.R. Rhinelander and J.E. Dekay *Report of the Commissioners Employed to Investigate the Origin and Nature of the Epidemic Cholera of Canada* (New York 1834) 54; Sylvio LeBlond 'Quebec en 1832' *Laval Médical* 38 (Feb. 1967) 184–5;

15 June 1832 Montreal General Hospital Minutes, McGill U. Archives
1501/3A
20 20 March, 17 April, 8, 25 May 1832, QCHA Minute Book, Board of
Health, Quebec, 1; 18 May 1832 QBH to Sec. Craig, PAC RG4A1 S-282
11–14
21 15 June 1832 Lord Aylmer to Lord Goderich, PRO CO42/237; R. Nelson
Asiatic Cholera (New York 1866) 123
22 16 March, 5, 9, 28 April, 6 May 1832, QCHA Minutes vol 1, 30 July 1832,
Minutes vol 2
23 PAC RG4A1 S-279 130–1; 17 April 1832 L.-J. Papineau to Lord Aylmer,
7 April 1832 J. Leslie to Lord Aylmer, PAC RG4A1 S-280 pt I, 56, 57; 6
May 1832 PAC RG4A1 S-281 109–11
24 14, 20, 30 June 1832 Clerk of the Peace to E. McMahon, PAC RG5A1 vol
116–17 65,677–8, 65,931–2, vol 118 66,008; 27 June 1832 Provincial Sec. to
Brockville Police Board, PAC RG7G16C vol 26 80–1; 19 June 1832 Executive Council Report, PAC RG1E3 vol 16 28–30; 29 March, 4 April 1832,
PRO CO42/237; J.D. Douglas ed *Journals and Reminiscences of James
Douglas M.D.* (New York 1910) 134
25 31 March 1832 Thomas Clark to James Hamilton, PAC MG24D45 no. 198;
26 March 1832 Dr W. Telfer to J. Muirhead, PAC RG5A1 vol 115, 64,640,
64,746–7; 26 March 1832 J. Skelton to Capt. Forbes, PAC RG5A1 vol 114,
64,642–5; *Canadian Freeman* 29 March 1832; *Montreal Gazette* 23 April 1832
26 R.J. Morris *Cholera 1832* (London 1976) passim; *Colonial Advocate* 23 Feb.,
19 April 1832

CHAPTER 2 'Calculated to unman the ... strongest': Lower Canada 1832

1 6–8 June 1832, QCHA Minutes vol 1
2 15 June 1832 Dr Skey to Lord Aylmer, PRO CO42/237; *Quebec Mercury* 9,
16 June 1832
3 *Canadian Courant* 16 June 1832
4 Figures can only be approximate as the statistics are unreliable. The board
of health reports give figures for deaths in hospitals, but many took place
outside. See PAC RG4A1 S-286–90 passim; PAC RG7G18 vol 16–17. J.M.
Le Moine *Quebec Past and Present: a History of Quebec 1608–1876* (Quebec
1876) 272–3 gives the daily rates quoted here. Lord Aylmer calculated
that by the end of June, 1,500 people had died in Quebec; 26, 30 June
1832 Lord Aylmer to Lord Goderich, PRO CO42/237.
5 9–11 June 1832, QCHA Minutes vol 2; Samuel Jackson, Charles Meigs,
and Richard Harlan *Report of the Commission Appointed by the Sanitary
Board of the City Councils to Visit Canada for the Investigation of the Epidemic
Cholera* (Philadelphia 1832) 2
6 19 June 1832 Alexander Hart to Moses Hart, ANQ Hart Papers Micro-reel
2GD

7 *Quebec Mercury* 14, 23 June 1832; *Montreal Gazette* 16 June 1832; 15 June 1832 Lord Aylmer to Lord Goderich, PRO CO42/237

8 13, 15, 16 June 1832, QCHA Minutes vol 2; 22 August, 29 Sept. 1832, QCHA Minutes vol 3; A.C. Buchanan *Report on Emigration to the Canadas in 1832* 12 Dec. 1832, PRO CO42/241; Jackson et al. *Commission* 6

9 28 June 1832 H. Stayner to J.S. Howard, AO Howard (Maclean) Papers II 40; 6 July 1832 Lord Aylmer to Lord Goderich, PRO CO42/237

10 13 June 1832 (the petition had thirteen pages of signatures), PAC RG4A1 S-283 98–109; *Quebec Mercury* quoted 16 June 1832 in *Montreal Gazette*; 11, 12 June 1832, QCHA Minutes vol 1; Le Moine *Quebec* 271

11 J.R. Rhinelander and J.E. Dekay *Report of the Commissioners Employed to Investigate the Origin and Nature of the Epidemic Cholera of Canada* (New York 1834) 33; Jackson et al. 11; *Canadian Courant* 20 June 1832; 22 June 1832, 7 Aug. 1832 Montreal General Hospital, committee on management, McGill U. Archives 1501/A

12 19 Nov. 1832 *Rapport du Comité permanent de la Faculté de Médecine de la Cité de Québec* (Québec 1832); Le Moine *Quebec* 271–2; *Montreal Gazette* 28, 30 June 1832; 12 June 1832, QCHA Minutes vol 2

13 20, 21 June 1832, QCHA Minutes vol 2; *Montreal Gazette* 26 June 1832; 20, 23 Oct. 1832, QCHA Minutes vol 3; 13 June 1832, QCHA Minutes vol 1

14 *Quebec Mercury* 23 June 1832; *Canadian Courant* 20 June 1832; *La Minerve* 22 June 1832; *Vindicator* 26 June 1832

15 30 Aug. 1832, QCHA Minutes vol 3

16 *Quebec Mercury* and *Canadian Courant* 23 June 1832

17 *La Minerve* 28 June, 30 July, 6 Aug. 1832; 17 July 1832 Lord Aylmer to Lord Goderich, PRO CO42/237

18 November 1832 Petition, PAC RG8C vol 301 122–5. In January 1835, Ayres returned to Canada for a visit to Kingston where he was an object of curiosity – but not of respect; Kingston *Chronicle* 24 Jan. 1835.

19 *Montreal Gazette* 16 June 1832

20 See, for example, regulations of MBH. *Montreal Gazette* 16 June 1832; 15 June 1832 Dr J.M. Skey to Sec. Craig PAC RG4A1 S-283 133

21 Samuel Neilson notes, PAC MG24B1 vol 42, 1747 for both quotations

22 11, 14 June, 16, 28 Aug. 1832 QCHA Minutes vols 1, 2, 3; *Montreal Gazette* 19 June 1832; *Vindicator* 17 July 1832; 19 June 1832 Alexander Hart to Moses Hart, ANQ Hart papers, microfilm reel 2Gd

23 'The Life and Times of Alfred Perry' 3, Chateau de Ramezay, Montreal, typescript

24 PAC RG4C2 1832 vol 12 102; PAC RG4A1 S-286 70

25 PAC RG4A1 S-286 23; *Montreal Gazette* 21 Aug. 1832

26 16, 27 June, 12 July 1832, QCHA Minutes vol 2; 25 June 1832 QBH to Sec. Craig, PAC RG4A1 S-284 106; *Canadien* reprinted *La Minerve* 5 July 1832; *Quebec Mercury* 5 July 1832

27 PAC RG4A1 S-286 14; PAC RG4C2 1832 vol 12 112, 147, 156; PAC RG4A1
   S-287 75; PAC RG4A1 S-288 75, 96; PAC RG4A1 S-290 2
28 27 June 1832, QCHA Minutes vol 2; 17, 18, 20, 21, 23, 25 Aug. 1832
   QCHA Minutes vol 3
29 10 May 1832, QCHA Minutes vol 1; 30 Dec. 1832 Dr Tessier to Col. Craig,
   PAC RG4A1 S-296 pt II 151–61; 1st, 2nd, 3rd Report of the Committee of
   the Board of Health, PAC RG4A1 S-292 138–60; Civil Secretary to Dr
   Tessier, PAC RG4C2 1832 vol 12 208; R. Christie *A History of the Late
   Province of Lower Canada, Parliamentary and Political* 3 (1850) 493
30 *Quebec Mercury* 23, 28 Aug; PAC RG4A1 S-290 161–4
31 PAC RG4A1 S-287 33; PAC RG4A1 S-289 43, 50
32 *Montreal Gazette* 23 June 1832; 24, 25, 26 June 1832, C.J. Forbes to Col.
   Craig, PAC RG4A1 S-284 91, 92, 105; 27 June 1832 Col. Craig to C.J.
   Forbes, PAC RG4C2 1832 vol 12, 87
33 *La Minerve* 25 June 1832; *Canadian Courant* 27 June 1832; 3 July
   1832 C.J. Forbes to Col. Craig, PAC RG4A1 S-285 18; *Vindicator* 4 June
   1833
34 *Montreal Gazette* 10 July; Resolution of the committee 7, 9, 11 Aug. 1832;
   Canadian Courant 1, 8 Aug. 1832
35 *Canadian Courant* 15, 18, 22 Aug. 1832; *Montreal Gazette* 23 Aug. 1832
36 *Canadian Courant* 28 July, 1 Aug. 1832; *Montreal Gazette* 14 Aug. 1832
37 *Quebec Mercury* 21 Aug. 1832; 22, 24, 25 Aug., 1, 13 Sept. 1832, QCHA
   Minutes vol 3
38 18 June 1832, PAC RG4A1 S-284 22; *La Minerve* 28 June, 9 July 1832;
   PAC RG4C2 1832 vol 12, 78
39 *Quebec Mercury* 19, 21, 31 July, 7 Aug. 1832. The figures were 188
   widows, 11 widowers, 348 children.
40 *Canadian Courant* 27 June, 7 July, 1832, 9 Oct. 1833; *Montreal Gazette* 1,
   20 Sept., 4 Oct. 1832, 17 Jan. 1833; Newton Bosworth *Hochelaga Depicta*
   (Montreal 1846) 184. The Montreal society gave outdoor relief to 41
   widows and more than 200 orphans in the winter of 1832–3; in March
   1833 the asylum held over 70 orphans and about 20 widows.
41 PAC RG4A1 S-283 113, 114, 119; PAC RG4A1 S-284 95–6, 164–164a; PAC
   RG4C2 1832 vol 12 92, 103, 180; *Canadien* 2 July 1832 reprinted
   La Minerve 5 July 1832; *Canadian Courant* 1 Sept. 1832; *La Minerve*
   14 July 1832; PAC RG4A1 S-289 54; PAC RG4A1 S-295 105
42 19 June, 13, 14 July, QCHA Minutes vol 2; 22 July 1832, QCHA Minutes
   vol 3
43 21 June 1832 Provincial Sec. to MBH, PAC RG4C2 1832 vol 12 75–6; for
   examples of the supervisory role over the board at William Henry see
   PAC RG4A1 S-286 162, and PAC RG4A1 S-287 26–7. By the end of the
   epidemic, boards had been set up at Gaspé, Trois-Rivières, Chambly,
   William Henry, St Johns, Soulanges, Berthier, La Prairie, Beauharnois, and
   St-Hyacinthe.

44 18 Oct. 1832, PAC RG4A1 S-292 23; *Bulletin des récherches historiques* 12 (1906) 88–92; J.J. Heagerty *Four Centuries of Medical History in Canada* I (Toronto 1928) 187; *Vindicator* 20 Nov. 1832; Buchanan *Report* 49

45 Louise Dechêne and Jean-Claude Robert 'Le choléra de 1832 dans le Bas Canada: mesure des inegalités devant la mort' (University of Montreal, mimeo 1977) (I should like to thank Professor Robert for providing me with a copy of this paper.) Fernand Ouellet *Le Bas-Canada 1791–1840* (Ottawa 1976) 215

46 28 June 1832, PAC RG4C2 1832 vol 12, 86; *Vindicator* 3 July 1832; *Canadian Courant* 15 Aug. 1832, 13 Feb. 1833

47 *La Minerve* 9 July 1832; *Vindicator* 20 Nov. 1832; *Montreal Gazette* 21 Aug. 1832 (as quoted in Ouellet *Le Bas-Canada* 216) and 14 Dec. 1832

48 This paragraph is based on Ouellet *Le Bas-Canada*.

CHAPTER 3 'Nothing is to be heard but the "Cholera"':
Upper Canada 1832

1 *Kingston Chronicle* 16 June 1832

2 5 Nov. 1832 Report of the Montreal Emigrant Society PAC RG4A1 S-289 9; 25 June Sec. McMahon to Proprietors of Steam Vessels, 30 June 1832 to Cheeseman Moe and John Patten, PAC RG7G16C vol 26 85, 91

3 C.M. Godfrey *The Cholera Epidemics in Upper Canada 1832–1866* (Toronto 1968) 15

4 13, 14 July 1832, AO Western District Quarter Sessions, Minutes 1821–1834 vol 166; 20 June 1832 Sec. McMahon to Chairman, Midland District Quarter Sessions, 2 July 1832 George Hamilton to Lt.Col. Rowan, PAC RG5A1 vol 118 65,977–8, 66,008; 20 June 1832, AO Home District Quarter Sessions, Minutes vol 7 363–4; 27 June 1832, AO Western District Quarter Sessions, Minutes 1821–1834 vol 166; Bytown Board of Health, PAC MG24I9 vol 21 5,628; *Brockville Gazette* 21 June 1832

5 25 June; 2 July John Mosier to Lt.Col. Rowan, 3 July 1832 Hugh Richardson to Lt.Col. Rowan, PAC RG5A1 vol 118, 66,125, 66,127–31, 66,133–4; 29 June 1832 Hugh Richardson to Lt.Col. Rowan, PAC RG5A1 vol 116–17 65,907–8; PAC RG4A1 vol 118 66,103–5, 66,116–20, 66,124, 66,107–10; 11 July 1832 Lt.Col. Rowan to Pres. BH Niagara, PAC RG7G16c vol 26 117–18; 25 July 1832 Dr Gillie to Chairman BH Bytown, PAC MG24I9 vol 19 4,725

6 22 June 1832, PAC MG24I9 vol 21 5,636–8; *Canadian Freeman* 17 May 1832

7 25 June 1832 Lt.Col. Dougall to Adjutant-General, PAC RG5A1 vol 116–17 66,829–32; Godfrey *Cholera* 35–6; 26 Aug. 1832 Surgeon J.M. Shortt to Lt.Col. MacDougall, PAC RG8C vol 300 no. 247

8 Rev. T. Radcliffe ed *Extracts from Authentic Letters from Upper Canada* quoted in *Continuation of Letters from Sussex Emigrants in Upper Canada for*

1833 (Petworth 1833); 18 Aug. 1832, AO Ottawa District Quarter Sessions RG21 vol 155; 12 July 1832 William Macaulay, 24 July 1832 London BH. 27 July 1832 John B. Askin to Lt.Col. Rowan, PAC RG5A1 vol 118 66,179–82, 66,327–8, 66,392–3; 2 Aug. 1832 James Clark to Lt.Col. Rowan, PAC RG5A1 vol 119–20 66,567–70

9 18 June 1832, Home District Quarter Sessions Minutes 1828–1833 AO RG21 vol 18 356–62; 18 June 1832, PAC RG5A1 vol 116–17 66,517–18; 20 June 1832 John Rolph to Ed. McMahon, ibid 66,739–40; 22 June 1832, TPL York Board of Health Papers B34

10 8 Aug. 1832, TPL York BH Minutes; PAC RG5A1 vol 121 67,001–5, 67,260–330; 30 Jan. 1833 Isaac Wilson to his brother, AO Isaac Wilson diary 67; 24 Sept. 1832 John Strachan to the bishop, AO John Strachan letter book no. 1, 204

11 22 June 1832, TPL York BH Minutes; Home District Quarter Sessions Minutes 1828–1833, AO RG21 vol 18 365–72

12 21 June 1832, PAC RG5A1 vol 116–17, 65,757–8; 24–29 June 1832, TPL York BH Minutes; 6 July 1832, Lt. Col. Rowan to Bishop McDowell, PAC RG7G16C vol 26 182

13 7, 11 July 1832 Home District Quarter Sessions Minutes 1828–1833, AO RG21 vol 18 378–9, 385–7

14 14 July 1832 John Carey to Sir John Colborne, 17 July 1832 York BH to Sir John Colborne, PAC RG5A1 vol 118 66,214–18; 3 Aug. 1832 John Rolph to York BH, TPL BH papers B34

15 6 Aug. 1832 Lt. Col. Rowan to Chairman York BH, PAC RG7G16C vol 27 5–9; 23 Aug. 1832 John Carey to Lt. Col. Rowan, PAC RG5A1 vol 119–20 66,824–5; *Canadian Correspondent* 20 April 1833

16 31 [sic] June 1832 Memorial of Debtors in York Jail, PAC RG5A1 vol 116–17 65,934–7; 26 June 1832 Catherine Merritt to her mother, AO Merritt papers, package 48; 30 June 1832 Anne Powell to her brother, AO William Dummer Powell correspondence vol 96; 24 Sept. 1832 John Strachan to the bishop, AO John Strachan letter book no. 1 204

17 8 Aug. 1832, TPL York BH Minutes; 10 Aug. 1832 Lt. Col. Rowan to Dr Baldwin, PAC RG7G16C vol 27 16–17

18 11 Aug. 1832, PAC RG7G16C vol 27 17; 14 Aug. 1832, PAC RG5A1 vol 119–20 66,704; York *Courier* 14 Aug. 1832

19 14 June 1832 Robert D. Cartwright to Sir John Colborne *Journal of the Legislative Assembly of Upper Canada* 3 Sess. 11 Parl. 1832–3, appendix, 82–3; 22 June 1832 John Kirby to Ed. McMahon, PAC RG5A1 vol 116–17 66,797–8; *Kingston Chronicle* 23 June 1832

20 PAC RG5A1 vol 121 67,035, 67,037, 67,047, 67,054, 67,065, 67,097, 67,126, 67,132, 67,150, 67,152, 67,162, 67,168, 67,190, 67,192

21 20 June 1832 William Steele to John Steele, AO John Steele papers; 23 June 1832 Handbill, PAC RG5A1 vol 116–17 65,822; 13 Aug. 1832 William Macaulay to Lt. Col. Rowan, PAC RG5A1 vol 119–20 66,675–8;

17 Aug. 1832 Lt. Col. Rowan to John Macaulay, PAC RG7G16C vol 27 27. The hospital had spent £420 by the second week of August. £220 was paid from the subscription of over £350; the balance of the subscription went toward relief.

22 2 July Circular letter, 12 July 1832 William Macaulay to Lt. Col. Rowan, PAC RG5A1 vol 118 66,007, 66,009–10, 66,179–82. Niagara District magistrates established branch boards at Queenston, Chippewa, Waterloo Ferry, Port Dalhousie; 25 June 1832 Public notice, special sessions, Niagara, PAC MG24 126 vol 47. London District magistrates established a branch board for the County of Norfolk; 30 June 1832 John B. Askin to Ed. McMahon, PAC RG5A1 vol 116–17 65,913. On 26 June 1832 Western District magistrates set fines of 5/- to 20/- for breaches of sanitary regulations; AO Western District Quarter Sessions, Minutes 1821–1834 vol 166. In York, most of the 30 people charged were not convicted; E. Firth *The Town of York 1815–1834* (Toronto 1966) lxiv.

23 5 Sept. 1832 J. Skey to Lt. Col. Clegg, PAC RG8C vol 301 no. 10–11; 16 July 1832 William Jones to Col. James Givens, AO William Jones, Indian Agent letter book, Baldon U.C., 27–8. There were cholera outbreaks in York, Kingston, Prescott, Brockville, Cornwall, Cobourg, Hallowell, Brantford, Bytown, Port Dalhousie, St Regis, and on the Welland Canal. The deaths figure is drawn from newspaper reports and board of health reports. It is, no doubt, an underestimate.

24 28 June 1832 H. Stayner to J.S. Howard, AO Howard (Maclean) Papers II 40; Godfrey *Cholera* 37

25 Anson Green *The Life and Times of the Reverend Anson Green* (Toronto 1877) 189; *Colonial Advocate* 2 Aug. 1832

26 M.A. Patterson 'The Cholera Epidemic of 1832, in York, Upper Canada' *Bulletin of the Medical Library Association* (April 1958) 165–84 suggests a possible link between government inadequacies revealed in this epidemic and the later political crisis. 24 Jan. 1833 *Journal of the Legislative Assembly of Upper Canada* 3 Sess. 11 Parl. 1832–3, appendix, 206

CHAPTER 4 'The ravages ... has been kept hid': Canada 1834

1 Joseph Signay: l'administration du Diocese de Quebec, mandements pour des actions de grace publiques *Mandements, lettres pastorales et circulaires des évêques de Québec* 3 (Québec 1888); *Quebec Mercury* 13 Feb. 1833 reprinted in *Canadian Courant*; PRO CO42/242 265–7

2 29 April, 3 May 1833, PAC RG7G18 vol 16–17; 9 May 1833 Governor's Medical Council to Lt. Col. Craig, 10 May 1833 G.A. Gore, John Bruce to Governor in Chief, 20 June 1833 Sec. Craig to Col. Gore, PAC RG7G18 vol 16–17

3 4 April 1833 PRO CO42/251 6–9, 81

4 26, 27 March, 7 April Report of the Committee of the whole council 1834, PAC RG4A S-320 134, 154, 202–3; PRO CO42/252 6–19

5 21 April 1834 Capt. Reid to Col. Craig, 24 April 1834 Report of the Committee of the whole council, PAC RG4A1 S-321 54, 78

6 1 Oct. 1834 J. Astle to Sec. State Colonies, PRO CO42/255 7; James Marr Brydon *Narrative of a Voyage with a Party of Emigrants to Upper Canada* (London 1834) 11–13

7 12 June, 23 June, 4 Aug. Capt. Reid to Col. Craig, PAC RG4A1 S-234 109 S-325 55–6, S-237 pt I 19–20; 24 Nov. 1834 Dr. Fortier memorial, PAC RG4A1 S-330 pt II 112

8 28 May, 11, 12, 6 June, 4 Aug. Capt. Reid to Col. Craig, PAC RG4A1 S-323 pt II 295; S-324 98, 109; S-234 55, 57; S-237 pt I 25–8

9 15 May, 21 June 1834, PAC RG7G18 vol 16–17; 11, 12 June, 4, 6, Aug. 1834 Capt. Reid to Col. Craig, 11 Aug. Col. Craig to Hon. Smith, PAC RG4A1 S-324 98, 109, S-327 pt I 19–20, 59, 92–4; 17 July 1834 Telegraph from Grosse Isle, PAC RG4A1 S-326 pt II 126–7; PAC RG4A1 S-329 177

10 7 April, Quebec Emigrant Society Memorial, 3 June 1834 petition, PAC RG4A1 S-234 150–3, 220; 1 May 1834, PAC RG4A1 S-323 pt II 329; 3 June 1834 Mayor of Quebec to Sec. Craig, PAC RG4A1 S-324 36–8; 28, 29 June, 3, 6 July 1834 Wm. Lyons to Col. Craig, PAC RG4A1 S-325 103, 115–15a, S-326 pt I 30, 46, 67; S-327 pt II 186; *Quebec Mercury* reprinted *Montreal Gazette* 14 June 1834; *Montreal Gazette* 16 Aug. 1834

11 14 Aug. 1834 Common Council of Quebec, PAC RG4A1 S-327 pt II 186; 28 Nov. 1834 Report of Sanitary Committee, PAC RG4A1 S-330 140

12 PAC RG4A1 S-327 pt II 186; *Quebec Mercury* 12 Aug. 1834 reprinted *Montreal Gazette* 28 Aug. 1834, 15 Aug. 1834 W. Steele to John Steele, AO John Steele Papers; *Montreal Herald* 1 Sept. 1834

13 11 Aug. 1834, PAC RG4A1 S-327 pt II 94, 95; *Vindicator* 15 Aug. 1834; 7 June 1834 Report of the Committee of the whole council, PAC RG4A1 S-231 84, 85; 18 March 1835 Aylmer to Spring-Rice, PRO CO42/256 296–301

14 12 July 1834 Executive Council PAC RG4A1 S-326 pt I 78; *Montreal Gazette* 30 Sept. 1834

15 *Quebec Mercury* 22, 31 July, 2 Aug. 1834; *Quebec Gazette* in *Montreal Gazette* 16 Aug. 1834; 21 July 1834 Sanitary Committee announcement, 21 July 1834 City Council to Col. Craig, PAC RG4A1 S-326 pt II 167, 196; 28 Nov. 1834 Report of the Sanitary Committee, PAC RG4A1 S-330 140

16 *Vindicator* 10 May, 4 June 1833; *Montreal Gazette* 5 July 1834; *Bye-laws, Rules and Regulations of the Common Council of the City of Montreal* (Montreal 1833); 1 July 1834 L. Gugy to Col. Craig, 9 Sept. 1834 Grand Jury presentment, PAC RG4A1 S-326 pt I 14; S-328 pt II 123

17 *Montreal Gazette* 3, 24 June 1834; 23 June 1834 Montreal Emigrant Society memorial, PAC RG4A1 S-325 51

18 12 July 1834 J. Viger to Col. Craig, PAC RG4A1 S-326 pt I 93–93c; *Montreal Herald* 22 July 1834; 'Return of total interments ... from 12th July ... to 29th August,' PAC RG4A1 S-328 pt I 36. Weekly totals of deaths by cholera were 60, 118, 258, 212, 150, 51, 33.

19 *Montreal Gazette* 19 July 1834; *Vindicator* 29 July 1834; *Montreal Herald* 7 Aug. 1834
20 *Report of the Special Sanitary Committee of Montreal upon Cholera and Emigration for the year 1834* (Montreal 1835) appendix, 3–5; *Montreal Herald* 22 July, 7 Aug. 1834; *Vindicator* 25 July, 1 Aug. 1834, *Montreal Gazette* 26, 31 July, 12 Aug., 23 Oct. 1834; 16 July 1834 Howell Paynter to J. Viger, PAC RG4A1 S-326 pt I 94–94a; *Montreal Gazette* 28 Aug. 1834 reported 47 deaths at Trois-Rivières; there were 14 dead at Soulanges, 22 at Lachine (*Report* appendix).
21 PRO CO42/252 gives immigration figures of 50,254 for 1832; 21,752 for 1833; 30,935 for 1834. 3 Sept. 1834 A.C. Buchanan to Col. Craig, PAC RG4A1 S-328 pt I 48; 8 July 1835 Aylmer to Lord Glenelg, PRO CO42/257 315–16; 18 March 1835 Aylmer to Spring-Rice, PRO CO42/256 296–301. Aylmer had advanced £4000 for Grosse Isle. Ouellet *Le Bas-Canada* 404–6, *Quebec Mercury* 31 July 1834; *Vindicator* 5, 16 Sept. 1834; *Montreal Gazette* 7, 16 Aug., 18, 30 Sept. 1834
22 Population in 1832: 261,000, in 1834: 320,693, PRO CO42/557; 3 April 1834 Petition House of Assembly U.C., PRO CO42/418 250–62; 31 March 1834 J. Colborne to Rt Hon. E.G. Stanley, PRO CO42/418 231; 23 Dec. 1834 Report of work of Kingston and Toronto hospitals, PRO CO42/423 340–53
23 In the course of 1834, boards were established at Toronto, Brockville, Kingston, Hamilton, Ancaster, Prescott, Dundas, Oakville, Sandwich, Port Credit, Peterborough, Bytown, Cornwall, Amherstburg, Niagara, the Eastern District, and Perth. They received a total of £2048.12.1, of which £685.19.11 went to Toronto and £260 to Kingston. 24 April 1835 Statement of Advances made by the Bank of Upper Canada to the various Boards of Health, PAC RG5A1 vol 152; 6 May 1834, AO Toronto City Council papers; 7 May 1834 W.L. Mackenzie to Col. Rowan, 14 May 1834 Col. Rowan to W.L. Mackenzie, PAC RG5A1 vol 41 76,923–6, 76,985
24 27 July 1834 Harriett Cartwright to Marianne, TPL Cartwright family correspondence; *Kingston Chronicle* 2 Aug. 1834
25 16 July 1834 Van Cortlandt to Capt. Baker, PAC MG24I9 vol 19 4,697; 18 July Bytown BH resolution, 19 July Brockville BH to Colborne, 21 July Arch. Mclean to Rowan, 31 July Peterborough BH resolution, 29 July 1834, Toronto BH to Rowan, PAC RG5A1 vol 143 78,133–4, 78,184–5, 78,196–7, 78,413–17, 78,377–81; Dr Thomas Rolph, 8 Aug. W.A. Dickson, 5 Aug. Hamilton Board of Police, 13 Aug. John Clarke Wm. Richardson to Rowan, 18 Aug. 1834 Prescott BH, PAC RG5A1 vol 144 78,429–30, 78,558–9, 78,478–9, 78,671, 78,691, 79,010; 18 Aug. 1834 Circular letter, PAC RG7G16C vol 31 221; 30 Aug. 1834 J. Colborne to R.W. Hay, PRO CO42/423 123–4; 4 Aug. 1834 Magistrates, Leeds to Craig, PAC RG4A1 S-237 pt I 31–2; *Kingston Gazette and Chronicle* 23 Aug. 1834

26 21 July Arch. Mclean, 29 July Toronto BH, 30 July John Cartwright, Wm.
    Macaulay to Col. Rowan, PAC RG5A1 vol 143 78,196–7, 78,377–81, 78,397,
    78,405–7; 5 Aug. A.H. Meyers, 18 Aug. Rector of Toronto, 26 Aug. 1834
    Charles Eliot to Rowan, PAC RG5A1 vol 144 78,482–3, 78,783, 78,953; 21
    Aug. 1834 J.D. Gellie and D. Scanlon to Bytown BH, PAC MG24I9 vol 22
    5,784; 30 Aug. 1834 Benjamin Tett to McIntosh, Queens U. Archives MGIII
    B-63 Tett Papers A vol I; 11 Aug. 1834 Wm. Stewart to McIntosh, AO William
    Stewart letter book; Report, Commissioners Kingston Hospital *Journal of the
    Legislative Assembly of Upper Canada* 1 Sess. 12 Parl. Appendix no. 2 Report
    no. 84; *Kingston Herald* 20 Aug. 1834
27 16, 18, 20 July 1834, PAC MG24I9 vol 22 5,757, 5,759, 5,764–5; 17, 18 July
    1834, PAC RG5A1 vol 143 78,133–4, 78,178; Van Cortlandt's resignation,
    PAC RG5A1 vol 145 79,190–4
28 25 July, 21 Aug. 1834 J.D. Gellie, D. Scanlon to Bytown BH, PAC MG24I9
    vol 22 5,771–2, 5,784; 2 Aug., 25 Sept. 1834 Col. Rowan to Bytown BH,
    PAC MG24I9 vol 19 4,727–8, 5789
29 11 Aug. 1834 Wm. Stewart, John Barrieville to Bytown BH, PAC MG24I9
    vol 22 5,776–7; 14 Aug. Special Session BH, 15 Aug. Capt. Boulton to
    Bytown BH, 23 Aug. 1834 Bytown BH to Boulton, PAC MG24I9 vol 19
    4,732, 4,734–5, 4,742
30 25 Sept. 1834, PAC MG24I9 vol 22 5,789; 4 Sept. 1834 C. Sherriff to Col.
    Rowan, a correspondence with enclosures from Van Cortlandt to Col.
    Rowan, PAC RG5A1 vol 145 79,179–81, 79,183–5, 79,188–94. Drs Gillie
    and Christie were the appointees offensive to Van Cortlandt; 20 Oct. 1834
    C. Sherriff to Col. Rowan, PAC RG5A1 vol 146 79,830–2.
31 17 July 1834 John Cartwright to Col. Rowan, PAC RG5A1 vol 143 78,115;
    21 July 1834 Executive Council Minutes, PAC RG1E2 vol 25
32 *Kingston Chronicle* 2, 23 Aug. 1834; *Upper Canada Herald* 30 July 1834;
    11 Aug. Wm. Macaulay, 16 Aug. 1834 H. Smith to Col. Rowan, PAC
    RG5A1 vol 144 78,612–13, 78,770–1; PAC RG7G vol 31 214
33 PAC RG5A1 vol 144 78,789–90, 78,814, 78,842, 78,849, 78,894, 78,976; PAC
    RG5A1 vol 143 78,383–96; *Kingston Chronicle* 6 Sept. 1834; 30 Aug. 1834
    J. Colborne to R.W. Hay, PRO CO42/423 123–4; *Kingston Herald* 14 Aug.,
    3 Sept. 1834
34 25 April 1835, PAC RG5A1 vol 152 83,516; *Kingston Chronicle* 26 July, 15
    Nov. 1834; *Kingston Herald* 27 Aug., 3, 24 Sept. 1834. The 21 widows and
    87 orphans were allowed 10/- and 5/- respectively per month.
35 F.H. Armstrong 'William Lyon MacKenzie, First Mayor of Toronto: a
    Study of a Critic in Power' *Canadian Historical Review* 48 (1967) 309–29
36 14 May 1834 Emigrant Officer to Mayor, 1 June 1834 committee recom-
    mendation, 14 June 1834 Emigrant Officer to Mayor, AO Toronto City
    Council Papers; 23 July 1834 Toronto BH to Col. Rowan, PAC RG5A1 vol
    143 78,267–9; 24 July Col. Rowan to C. Widmer, PAC RG7G16C vol 31
    169–70

37 29 July 1834 Toronto BH to Col. Rowan, PAC RG5A1 vol 143 78,377–81; 31 July 1834 Ch. Bernhard to Mayor, AO Toronto City Council Papers; 31 July Mr Spragge to Col. Rowan, PAC RG5A1 vol 143 78,419–20; *Canadian Correspondent* 16 Aug. 1834; PAC RG5A1 vol 145 79,303–4, 79,306–9, 79,323, 79,336, 79,344; 20 Sept. 1834 Dr Park to Col. Rowan, ibid 79,493; 3 Oct. 1834 J. Leslie to Col. Rowan, PAC RG5A1 vol 146 79,666–7

38 *Kingston Chronicle* 16 Aug. 1834; Armstrong 'Mackenzie' 322

39 1 Aug. 1834 R. Stanton to Macaulay, AO Macaulay Papers; 29 July 1834 Col. Rowan to Ald. Morrison, PAC RG7G16C vol 31 180; 29 July 1834 Toronto BH to Col. Rowan, PAC RG5A1 vol 143 78,377–81

40 7 Aug. Col. Rowan to Ald. Morrison, 9, 11 Aug. to Ald. Lesslie, 14 Aug., 2 Sept. to Drs C. Widmer et al., 5 Sept. to Sheward, 6 Sept. 1834 to George Parke, PAC RG7G16C vol 31 200, 204–6, 215, 253, 258, vol 32 3; 9 Aug. Toronto BH resolution, 9, 11 Aug. Ald. Lesslie to Col. Rowan, 30 Aug. C. Widmer to Ald. Lesslie, 5 Sept. Ald. Lesslie, 6 Sept. 1834 George Parke to Col. Rowan, PAC RG5A1 vol 144 78,570–4, 78,596–8, 78,606–10, 79,025–6, vol 145 79,210, 79,239–43; 12 Dec. 1834 Petition Dr Charles E. Sheward, PAC RG1E3 vol 83 18–29; 20 Dec. 1834 Executive Council Minutes, PAC RG1E2 vol 25; the work of helping widows and orphans was done by the churches. John Strachan noted that Church of England members subscribed £712.6.3 in 1832 and £463.14.0 in 1834; in 1834 the Church of England was the only denomination which subscribed anything (AO Strachan papers – unbound papers 1834).

CHAPTER 5 'Distance is no security': The Maritimes 1832–4

1 J.S. Martell *Immigration to and Emigration from Nova Scotia 1815–1838* (Halifax 1942) 94 gives the figures of 3,136 in 1831, 2,925 in 1832, and 1,285 in 1834. Helen I. Cowan *British Emigration to British North America 1783–1837* (Toronto 1928) 207; 9 April, 1832 Expenses of the establishment, PANS RG5 Series R vol 16

2 C. Bruce Fergusson 'A Coke's Tour to Halifax' *The Dalhousie Review* 29 (1950) 51–61; *Journal of the Proceedings of the House of Assembly* 17 (1832) Appendix 49

3 *Journal House of Assembly* 16 1832. The quarantine act was introduced 21 March 1832 and received assent 14 April 1832. The infectious diseases act was introduced 29 March 1832, received assent 14 April 1832. Cowan *British Emigration* 215–16; 17 April 1832 Minutes of the Council, PANS RG1 vol 214½B

4 26 June, 31 July 1832 Minutes of the Council, PANS RG1 vol 214½B; 27 June 1832 Provincial Sec., circular letter to Halifax MDs and local magistrates, PANS RG1 vol 148; 18 July 1832 J. Richie to Provincial Sec., PANS RG7 vol 6; n.d. Minutes of the Central Board of Health, PANS MS Documents vol 240

5   13 Aug. 1832 Provincial Sec. to Doctors of cholera hospitals, PANS RG1 vol 148
6   27 April 1832 Provincial Sec. to Messrs Albro, Tobin, and Howe, ibid; PANS RG7 vol 6
7   9 July Sydney, 27 July Fort Lawrence. At Parrsboro the health officer visited 118 vessels in August 1832; PANS RG7 vol 6. 13 July Arichat, 17 July Parrsboro, 31 July Truro, 2 Aug. Picton, 21 Aug. 1832, PANS RG1 vol 148. At Halifax the boats made 2,701 visits between April and September; 20 Sept., 10 Dec. 1832, PANS RG1 vol 214½B.
8   10 April 1833 Committee of House of Assembly report, PANS RG25 Series C vol 2. The final figures were for expenditures of £2887.11.4. Lieutenant-governors paid £1135.11.7½; shipping fees £413.6.10; sale of manure £38.4.2. 17 April 1832 Committee of House of Assembly report, PANS RG5 Series R vol 17; 12 April 1834 Committee of House of Assembly recommendation, PANS RG5 Series R vol 19
9   *Acadian Recorder* 5, 12 July, 9 Aug. 1834; 11 Aug. 1834 Record Book Commissioners of the Halifax Poor Asylum, PANS RG25 Series C vol 40
10 9 April, 6 Aug. 1834 Minutes of Council, PANS RG1 vol 214½C; 29 July 1834 President of PEI to Lt. Gov. Sir Colin Campbell, PANS MS documents vol 240; Sept. Sir Colin Campbell to Spring-Rice, PANS RG1 vol 114
11 19, 23, 27, Aug., 9, 27 Sept. 1834 General Orders, PANS HQ30
12 Sept. Sir Colin Campbell to Spring-Rice, PANS RG1 vol 114; *Acadian Recorder* 16, 30 Aug. 1834; Record Book, Commissioners of the Halifax Poor Asylum, PANS RG25 Series C vol 4a
13 *Acadian Recorder* 6 Sept., 11 Oct. 1834; 4, 6 Sept. 1834 Minutes of the Council, PANS RG1 vol 214½C; 31 March 1835 Provincial Sec. to T.N. Jeffery, PANS RG1 vol 149; Sept. Sir Colin Campbell to T. Spring-Rice, PANS RG1 vol 114; 7 Nov. 1834 Record Book, Commissioners of the Poor Asylum, PANS RG25 Series C vol 4a
14 10 Dec. 1834 Petition of Dr John Adamson, PANS RG5 Series R vol 20. Adamson tended to call all sickness cholera during the epidemic, but the death figures seem acceptable. The cases are, naturally, concentrated near his drugstore on Water Street, but he did deal with cases in more distant parts of town. *Report of the Society for the Propagation of the Gospel* (London 1833) 97–101; *Report* (1834–5) 101–2. St Paul's Anglican church, burial register, PANS MG4 (microfilm): the records suggest that the burials were of parishioners, not of the dead from Dalhousie.
15 6 Sept. 1834 John Bell to his parents, quoted in Winthrop Bell 'A Halifax Boyhood of One Hundred and Twenty Years ago' *Collections of N.S. Historical Society* 28 (1949) 128
16 3 Sept. 1834 Provincial Sec. to H.H. Cogswell, PANS RG1 vol 149; *Acadian Recorder* 13 Sept. 1834; 31 Dec. 1834 Report of a committee of the House of Assembly, PANS RG5 Series R vol 20; 25 Aug., 6 Sept. 1834

Minutes of the Council, PANS RG1 vol 214½C; 19 Sept. 1834 Minutes of
the Board of Health, PANS MS Documents vol 237
17 C.B. Fergusson *A Documentary Study of the Establishment of the Negroes in
    Nova Scotia between the War of 1812 and the Winning of Responsible Govern-
    ment, 1848* (Halifax 1948) 45; 19, 20 Sept. 1834 Minutes of the Board of
    Health, PANS MS Documents vol 237; Sept. Sir Colin Campbell to
    Spring-Rice, PANS RG1 vol 114
18 N.d. Sec. Windsor BH, 6 Sept. 1834 Guysborough BH to Provincial Sec.,
    PANS MS documents vol 240; 30 Aug. 1834 Provincial Sec. to Rev. James
    Shreve, Chester, PANS RG1 vol 149; 26 Sept. 1834 Minutes of Council,
    PANS RG1 vol 214½C
19 29 Nov. 1834 Minutes of Council, PANS RG1 vol 214½C; *Journal House of
    Assembly* 16, 1834–35 Appendix 31; *Acadian Recorder* 15 Nov. 1834
20 24 March 1832, PANB General Sessions of Saint John, 1832, 269–71;
    6 April 1832 Provincial Sec. to Magistrates of Saint John, PANB Provincial
    Sec.'s letter book
21 4 June 1832 Provincial Sec. to Provincial Sec. of Quebec, ibid; *Gleaner* 7,
    17 July, 14 Aug. 1832
22 23 June, 21 July, 6 Aug., 8 Sept. 1832 St John *Courier*; 27 July 1832
    Provincial Sec. to Chas Simonds, Saint John, and others, PANB Provincial
    Sec.'s letter book. 31 Jan. 1833 Abstract of expenditures, PANB RLE/833
    RE1/5 House of Assembly Papers – the total was £1634.5.10. 12 July,
    petition BH Saint John, 14 July 1832 Minutes BH Saint John, PANB
    MG9A1 vol 116
23 26 Feb. 1833 Report of Committee of House of Assembly, *Journal House of
    Assembly N.B.* 1833, 30–1; *Statutes of New Brunswick* 3 William IV C21; 3
    William IV C28
24 21 March, 7 June, 6 Sept. 1834 Grand Jury presentment, PANB General
    Sessions 1833–5 179–80, 219, 282–95; 3 Sept. 1834 Provincial Sec. to Brig.
    L. Peters, PANB Provincial Sec.'s letter book, additional papers;
    A. Douglas Gibbon 'The Kent Marine Hospital, St John N.B.' *Collections of
    the New Brunswick Historical Society* 14 (1955) 2; *Courier* 7, 28 June 1834
25 25 Sept., 2 Oct. 1834, PANB REX/pa Health and sickness box 1; 16 Jan.
    1835 Accounts of St John, PANB MG9A1 vol 116 806–11; *Courier* 4 Oct. 1,
    8 Nov. 1834; *The Islander* Charlottetown 11 Aug. 1854 (reviewing the
    epidemic of 1834)
26 In July BHs were operating in Saint John, Kent County, Northumberland
    County, Charlotte County, and Gloucester County; PRO CO 188/50
    57–77; 17, 20 Nov. 1834 Fredericton BH, PANB REX/pa Health and sick-
    ness box 1; *Courier* 4 Oct., 1, 8 Nov. 1834; *The Islander* 11 Aug. 1854
27 The 1833 census reported a population of 22,292 with 1,965 in Charlotte-
    town *Journal House Assembly P.E.I.* 4 Sess. 13 Gen. Ass. 1834, Appendix C.
    Revised Statutes P.E.I. 2 William IV C13; 5, 28 April 1832 Col. Sec. to B. de
    St Croix, 28 April 1832 to Robert Small, PAPEI Col. Sec. correspondence

1831–6, 21 May 1832 Lt. Gov. to Viscount Howick, PRO CO226/49 261–4; *Royal Gazette* 1, 15 May 1832.

28 20 Sept. 1832 E.J. Jarvis to Wm. Jarvis, NB Museum, Jarvis papers (typescript); 13 Oct. 1832 Lt. Gov. to B. de St. Croix, PAPEI Col. Sec. correspondence 1831–6; *Royal Gazette* 3 July, 13 Nov. 1832, 5 Feb. 1833. The total expenditure was £201.1.4½d.

29 PEI 3 William IV C25; *Royal Gazette* 21 May 1833

30 *Royal Gazette* 9 Sept., 7 Oct. 1834; 22 Sept. Col. Sec. to B. de St Croix, 29 Sept. to Wm. Compton, 17 Sept. 1834 to Peter Emery, PAPEI Col. Sec. correspondence 1831–6; 9 June 1834 President G.W. Wright to Stanley, PRO CO226/51 247–50. St Croix was paid £10.10.0. for visiting the steamer nine times, a sum which the House of Assembly later said should be paid by the ship owners as the act provided. They also objected to payments made to St Croix and Dr Mackieson for visiting country districts, which the house thought 'most exorbitant'; *Journal House of Assembly* 1 Sess. 14 Gen. Ass. 1835, 24 Feb. 1835.

31 *Royal Gazette* 29 July 1834; 29 July 1834 Col. Sec. to M. MacDonald, PAPEI Col. Sec. correspondence 1831–6. Expenses for protection against the cholera amounted to £154.18.9½d, almost half of it for boat hire. *Journal House Assembly* 1 Sess. 14 Gen. Ass. 1835; John Mackieson, Sketches of Medical and Surgical Cases, ms in the possession of Dr R.G. Lea of Charlottetown, PEI

32 20 Aug. 1831, 31 March 1832 Col. Sec. to Magistrates, ANfld CSI/38; *Public Ledger* 29 June, 3, 10, 24 July 1832, 1, 22 Jan., 29 March, 5 April, 6 Aug. 1833, 6 May, 19 Aug., 23 Sept. 1834, 11 Aug. 1835

CHAPTER 6 'Ample room ... for further improvements': Later Epidemics

1 *Globe* 26 July 1849; *Morning Chronicle* Halifax 22 Nov. 1871

2 J.J. Heagerty 'Public Health in Canada' R.D. Defries ed *The Development of Public Health in Canada* (Toronto 1940) vii

3 Oliver Macdonagh 'The Irish Famine Emigration to the United States' *Perspectives in American History* 10 (1976) 394, 414; 2 March 1849 Elgin to Grey PRO CO42/558 1–3. The tax was cut from 10/- to 7/6 per adult and 5/- per child between 5 and 15. David Coleman Lyne 'The Irish in the Province of Canada in the Decade Leading to Confederation' (MA Thesis McGill University 1960) 34; K.F. Brandon 'Public Health in Upper Canada' Defries ed *Public Health* 63

4 *BAJ* 5 (1849–50) 76–7. The members were Drs Wolfred Nelson (chairman), Guillaume Deschambault, Robert L. McDonnell, and Messrs Olivier Bertholet, William Workman, John James Day, Moses J. Hays; Dr A. David was secretary. Sylvio LeBlond 'Cholera in Quebec 1849' *Canadian Medical Association Journal* 71 (1954) 289; *Montreal Gazette* 15 June 1849; *British Whig* 20 June 1849; *Spectator* 27 June 1849

5 14 June 1849 CBH regulations, *BAJ* 5 (1849–50) 76–7
6 *BAJ* 5 (1849–50) 108; 7 Aug. 1849 Circular letter printed *Montreal Chronicle* 17 Aug. 1849
7 17, 19 April 1849 T.E. Cambell to Capt. Kirkland, PAC RG7C 17C vol 14 151; *Quebec Mercury* 8, 17 May 1849; 16 May 1849, QCHA QBH Minutes 1848; 27 June Drs Parrant & Nault to J. Leslie, 30 June 1849 J. Leslie to Drs Parrant & Nault, PAC RG4C1 vol 261 no. 2098; 8 Nov. 1849 Commissariat Clerk Harris to Commissary General, PAC RG7G20 vol 48 no. 5231
8 3 July J.R. Sexton to J. Leslie, 6 July 1849 J. Leslie to J.R. Sexton, PAC RG4C1 vol 267 no. 2160 (filed with 2833); 2 July 1849 AO TCC papers 1849; City of Hamilton Minutes, AO RG21 Section A (microfilm GS1603); 20 July 1849 J. Leslie to W.L. Distin, PAC RG5C2 vol 18 295–6; Hamilton *Spectator* 27 Aug. 1849; 12 May 1849 R. Buritt to J. Leslie, PAC RG5C1 vol 262 no. 1107; 30 Jan., 21 April J. Crawford, 15 Feb. 1849 B. Richards to J. Leslie, 28 Feb. Exec. Council, 24 April 1849 J. Leslie to J. Crawford, PAC RG5C1 vol 247 no. 203
9 *BAJ* 4 (1848–9) 220, 314; 16 April, 23 July 1849 AO TCC Papers 1849; *Gazette* 30 May 1849 reprinted Kingston *British Whig*; *Quebec Mercury* 26 July 1849; LeBlond 'Cholera 1849' 289; *Montreal Gazette* 23 June 1849; G.P. de T. Glazebrook *The Story of Toronto* (Toronto 1971) 174
10 15 Dec. 1848, 10 May 1849, QCHA QBH Minutes 1848; *Quebec Mercury* 26 May 1849; 28 Dec. 1848 Arthur Palmer to J. Leslie, 2 Jan. 1849 J. Leslie to A. Palmer 4, 10, 13, 24 Jan. 1849, PAC RG5C1 vol 244 no. 2, 21, 61; 2 July 1849, AO TCC Papers 1849; 28 July 1849 PAC RG5C1 vol 255 no. 640. Local boards were established at Quebec, Montreal, Berthier, Hamilton, Kingston, Toronto, Port Dover, St Thomas, Ancaster, Stratford, Brockville, Sarnia, Niagara, Woodstock, Prescott, Port Dalhousie, Ingersoll, Port Maitland, Stuartville, Simcoe, Gaspé; 19 June 1849 J. Leslie to J.V. Ham, PAC RG5C2 vol 18 PAC RG5C1 vol 256 no. 703, PAC RG4C1 vol 267 no. 2361 (filed with 2833).
11 *Chronicle* 18 Sept. 1849; *Quebec Gazette* 24 Sept. 1849
12 24 Dec. 1849, AO RG21 Section A Town of Dundas Minute Book (Microfilm GS1442); *Globe* 4 Sept. 1849; *Quebec Mercury* 9 June, 13 July 1849
13 *British Colonist* 20 July, 24 Aug. 1849; *Globe* 19 July, 23 Aug. 1849
14 30 June 1849 J.P. Sexton to J. Leslie, PAC RG4C1 vol 267 no. 2114 (filed with 2833); 30 June 1849 Minutes Committee of Management MGH, McGill U. Archives 1501/D; 6 July 1849 J. Leslie to A.B. Hawke, PAC RG5C2 vol 18 268–9; 2, 11 June 1849 J. Leslie to A.B. Hawke, 5 June 1849 A.B. Hawke to J. Leslie, PAC RG5C1 vol 266 no. 1307, 1309; 10 Dec. 1849, AO RG21 City of Hamilton Minutes Section A (microfilm GS1603); 5 Dec. 1849 J. Leslie to A.B. Hawke, PAC RG5C2 vol 18 430; W.G. Cosbie *The Toronto General Hospital* (Toronto 1975) 33; 18, 20 June 1849 Petitions of

residents of West End, AO TCC Papers 1849; PAC RG5C1 vol 256 no. 686; *Royal Gazette* PEI 11 Sept. 1849

15 11, 12, 18 July 1849, QCHA QBH Minutes 1849; *Quebec Mercury* 12 July 1849; *Chronicle* 18 Sept. 1849; *Gazette* 1 Sept. 1849

16 *Quebec Mercury* 19 May 1849; *BAJ* 5 (1849–50) 90; 2 June J. Leslie to A.B. Hawke, 5 June 1849 A.B. Hawke to J. Leslie, PAC RG5C1 vol 266 no. 1307; 6 June 1849, PAC RG1E7 vol 33; 4 June D.E. MacDonnell, 5 June 1849 Wm. Ford to J. Leslie, PAC RG5C1 vol 266 no. 1,311, 1,318; 12 June 1849 J. Leslie to Mayor, Kingston, PAC RG5C2 vol 18 223; *British Whig* 4 June, 26 Aug. 1849

17 30 June, 17 July 1849 A.J. Jackson to Major-General Commanding, Canada, to Inspector General Hospitals, 17 July 1849 Wm. Odell to Lt. Col. Hay, PAC RG8C vol 309 no. 87, 91, 93–5; *Montreal Gazette* 22 June 1849; *BAJ* 5 (1849–50) 107, 135, 165

18 *Quebec Mercury* 7 July 1849. 31 Aug. 1849, QCHA QBH Minutes show 1,066 dead; 284 had French-Canadian names. *Report of the Central Board of Health* (Quebec 1854) 21–2 shows 1,052 dead in the 1849 epidemic. 'Extracts from the Journal of Rev. T.S. Chapman' in *Annual Report of the Incorporated Church Society of the Diocese of Quebec 1850* 8 (Quebec 1850) reports cholera at Grosse Isle from the end of August to 7 Sept.

19 7, 9 July 1849 Dr. John King to Mayor, AO TCC Papers 1849; *Globe* 10, 19 July, 23 Aug., 4 Sept. 1849; *British Colonist* 17 July, 3 Aug. 1849; *Examiner* 1 Aug. 1849; Ontario Provincial Board of Health *Annual Report* 10 (1891) 15

20 *Quebec Mercury* 2 June, 14 July 1849; *Spectator* throughout the summer; *Transcript* 4 Aug. 1849; *Morning Chronicle* 18 Sept. 1849

21 J.D. Douglas ed *Journals and Reminiscences of James Douglas* (New York 1910) 148–9; *Quebec Mercury* 28, 31 July, 2 Aug. 1849; *Globe* 26 July 1849; *Transcript* 7, 11, 16 Aug. 1849; 24 Dec. 1849 *Mandements, lettres pastorales et circulaires des Évêques de Québec* 3 (Québec 1888) 561; 11 Dec. 1849, PAC RG1E7 vol 34

22 See note 18 to this chapter. *Quebec Mercury* 11 Aug. 1849; 26 Oct. 1849 J. Leslie to A. David, PAC RG4C1 vol 267 no. 2833

23 *Report of the Central Board of Health, 1854* 8; LeBlond 'Quebec, 1849' 292; *Report of the Water Committee Submitting the Report of the Engineers on the New Water Works of Montreal* (Montreal 1854) quotations from p. 84

24 *Proceedings of the Sanitary Committee on Fire, Water and Gas of the City of Toronto in Connection with the Supply of Water to the City* (Toronto 1854); 7 July 1854 Village of Galt Minutes, AO RG21 Section A (microfilm GS2982)

25 'On the Propagation of Cholera by Emigration' *Medical Chronicle* 2 (1855) 411; M. Charlton 'Outline of the History of Medicine in Lower Canada' *Annals of Medicine* 6 (1924) 343; 12 July 1849 T. Blatherwick to P.J.O.

Chauveau, PAC RG4C1 vol 350 no. 1123; *Report of the Central Board 1854* 9, 10–14

26 8, 11 July 1854 T. Blatherwick to P.J.O. Chauveau, to Insp. General of Military Hospitals, PAC RG17AV vol 2432 no. 1, 3; 12, 17 July 1854 Insp. General to T. Blatherwick, to P.J.O. Chauveau, PAC RG17AV vol 2433 no. 3, vol 2432 no. 14; *Report, 1854*; 10 July 1854 Wm. Marsden to Governor-General, PAC RG4B66

27 Quebec reported 734 deaths between 20 June and 31 August. This is inconsistent with the breakdown given: 494 males, 220 females; 461 residents, 163 seamen, 100 immigrants. Final figures were Quebec 748, Montreal 1,039, Hamilton 547, Kingston 186, for a total in these cities of 2,520. *Report, 1854* 9–14, 24–7; Godfrey *The Cholera Epidemics* 58; 6 Nov. 1854 Town of Dundas, Minutes, AO RG21 Section A (microfilm GS1442)

28 G. Bilson 'The Cholera Epidemic in St. John, N.B., 1854' *Acadiensis* (autumn 1974) 86–99; W.W. Warwick 'Public Health in New Brunswick' Defries ed *Public Health* 48–9

29 P.S. Campbell & H.L. Scammell 'Public Health in Nova Scotia' Defries ed *Public Health* 30; *Public Ledger* 19 Sept., 10 Oct. 1854, 26 Jan., 2 Feb. 1855; 19 Nov. 1854 Robert M. Pretient to Col. Sec., ANfld CS2/68; 17 July 1855 Report of the District Surgeon of Conception Bay *Journal House of Assembly* 1 sess. 6 gen. ass. 1855; *The Times* St John's 27 Dec. 1854

30 *Memorandum on Cholera* (Ottawa 1866) 13–14

31 22 Feb. 1866, E.S. Meredith circular letter, PAC RG5C1 vol 835 no. 214; 20 Feb. 1866, PAC RG17A vol 8 no. 641; 10 March 1866, PAC RG17A vol 9 no. 663; Minutes of medical conference on cholera, PAC RG17AV vol 2430. The conferences debated Dr J.C. Taché's draft and accepted most of it. One of the few divisions was on the question of whether to include Sisters of Charity in the list of those intimately connected with the sick. They were listed by a vote of 5 to 3.

32 Members were Drs R.L. McDonnell (Montreal, chairman), G.B. Badeau (Trois-Rivières), E. Van Cortlandt, H. Hill, G.A. Grant, G.T. Beaubien, J.C. Taché (Ottawa), W.J. Atkins (Toronto), G.R. Dickinson (Kingston), G.D. MacDonald (Hamilton), C.G. More (Toronto), and J.E. Landry (Quebec). Minutes of CBH and Final Report, PAC RG17AV no. 2431; 17 Nov. 1866, AO TCC Papers report no. 5 quoted in Godfrey *The Cholera Epidemics* 62; 19 Feb., 5 March, 2, 23 April, 7, 14, 21 May, 6 Aug. 5 Nov. 1866, Minutes City of Ottawa, AO RG21 Section A; 12 Dec. 1866 Annual Return from Grosse Isle, PAC RG17A vol 13, no. 1015; W. Marsden 'Plan of Quarantine for Cholera' *Canada Medical Journal* 2 (1866) 344; *Morning News* 12 Sept. 1866

33 This discussion is based on my 'Two Cholera Ships in Halifax' *Dalhousie Review* (autumn 1973) 449–59. *Mandements des évêques* 4, 537

34 Bye-law 431, 27 April 1866 (Toronto 1866); *Canada Medical Journal* 5 (1868–9) 92

35 After 1867, quarantine was governed by 31 Vic. 63 (1868), 32 Vic. 10, and 33
Vic. 10 and by regulations promulgated by the Governor-in-Council. Quarantine references can be found in PAC RG17A1 vol 1502. For the special
impact of cholera see e.g. *Canada Medical Journal* 7 (1871) 286;
J.T. McPhair 'Public Health in Ontario' Defries ed *Public Health* 67.
36 This is based on my 'Two Cholera Ships.'
37 Robert Wilson *A Retrospect* (Toronto 1954) 32
38 *Canada Medical and Surgical Journal* 1 (1873) 182; 2 (1874) 105-7, 476; *The
Canada Lancet* (1873) 524, (1874) 169-70; Ontario Board of Health *Annual
Report* 10 (1891) 12

CHAPTER 7 'Charlatanism of every description'

1 On fees: in 1839 a fee schedule agreed by 16 practitioners in Toronto
shows charges of 5/- a visit within the city and 5/- a mile outside for both
the 'highest class' and the 'lowest class' of patient. Fees for blood-letting
for both classes were 2/6, but cupping cost the highest class 7/6 and the
lowest 5/-; a blister cost 2/6. Despite these efforts to distinguish between
classes of customer the fees were high for the working man. The percent-
age of bad debts in any doctor's practice would require separate investigation but the fees must have discouraged calls on the doctor (fee schedule in Academy of Medicine Library, Toronto).
2 Maude E. Abbott *History of Medicine in the Province of Quebec* (Montreal
1931) 72; Sylvio LeBlond 'La Médecine dans la Province de Québec
avant 1847' *Les Cahiers des Dix* 35 (1970) 81; H.E. MacDermott *History of
the Canadian Medical Association 1867-1921* (Toronto 1935) 3
3 3 May 1834 C. Widmer to Lt. Col. Rowan, PRO CO42/419 31-42
4 Ibid; William Caniff *The Medical Profession in Upper Canada 1783-1850*
(Toronto 1894) 20-1, 31, 36, 62, 64, 67, 153
5 *Canada Medical Journal* (July 1852) quoted in George W. Spragge 'The
Trinity Medical College' *Ontario History* 58 (1966) 64; McDermott *History*
8. Homeopaths were recognized in 1859, eclectics in 1861; MacNab
A Legal History of the Health Professions in Ontario (Toronto 1970) 9.
6 Abbott *History* 49; Caniff *Medical Profession* 53, 176; William G. Rothstein
American Physicians in the Nineteenth Century (Baltimore 1972) 85
7 Caniff *Medical Profession* 185; Spragge 'Trinity Medical College' 69;
Charles G. Roland ed 'Diary of a Canadian Country Physician: Jonathan
Wolverston (1811-1883)' *Medical History* 15 (1971) 168-79; 7 July 1835
C. Widmer to Col. Rowan, PAC RG5A1 vol 155 84,806-8; 7 June 1834
Col. Rowan to President, Student Medical Society, Toronto, PAC
RG7G16C vol 31 99,107
8 C.M. Boissonault 'Charles-Jacques Fremont' *Dictionary of Canadian Bio-
graphy* 9 (Toronto 1976); Harvey Cushing *The Life of Sir William Osler* 1
(Oxford 1925) 70-1, 144

9 Heagerty 1, 282–3; McDermott *History* 17, 19
10 E.H. Bensley 'Archibald Hall' *DCB* 9
11 J.K. Crellin 'The Dawn of Germ Theory: Particles, Infection and Biology'
   F.N.L. Poynter ed *Medicine and Society in the 1860s* (London 1968)
12 N. Howard-Jones 'The Scientific Background of the International Sanitary
   Conferences 1851–1938' *WHO Chronicle* 28 (1974) 4 pts
13 J.R. Rhinelander and J.E. De Kay *Report of the Commissioners Employed to
   Investigate the Origin and Nature of the Epidemic Cholera of Canada* (New
   York 1834); 31 May 1831 Dr George Roberts to Lord Aylmer, PAC
   RG7G18 vol 16–17; *Rapport du Comité permanent de la Faculté de médecine
   de la Cité de Québec* (Québec 1832) 11; Martin Paine 'History of the
   Cholera at Montreal' *Boston Medical and Surgical Journal* 4 and 5 (1833)
   54–5. Dr. Holmes was replying to a questionnaire.
14 Joseph Workman 'Cholera in 1832 and 1834' *Canada Medical Journal* 2
   (1865–6) 485–9; George Douglas 'Asiatic Cholera' *BAJ* 3 (1847–8) 262;
   BAJ 5 (1849–50) 108, 178–83, 198–200, 209; W. Marsden 'An Essay on the
   Contagion, Infection, Portability and Communicability of the Asiatic
   Cholera' *Canada Medical Journal* 4 (1868) 529–37, 5 (1869) 1–7, 49–53,
   101–8, 146–51, 196–203, 243–50; Bilson 'The Cholera Epidemic in St. John,
   N.B., 1854' *Acadiensis* (autumn 1974) 95
15 *Canada Medical and Surgical Journal* 9 (1873) 426; W. Marsden 'Plans of a
   Hospital and Cleansing Establishment for the Treatment of Cholera'
   American Public Health Association *Public Health Papers and Reports* 1
   (1875) 183–7; 1 Aug. 1884 Peter H. Bryce to David H. Ledane, enclosing
   Resolutions of the Provincial Board of Health, PANB Executive Council
   Papers
16 *BAJ* 4 (1848–9) 255–6; *Report of the Central Board of Health* (Quebec 1855)
   9, 17; Bilson 'St. John'; Wolfred Nelson *Practical Views on Cholera* (Montreal 1854) 1, 6–7; Francis W. Campbell 'The Present Epidemic of
   Cholera – its Origin and Progress' *Canada Medical Journal* 2 (1865–6) 202,
   211; *The Canada Lancet* June 1873 523–5
17 William Kelly MD 'On the Medical Statistics of Lower Canada' read 19
   April 1834 *Transactions of the Literary and Historical Society of Quebec* 3, 1st
   series (reprinted 1927) 193–221; *Report, 1854* 20; G.E. Fenwick 'The Medical Statistics of the City of Montreal' *BAJ* 1 (1861) 390–4, 439–42, 489–93,
   2 (1862) 2–37
18 Samuel Jackson, Charles Meigs, and Richard Harlan *Report of the Commission Appointed by the Sanitary Board of the City Councils to Visit Canada for
   the Investigation of the Epidemic Cholera* (Philadelphia 1832) 2–3; R. Nelson
   Asiatic Cholera (New York 1866) 64; W. Nelson *Views* 2–3; *Memorandum
   on Cholera* (Ottawa 1866) 4, 23; *Canada Medical Journal* (1872) 376–7; J.B.
   McConnell *Cholera, its Nature, Symptoms, History, Cause and Prevention*
   (Montreal 1885) 24–5

19 Jackson et al. *Commission* 21–2; George Griffin 'Observations'; G. Russell 'On the Operation of Physical Agencies with Suggestions as to the Nature of Cholera' *BAJ* 4 (1848–9) 293, 323; A. Hall 'On the Calomel Treatment in Algide or Asiatic Cholera' *BAJ* 5 (1849–50) 85–6; L.F. Chaperon 'Essai sur la nature et le traitment du Choléra asiatique' *Canada Medical Journal* 1 (1852) 522–3; R. Nelson *Asiatic Cholera* 158–60; for the dominance of cholera see *Memorandum* 5.
20 Norman Howard-Jones 'Cholera Therapy in the Nineteenth Century' *Journal of the History of Medicine and Allied Sciences* 27 (1972) 373–95
21 Griffin 'Observations' 269, 295; Walter Henry *Surgeon Henry's Trifles* (London 1970) 238, Caniff *The Medical Profession* 517; William Marsden 'On Bloodletting in Cholera'; A. van Iffland 'The Quebec Board of Health' *BAJ* 5 (1849–50) 141–5, 198, 222; George Johnson 'How Shall We Treat the Cholera?'; Ewing Whittle 'Bleeding in Cholera' *Canada Medical Journal* 2 (1866) 518–19, 565, 569–70; Hall 'On the Calomel Treatment' 86; George D. Gibb 'On the Successful Treatment of Cholera in Canada' *Lancet* (1854) 5; *Memorandum* 33
22 Charles E. Rosenberg *The Cholera Years* (Chicago 1962) 70–2; *BAJ* 4 (1848–9) 388; Margaret Pelling *Cholera, Fever and English Medicine 1825–1865* (Oxford 1978) 310

CHAPTER 8 'Shortcomings ... exposed relentlessly'

1 6 Aug. 1832, AO Thomas Need Papers D Diary
2 Tom Harrison *Living through the Blitz* (London 1976)
3 Asa Briggs 'Cholera and Society in the Nineteenth Century' *Past and Present* 19 (1961) 76–96. Much has been written on cholera in nineteenth-century society. Some studies which I have found useful include Charles E. Rosenberg *Cholera Years* (Chicago 1962); R.M. Mcgrew *Cholera in Russia* (Madison 1965), L. Chevalier *Labouring and Dangerous Classes in Paris during the Nineteenth Century* (New York 1973), Catherine Rollett and Catherine Souriac 'Epidémies et Mentalités: le choléra de 1832 en Seine-et-Oise' *Annales* 29 (1974) 935–65; R.J. Morris *Cholera 1832* (London 1976). See also the bibliography and bibliographical essay.
4 Helen I. Cowan *British Emigration to British North America 1783–1837* (Toronto 1928) 215
5 Herbert Brown Ames *The City Below the Hill* (Toronto 1972); Elwood Jones and Douglas McCalla 'Toronto Waterworks, 1840–1877: Continuity and Change in Nineteenth Century Toronto Politics' *Canadian Historical Review* 60 (1979) 300–23
6 Green *The Life and Times of Reverend Anson Green* (Toronto 1877) 186–7

Selected Bibliography

PRIMARY SOURCES

I have examined public and personal papers in the Public Archives of Canada, les Archives nationales du Québec, the Archives of Ontario, the Public Archives of Nova Scotia, the Provincial Archives, New Brunswick, the Public Archives of Prince Edward Island, the Newfoundland Archives, the Toronto Public Library, Queen's University Archives, McGill University Archives, the Academy of Medicine in Toronto, the Château de Ramezay in Montreal, and the Public Record Office in London, England.

The printed journals of colonial and provincial assemblies and of the federal Parliament were consulted, as were files of the following newspapers: *Acadian Recorder, British Colonist, British Whig, Brockville Gazette, Canadian Correspondent, Canadian Courant, Canadian Freeman, Canadien,* Kingston *Chronicle,* Montreal *Chronicle, Colonial Advocate,* York *Courier,* Toronto *Examiner,* Quebec *Gazette,* Montreal *Gazette,* Kingston *Gazette and Chronicle,* Miramichi *Gleaner, Globe,* Kingston *Herald,* Montreal *Herald, Islander, La Minerve,* Saint John *Morning News, Public Ledger, Royal Gazette,* Hamilton *Spectator,* St John's *Times, Transcript, Upper Canada Herald,* and *Vindicator.* I also examined files of these journals: *Boston Medical and Surgical Journal, British American Journal, Canada Lancet, Canada Medical Journal,* and *Lancet.*

Official Reports

Orders and Directions made by the Board of Health for the Regulation of Pilots Quebec 1832
Rapport du Comité permanent de la Faculté de médecine de la Cité de Québec Quebec 1832
Bye-laws, Rules and Regulations of the Common Council of the City of Montreal Montreal 1833
Report of the Society for the Propagation of the Gospel London 1833
Report of the Special Sanitary Committee of Montreal upon the Cholera and Emigration for the year 1834 Montreal 1835
Annual Report of the Incorporated Church Society of the Diocese of Quebec 8, Quebec 1850
Proceedings of the Sanitary Committee ... of Toronto ... Toronto 1854
Report of the Water Committee ... of Montreal Montreal 1854
Report of the Central Board of Health, 1854 Quebec 1855
Ontario Board of Health, Annual Report 10, Toronto 1891

Books and Articles

Bell, Winthrop 'A Halifax Boyhood of One Hundred and Twenty Years ago' *Collections of the N.S. Historical Society* 28 (1949)
Bosworth, Newton *Hochelga Depicta* Montreal 1846
Brydon, Joseph Marr *Narrative of a Voyage with a Party of Emigrants ... to Upper Canada* London 1834
Campbell, Francis W. 'The Present Epidemic of Cholera: Its Origin and Progress' *Canada Medical Journal* 2 (1865–6) 202, 211
Chaperon, L.F. 'Essai sur la nature et le traitement du Choléra asiatique' *Canada Medical Journal* 1 (1852) 522–3
Douglas, George 'Asiatic Cholera' *BAJ* 3 (1847–8) 262, 4 (1848–9) 220
Douglas, J.D. ed *Journals and Reminiscences of James Douglas* New York 1910
Fenwick, G.F. 'The Medical Statistics of the City of Montreal' *BAJ* 1 (1861) 390–4, 2 (1862) 2–37
Gibb, George D. 'On the Successful Treatment of Cholera in Canada' *Lancet* (1854) 5

Green, Anson *The Life and Times of Reverend Anson Green* Toronto 1877

Hall, A. 'On the Calomel Treatment in Algide or Asiatic Cholera' *BAJ* 5 (1849–50) 85–6

Henry, Walter *Surgeon Henry's Trifles* London 1970

Iffland, A. van 'The Quebec Board of Health, The Cholera at Beauport and Its Treatment' *BAJ* 5 (1849–50) 199–200

Jackson, Samuel, Charles Meigs and Richard Harlan *Report of the Commission Appointed by the Sanitary Board of the City Councils to Visit Canada for the Investigation of the Epidemic Cholera* Philadelphia 1832

Johnson, George 'How Shall We Treat the Cholera?' *Canada Medical Journal* 2(1866) 565

Kelly, William 'On the Medical Statistics of Lower Canada' *Transactions of the Literary and Historical Society of Quebec* 3, 1st Series (reprinted 1927)

McConnell, J.A. *Cholera, Its Nature, Symptoms, History, Cause and Prevention* Montreal 1885

– *Mandements, lettres pastorales et circulaires des Évêques de Québec* vols 3, 4, Québec 1888

Marsden, William 'On Bloodletting in Cholera' *BAJ* 5 (1849–50) 141–5

– 'Plan of Quarantine for Cholera' *Canada Medical Journal* 2 (1866) 344

– 'An Essay on the Contagion, Infection, Portability and Communicability of the Asiatic Cholera' *Canada Medical Journal* 4 (1868) 529–37, 5 (1869) 1–7, 49–53, 101–8, 146–51, 196–203, 243–50

– 'Plans for a Hospital and Cleaning Establishment for the Treatment of Cholera ...' American Public Health Association *Public Health Papers and Reports* 1 (1875) 183–7

Memorandum on Cholera Ottawa 1866

Moodie, Susanna *Roughing It in the Bush* Toronto 1916

Nelson, Robert *Asiatic Cholera* New York 1866

Nelson, Wolfred *Practical Views on Cholera* Montreal 1854

Paine, Martin 'History of the Cholera at Montreal' *Boston Medical and Surgical Journal* 4 and 5 (1833) 54–5

Radcliffe, R.T. ed *Extracts from Authentic Letters from Upper Canada* in

Continuation of Letters from Sussex Emigrants in Upper Canada for 1833 Petworth 1833

Rhinelander, J.R. and J.E. De Kay *Report of the Commissioners Employed to Investigate the Origin and Nature of the Epidemic Cholera of Canada* New York 1834

Roland, Charles G. ed 'Diary of a Canadian Country Physician: Jonathan Wolverton (1811–1883)' *Medical History* 15 (1971) 168–79

Russell, G. 'On the Operation of Physical Agencies with Suggestions as to the Nature of Cholera' *BAJ* 4 (1848–9) 293–323

Whittle, Ewing, 'Bleeding in Cholera' *Canada Medical Journal* 2 (1866) 569–70

Workman, Joseph 'Cholera in 1832 and 1834' *Canada Medical Journal* 2 (1865–6) 485–9

SECONDARY SOURCES

Abbott, Maude E. *History of Medicine in the Province of Quebec* Montreal 1931

Allen, Phyllis 'Etiological Theory in America Prior to the Civil War' *Journal of the History of Medicine and Allied Sciences* II (1947) 489–520

Armstrong, F.H. 'William Lyon Mackenzie, First Mayor of Toronto: a Study of a Critic in Power' *Canadian Historical Review* 68 (1967) 209–329

Bilson, Geoffrey 'The Cholera Epidemic in St John, N.B., 1854' *Acadiensis* (autumn 1974) 86–99

– 'Two Cholera Ships in Halifax' *Dalhousie Review* (autumn 1973) 449–59

Briggs, Asa 'Cholera and Society in the Nineteenth Century' *Past and Present* 19 (1961) 76–96

Burria, D. and W. Burrows eds *Cholera* Philadelphia 1974

Caniff, W. *The Medical Profession in Upper Canada 1783–1850* Toronto 1894

Charlton, M. 'Outlines of the History of Medicine in Lower Canada' *Annals of Medicine* 6 (1924) 343

Chevalier, L. *Labouring and Dangerous Classes in Paris during the First Half of the Nineteenth Century* New York 1973

Christie, R. *A History of the Late Province of Lower Canada, Parliamentary and Political* 3 vols Quebec 1850

Cosbie, W.G. *The Toronto General Hospital, A Chronicle* Toronto 1975

Cowan, Helen I. *British Emigration to British North America 1783–1837* Toronto 1928

Crellin, J.K. 'The Dawn of the Germ Theory: Particles, Infection and Biology' in F.N.L. Poynter ed *Medicine and Society in the 1860s* London 1968

Cushing, H. *The Life of Sir William Osler* Oxford 1925

Dechêne, Louise and Jean-Claude Robert 'Le choléra de 1832 dans le Bas-Canada: mesure des inégalités devant la mort' U of Montreal mimeograph 1977

Defries, R.D. ed *The Development of Public Health in Canada* Toronto 1940

Fergusson, C.B. 'A Coke's Tour to Halifax' *Dalhousie Review* 29 (1950) 51–61

– *A Documentary Study of the Establishment of the Negroes in Nova Scotia between the War of 1812 and the Winning of Responsible Government, 1848* Halifax 1948

Firth, E. *The Town of York 1815–1834* Toronto 1966

Frieden, Nancy M. 'The Russian Cholera Epidemic 1891–93 and Medical Professionalisation' *Journal of Social History* 10 (1977) 538–59

Gibbon, A. Douglas 'The Kent Marine Hospital, St. John, N.B.' *Collections of the New Brunswick Historical Society* 14 (1955)

Glazebrook, G.P. de T. *The Story of Toronto* Toronto 1971

Godfrey, C.M. *The Cholera Epidemics in Upper Canada 1832–1866* Toronto 1968

Heagerty, J.S. *Four Centuries of Medical History in Canada* Toronto 1928

Howard-Jones, N. 'Cholera Therapy in the Nineteenth Century' *Journal of the History of Medicine and Allied Sciences* 27 (1972) 373–95

– 'The Scientific Background of the International Sanitary Conferences 1851–1938' *WHO Chronicle* 28 (1974) 159–71, 229–47, 369–84, 414–61

LeBlond, Sylvio 'Cholera in Quebec 1849' *Canadian Medical Association Journal* 71 (1954) 289

- 'La Médecine dans la Province de Québec avant 1847' *Les Cahiers des Dix* 35 (1970) 69–75
- 'Quebec en 1832' *Laval Médicale* 38 (1967) 183–91
Longmate, N. *King Cholera* London 1966
Lyne, David Coleman 'The Irish in the Province of Canada in the Decades Leading to Confederation' MA thesis, McGill University, 1960
MacDermott, H.E. *History of the Canadian Medical Association 1867–1921* Toronto 1935
Macdonagh, Oliver 'The Irish Famine Emigration to the United States' *Perspectives in American History* 10 (1976) 357–446
McGrew, R.E. *Russia and the Cholera 1823–1831* Madison 1965
MacNab, Elizabeth *A Legal History of the Health Professions in Ontario* Toronto 1970
Martell, J.S. *Immigration to and Emigration from Nova Scotia 1815–1838* Halifax 1942
Moine, J.M. *Quebec Past and Present: a History of Quebec 1608–1876* Quebec 1876
Morris, R.J. *Cholera, 1832* London 1976
Ouellet, Fernand *Le Bas-Canada 1791–1840. Changements structuraux et crise* Ottawa 1976
Paterson, M.A. 'The Cholera Epidemic of 1832, in York, Upper Canada' *Bulletin of the Medical Library Association* (April 1958) 165–184
Pelling, M. *Cholera, Fever and English Medicine* Oxford 1978
Pollitzer, R. *Cholera* Geneva 1959
Rollet, Catherine and Catherine Souriac 'Epidémics et Mentalités: le choléra de 1832 en Seine-et-Oise' *Annales* 29 (1974) 935–65
Rosenberg, Charles E. *The Cholera Years* Chicago 1962
Rothstein, William G. *American Physicians in the Nineteenth Century* Baltimore 1972
Spragge, George W. 'The Trinity Medical College' *Ontario History* 58 (1966) 63–98
Wilson, Robert *A Retrospect* Toronto 1954

A Bibliographical Essay

Cholera is one of the most widely studied diseases. A stream of articles, pamphlets, and books began appearing from the beginning of the nineteenth century pandemics, rising and falling as the disease approached and receded. Most of the material asked what the disease was, how it spread, and how its victims might be cured. In Canada, Elam Stimson was one of the first commentators, publishing *The Cholera Beacon* at Dundas, Upper Canada, in 1835. I have used most of the Canadian material of this sort in this book. For historians of medicine, John Snow's 'on the Mode of Communication of Cholera,' which first appeared in 1849, is one of the most important works of this kind. It can be found in W.H. Frost ed *Snow on Cholera* (New York 1936). In 1849, Thomas Shapter published *The History of Cholera in Exeter in 1832* (London 1849). Shapter, like Snow, plotted the deaths on a street map but concluded that the disease was normally airborne. He wrote to encourage his fellow citizens to maintain public health measures introduced since 1832. His book contains many details of the emotional impact of the first epidemic.

The problem of the impact of disease on society attracted French historians in the middle of the twentieth century. Louis Chevalier's *Le Choléra* (La Roche sur yon 1958) brought together essays by a number of authors discussing the epidemic of 1831–2 in Paris, the French provinces, Russia, and England. The essayists studied the demographic effects of cholera and the responses it provoked among populations hit with differing force by the disease. In *Labouring and Dangerous Classes*

(New York 1973) Chevalier again pointed to the role of cholera in periods of social unrest when it helped to intensify awareness of inequalities. The French historians influenced French-Canadian students who followed their lead in exploring Quebec's history. Fernand Ouellet *Le Bas-Canada* (Ottawa 1976) considers the demographic and social effects of the cholera epidemics in the 1830s.

English-language historians were beginning at this time to look at disease and its effects on society. For many years medical historians such as Erwin H. Ackernecht, George Rosen, Richard Shryock, and Owsei Temkin had urged medical historians to be aware of the social context in which medicine developed. Social historians were now reminded that disease was a fundamental part of human history. Asa Briggs, in 'Cholera and Society' *Past and Present* (1961), said that cholera offered one way of understanding social problems. Charles E. Rosenberg *The Cholera Years* (Chicago 1962) used cholera as 'a constant and ... randomly recurring stimulus against which the varying reactions of Americans could be judged' on religious, scientific, intellectual, and social questions in the years between 1832 and 1866. He drew general conclusions from a study mainly confined to the disease in New York City. Roderick E. McGrew *Russia and the Cholera 1823–1832* (Madison 1965) was influenced by Chevalier in his analysis of the social and administrative response to the disease. R.J. Morris's *Cholera, 1832* (London 1976) is a recent attempt to discuss the English epidemic and to assess 'the social response to an epidemic.' Canadian historians outside Quebec have not been much affected by these historical developments. Charles M. Godfrey's account, *The Cholera Epidemics in Upper Canada 1832–1866* (Toronto 1968), is the fullest narrative but does not contain an extensive discussion of the social response to the epidemic.

Social historians have barely touched on questions of health and medicine in nineteenth-century Canada. The demographic impact of disease, its influence on patterns of settlement and urban development and on the standard of living of the population all await full investigation. The provision of medical help, the development of a medical profession and the role of education, and the development of public health measures are all topics needing fuller study. Professor Charles G. Roland is preparing a bibliography of the history of Canadian medicine. Until that appears, the *Bibliography of the History of Medicine*

1964–69 and *1970–74* and yearly since (Washington, DC) and *Current Works in the History of Medicine* (London, The Wellcome Foundation) which appears eight times a year are the best guides to current work in the field. For the years before 1964, see G. Miller *Bibliography of the History of Medicine in the US and Canada 1939–1960* (Baltimore 1964) and annual bibliographies in *Bulletin of the History of Medicine*. Standard reference works are William Caniff *The Medical Profession in Upper Canada* (Toronto 1894), J.J. Heagerty *Four Centuries of the Medical History of Canada* 2 vols (Toronto 1928), and Maude E. Abbot *The History of Medicine in the Province of Quebec* (Toronto 1931). In addition to these older works, there are some more recent surveys of particular regions and topics. These include *One Hundred Years of Pharmacy in Canada* (Toronto 1967), D.W. Gillett *A History of Dentistry in Canada* (Toronto 1971), E. MacNab *A Legal History of the Health Professions in Ontario* (Toronto 1970), H.E. MacDermott *One Hundred Years of Medicine in Canada 1867–1967* (Toronto 1967) and *History of the CMA* (Toronto 1958), T.F. Ross *From Shaman to Modern Medicine, a Century of the Healing Arts in B.C.* (Vancouver 1972), and W.B. Stewart *Medicine in New Brunswick* (Saint John 1974).

The impact of disease on Canadian life has interested some anthropologists and historical geographers, but few historians. G. Graham-Cumming made use of a historical thesis when preparing 'Health of the Original Canadians 1867–1967' *Medical Services Journal of Canada* 23 (1967) 115–66. G.J. Wherrett *The Miracle of the Empty Beds: A History of Tuberculosis in Canada* (Toronto 1977) deals with a disease devastating to the native population, but most of his work is set in the twentieth century. Cholera is, for Canada as elsewhere, one of the most fully discussed diseases, but there is room for studies of the major killer diseases as part of any analysis of life in nineteenth-century Canada. How did malaria affect settlement, what pattern did the child-killers measles, diphtheria, and the milk- and water-borne diseases take in the growing cities of the period? What part did smallpox play in Canadian settlement and urban growth? What part did nutrition play in different places and among different groups in the pattern of health and sickness? There are some suggestions that in other countries improved nutrition did as much as, or more than, improved medicine in conquering disease.

The history of medicine in Canada, as far as it exists, is still very much the history of doctors – and regular doctors at that. This is a natural consequence of the fact that most of the history has been written by medical men viewing the question from inside the profession. Material on individual doctors is appearing in each volume of the *Dictionary of Canadian Biography*. In Quebec, Edouard Desjardins and Sylvio LeBlond have published many useful articles on particular doctors and on developments in the medical profession to be found in *Union Médicale*, *Laval Médicale*, and the *Canadian Medical Association Journal*. Both in Quebec and outside there is still much to be written about the development of the medical profession. The question of how the regular medical profession achieved its particular status in competition with the irregulars needs study. The peculiar problems of achieving professional control in a colony where the imperial government was influenced by the British professional colleges needs consideration. The nature of professional practice, who entered, why they chose medicine, how much money they made, the doctor's standing in the community, how he treated his patients (there was often a gap between what was taught and what was done), why his patient chose a regular doctor rather than a sectarian, and the place of domestic and folk medicine in nineteenth-century Canada are all worthy of investigation. At the moment, one commentator has said, the veterinary profession is the best studied one in Ontario; D.A. Lawr *Canadian Historical Review* (1977) 506. G.W.L. Nicholson has recently written on *Canada's Nursing Sisters* (Toronto 1975) but there is no modern, comprehensive study of the medical profession in nineteenth-century Canada.

Regular doctors rested their claim to special status on their education. Canadian medical education was closely tied to the universities and thus differed from United States experience. Each university has its historians and some of the medical schools have been separately studied. C.M. Boissonault 'Créations de deux écoles de médecine au Québec' *Laval Médicale* 39 (1968) 547–9; E. Desjardins 'La vielle Ecole de Médecine Victoria' *Union Médicale* 103 (1974) 117–25, and 'L'enseignement médicale à Montréal au milieu du xixieme siècle' *Union Médicale* 100 (1971) 305–9; C.M. Godfrey 'Trinity Medical School' *Applied Therapeutics* 8 (1966) 1024–8, and 'The Origins of Medical Education of Women in Ontario' *Medical History* 17 (1973) 89–94; and G.W.

Spragge 'The Trinity Medical College' *Ontario History* 58 (1966) 63–98
are useful. J.F. Kett 'American and Canadian Medical Institutions
1800–1870' *Journal of the History of Medicine and Allied Sciences* 22
(1967) 343–56 makes some comparative remarks. The question of how
education was linked with professionalization can be more fully
explored. To what extent was education used to restrict entry and raise
the social standing of the profession, for example, by requiring a 'gen-
tlemanly' knowledge of Latin as a condition of entry? What was taught
and what was learned, how quickly did Canadian schools accept the
new ideas of the nineteenth century, and what were the relative importance of British, Continental European, and American influences on
Canadian medical schools? Two studies of the way in which medical
knowledge reached Canada are M. Ewing 'Influences of the Edinburgh
Medical School on the Early Development of McGill University' *Canadian Journal of Surgery* 18 (1975) 287–96 and C.G. Roland 'The Early
Years of Antiseptic Surgery in Canada' *Journal of the History of Medicine
and Allied Sciences* 22 (1967) 380–91. There is room for further studies
of this process and of the influence of foreign studies and immigrants
on the profession.

Doctoring came gradually to be associated with hospitals and the
development of the hospital as a social institution needs study by historians of nineteenth-century Canada. They might consider questions of
public support and public attitudes toward hospitals. The existing his-
tories tend to be concerned with the interior history of the institution,
and most of the older hospitals have a published history. These include
L'Hôtel-Dieu de Montréal 1642–1973 (Montreal 1973), W.G. Cosbie *The
Toronto General Hospital 1887–1947* (Toronto 1975), D.S. Lewis *Royal
Victoria Hospital 1887–1947* (Montreal 1969), and H.E. MacDermott *A
History of the Montreal General Hospital* (Montreal 1950). Medical provision outside the hospital needs investigation, as does the development
of public health. Neil Sutherland *Children in English-Canadian Society*
(Toronto 1976) has looked at some aspects of this question for the last
years of the century. Much of the material for Canadian medical history
lies almost untouched in provincial archives and the Public Archives of
Canada in Ottawa and in hospital and university archives. A thorough
investigation of those boxes would help bring a deeper knowledge of
what life was like for nineteenth-century Canadians.

Index

The Social History of Canada

General Editors:
Michael Bliss 1971–7
H.V. Nelles 1978–